WAYS OF LIFE

WAYS OF LIFE

On Places, Painters and Poets

Selected Essays and Reviews
1994–2008

ANDREW MOTION

faber and faber

First published in 2008
by Faber and Faber Limited
3 Queen Square London WC1N 3AU

Typeset in Minion by Faber and Faber Ltd
Printed in England by CPI Mackays, Chatham, ME5 8TD

A CIP record for this book
is available from the British Library

ISBN 978-0-571-22365-7

2 4 6 8 10 9 7 5 3 1

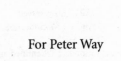

For Peter Way

Contents

FOREWORD

I began writing reviews in 1976, when John Gross invited me to
contribute some short pieces about contemporary novels and
poetry to *The Times Literary Supplement*; at the time I was a graduate student at Oxford, finishing my thesis on Edward Thomas.
Soon afterwards I also started writing occasional pieces for Ian
Hamilton at the *New Review*, and more regular poetry round-ups
for Martin Amis then Julian Barnes at the *New Statesman*. If I had
to characterize the kind of approach I tried to take, I'd call it an
evolution of Practical Criticism: close concentration on the printed page, but with a special interest in historical context. Structural-
ism (which at this time was beginning to take root in British
academies) interested me – but it troubled me too. I wanted to
write prose that was free of jargon, and spoke as directly as possible to the general reader.

Over the next thirty years I've continued to write for various
newspapers and journals at a steady rate: I enjoy the work, the
primitive thrill of reading books hot off the press, and the extra
money it brings into my bank account. My thinking has inevitably
been given more substance by the growth of my reading, but my
intentions have remained essentially the same. I especially admire
critics who combine the rigour of the seminar room with the flair
of good journalism. That mixture has been and remains my ideal.

I began preparing this book by gathering together as many of
my reviews as I could lay my hands on, then added the various lec-
tures and essays I've written over the years. They amounted to
nearly two thousand pages: an *omnium gatherum* was clearly out
of the question. All the same, I wanted to show the variety of subjects I'd written about, so my next step was to divide the pieces into
distinct categories: one that contained essays about journeys and

places; one that looked at painters and paintings; and one given over entirely to my 'imaginary life' of Edward Thomas. This piece first saw the light of day as a lecture at the National Portrait Gallery in 2004; it was one of a series of talks I helped to organize, in which speakers were invited to imagine what certain writers might have achieved if they hadn't died young. In my own case, I allowed Thomas (who was killed at the Battle of Arras in 1917) to survive the war and continue writing into the late 1920s. I wanted to reflect on the losses entailed in his early death, to make some plausible suggestions about what might have happened to him had he lived longer, to find a way of re-evaluating what did actually occur during his life, and to raise some questions about conventional biographical form. In these ways, the essay is a partner to my novella *The Invention of Dr Cake* (2003), which imagines that Keats didn't die in Rome in 1821 but returned to England and resumed his career as a doctor.

It remained for me to work out what to do with the large number of pieces I'd produced about poets, poetry, and other kinds of writing. My first instinct (again, to show variety) was to compile a section on modernism, a section on writing by women (including the Chatterton Lecture on Elizabeth Bishop, which I gave in 1984), a section on recent fiction, a section on contemporary culture, and a section on writers who belong to 'the English line' – in which I have a particular interest. I soon realized this structure was more likely to produce bagginess than variety, and abandoned it. Eventually, after more chopping and changing, I decided to choose pieces concentrating mainly on writers and topics which have not always been valued as highly as I think they deserve to be. On poets who have a history of neglect (John Clare, William Barnes, Ivor Gurney, W. S. Graham), on other kinds of side-lined literary figures (the 'Romantic Sisterhood', Leigh Hunt, Joseph Severn), on less popular works by generally celebrated poets (John Donne's *Devotions Upon Emergent Occasions*, Christina Rossetti's short stories, Thomas Hardy's *The Dynasts*), and on overlooked aspects of writers' personalities and styles (John Betjeman's camp). My intention is to show the intrinsic interest of these things, but also to use them as a kind of lamp to illuminate better-known (and more frequently discussed) work that lies adjacent.

Several of the twenty-three pieces in this section began life as reviews, and are therefore shorter than the essays, etc., which appear elsewhere – for the simple reason that they were written to fit the requirements of a newspaper's Books Pages. The effect, inevitably, is to make the rhythm of reading feel choppier. I've tried to minimize this by adding a few articles about writers (such as Robert Frost and Sylvia Plath) who are not and never have been neglected – in the hope that they will give a sense of continuity by showing the development of certain techniques and attitudes across a spread of time. Readers may well choose to read these articles at random. If they read consecutively I hope they will feel they are making surprising connections, and extending familiar definitions.

Literary journalists, like other kinds of reporters, are often stigmatized as hacks – and sometimes even embrace this definition themselves, to diminish their sense of responsibility for what they write. For my own part, I've always thought reviewers need to have a proper sense of modesty in the face of other people's effort and newness, while at the same time taking their job absolutely seriously. Reviewers, after all, stand at the gate between the solitary creator and the wide world: their response to a book not only affects its short-term life, but plays a pivotal part in the establishment or otherwise of its long-term future. Sometimes reviewers get things wrong, or show unreasonable prejudice, or prove unequal to the task, and often they find that readers disagree with them. But this doesn't mean their work is fatally compromised. Reviewing is a way of life as well as a way of giving life, and in both respects it requires self-assertion as well as self-surrender.

Acknowledgements

The pieces in this book first appeared in the following places, usually in slightly different versions, and with different titles; I'm grateful to the editors who commissioned them, to Alan Hollinghurst and Sarah Emily Miano for reading and commenting on them, and to Katherine Baxter for her help in collecting them: 'Stisted: A Homecoming' in the *Observer* (6 June 1999); 'Spurn Point: A Drive' in the *Independent on Sunday* (9 January 1994); 'Normandy: An Anniversary' in the *Guardian* (12 June 2004); 'Sailing to Italy: A Diary' in *Salt Water* (Faber and Faber, 1997); 'Haydon Bridge: A Break-in' in *Granta* (spring 1993); 'Jacob van Ruisdael: True Understanding' in the *Guardian* (25 February 2006); 'Samuel Palmer: Shadowlands' in the *Guardian* (27 September 2005); 'John Constable: Another Word for Feeling' in the *Guardian* (22 November 2003); 'J. M. W. Turner: In Venice' in the *Guardian* (11 October 2003); 'Pierre Bonnard: Adventures of the Optic Nerve' in the *Sunday Telegraph Magazine* (1 February 1998); 'Howard Hodgkin: Emotional Situations' in *Modern Painters* (vol. 7 no. 4, winter 1994); 'Edward Thomas: An Imaginary Life' in *Interrupted Lives* (National Portrait Gallery, 2004); 'John Donne: A Melancholy Lover' in the *Guardian* (22 July 2006), and *Devotions Upon Emergent Occasions* and *Death's Duel* (Vintage, New York, 1999); 'The Romantic Sisterhood: Iron Hinges' in the *Financial Times* (22 June 1997) and 'How Deep a Blessing' in the *Guardian* (8 March 2008); 'John Clare: A Life at Last' in the *Guardian* (18 October 2003), and 'Images from Nature' in the *Observer* (9 August 1998); 'Leigh Hunt: In the Political World' in the *Guardian* (8 January 2005); 'Joseph Severn: Painter, Friend, Consul' in the *Guardian* (7 May 2005); 'Christina Rossetti: Stories and Secrets' in *Christina Rossetti: Commonplace* (Hesperus, 2005); 'William

Barnes: An Introduction' in *William Barnes: Selected Poems* (Faber and Faber, 2007); 'Thomas Hardy: *The Dynasts*' in *The Times Literary Supplement* (7 July 1995); 'Robert Frost: Accounts of the Life' in *The Times Literary Supplement* (29 January 1999) and 'The Secret Places' in *The Times Literary Supplement* (26 March 1982); 'Ivor Gurney: Beaten Down Continually' in *The Times Literary Supplement* (15 October 1982); 'Wilfred Owen: The Last Two Years' in *The Times Literary Supplement* (6 November 1992); 'John Betjeman: Serious Feelings' in *Collected Poems of John Betjeman* (Murray, 2006); 'Robert Lowell: Like a Tennis Match' in the *Guardian* (13 August 2005); 'W. S. Graham: It is Myself' in the *Observer* (30 January 1997) and 'The Blue Crevasse' in the *Guardian* (13 March 2004); 'Sylvia Plath: Weirdness' in the *Financial Times* (8 April 2000); 'Anne Stevenson: Putting the Bones to Bed' in *Anne Stevenson: Selected Poems* (The Library of America, 2008); 'Bob Dylan: Going Electric' in the *Daily Telegraph* (10 October 1998) and 'Drawn Blank' in *The Drawn Blank Series* (Halcyon Gallery, 2008).

PLACES

STISTED
A Homecoming

Across the valley, a few dozen houses among bare branches and clumps of evergreen. In fields below, the Blackwater – black as its name, but also peat-brown, hazel, silver, white, pewter and cobalt as it reflects the winter sky. I am staring from my car on the top road, putting everything in its place: the grey farmhouse in the foreground, wearing a patch of ivy over one eye; the Victorian Hall with its sour yellow brickwork; the wooden church spire; the pale sores of the golf course; the windscreens flashing in the main street. Further off, beyond the crown of the hill and invisible, the house my father and mother bought thirty-five years ago, when I was twelve – the house where I first paid attention to the world.

The Hall has a long south front, and a heavy-legged portico darkening the front door. My great-grandparents lived here in the 1920s: Andrew and Jessie – Andrew the self-made man and proud of it, Jessie with asthma, wanting to live on high ground. When I knew it first, they were long gone and the house was an Old People's Home. The gardens had run wild, and were a part of every walk I took: across the field from my parents' house half a mile away, over the lane, and in through the hedge. Then open ground, where contractors were sketching out bunkers and fairways, and might ask me what I was doing. After that, I was safe.

First came the stable block, smeared green by overhanging trees, with one small window in the back wall. If I huffed on the cobwebby glass and rubbed with my sleeve, I could see a mattress on the floor, and a blanket someone had peeled back in a hurry, then abandoned. The window frame smelled of mushrooms.

On again, with the stables behind me. It was easy to see how the lawn must have looked in the old days: silver where the wind brushed it; sparse and silent under the cedar, round the laurel and

3

rhododendron. Even with branches smashed off the big trees, and bushes looming shaggily, the wide grass made room for its ghosts. Andrew in his wicker chair, retired from business and fuddled with Alzheimer's. Jessie in her trailing blacks, out of date by fifty years. My grandfather, their only son, pacing after her. Next, my father – a child – his head bowed and his hands clasped behind his back like a little man.

Their shadows melted where the lawn ran out, and I followed. The yew-tree walk. Storms had lashed the high branches together, snapping some into each other's arms and leaving them to a sky burial. Within a few yards I was in the dark, stumbling over roots. Here and there an entire yew tree had been lifted out of the ground, and the jagged edges of the bark showed blood-red around the wood proper, which was pure white like chicken. These fallen trees looked so enormous, with their mush of red berry-wreckage and their feathery mourning-plumes, I felt they might have fallen only a moment before, or were still falling as I watched, catching me in their downdraft.

But that was all in the past; it was over and done with. As soon as I wanted, I could be away from that part of the garden, putting the open sky above me again. I found the Church Walk, the path Andrew and Jessie had taken every Sunday, when they followed its curve to the end-wall, and the gate into the graveyard. A honey-suckle had gone mad over the holly bush which marked the beginning. Heavy grass-swags flopped across the brick borders on either side. Brambles blocked the entrance, swaying whenever the wind touched them.

I might have pushed at them with a stick, but it would have made no difference. The only way forward was on a parallel line, wading through a battery of dead nettles, my hands above my head as if I had surrendered, then along the back of the rhododendrons, and eventually out by the wreck of the summer house. A dark-green drum, open on the south to take in the view of the Blackwa-ter – except the roof had slipped forward like a hat over a sleeping face. This was where Jessie filled the long afternoons after Andrew had died, and where the soldiers sat too, when the Army took over

the Hall at the beginning of the war, and Jessie moved out. She
never came back, and it was the soldiers' names I saw carved in the
walls of the summer house when I crouched there myself, thinking
about their fear of dying and their excitement. I never stayed long.
It was too easy to imagine someone rustling up behind me, darting
their head round the corner into my twilight.

Then, as a last thing, the pond. I shoved along the wall of the
kitchen garden – red brick, and always warm to look at – not
knowing what lay inside. The wall was too high, and the gates
upright and locked. But here on my left the water-garden still
showed clear, in spite of the elm crashed head-over-heels at the far
end, and the freakish saplings quivering on mud-humps. There
was no depth any more, only slicks of olive green, and a weed-cov-
ering that continually threatened to close. Was I inventing it, or
were there goldfish? The water was alive with odd twitches and
pulses, waiting for me to turn my back so that it could continue its
journey through the iron trap under the sleeper-bridge, down the
ornamental ravine, then flatten into the lower pool under the
plane trees, where I couldn't find a way through the brambles.

I could today, if I wanted. I could, now that I've left the top road,
bounced over the hump-backed bridge, and slowed to a standstill
alongside the Hall's boundary hedge. I could, but I don't. Instead,
I crank down my window and leave the engine of my car running,
looking on. In the distance, outside the stables, and again beneath
the front portico, cement mixers – their orange bird-mouths tilted
towards me. What has my father told me? The Freemasons have
bought the Hall; they're turning it into a retirement home. Even
now, the front door is open and there are men inside, stooping or
lounging about. They seem to be laying a new floor. The gardens
have been taken in hand, too. Where the yew-tree walk begins, the
cinder track has been chewed by the wheels of a digger. That broad
pale heap must be sawdust – wisps blowing off the top like sand off
a dune.

I edge the car forward again. Fawn gravel and winter sky. Brown
shadows, like falling sticks. Nothing else. No, something. My father.
On one of the times we walked through the gardens together years

ago, just after the hurricane. A big flat hand of the cedar had smashed onto the lawn, and the rhododendrons were out of their wits. The whole top half of the Wellingtonia was snapped off, and the tulip tree uprooted, like a girl with her dress blown over her head. My father went first, lifting his arms from his sides then letting them fall heavily. Slops of new light splashed on his shoulders and grey head. I followed marvelling, wanting him to turn round and show me his face, but grateful that he would not.

*

Today I am on my way to visit my father again – no reason in particular; just to see him. Even with my wait on the top road, and then outside the Hall, it's still early. I follow the lane alongside a thick curving hedge and come to the churchyard, park by the lichgate, then walk past the grave of the Victorian chimney-builder and reach the door which connects with the Hall. This is my great-grandparents' world from the other side. If I heave myself up, I can look over the wall into the water-garden, where the trees have been cut back, and the pool cleared. Those are definitely goldfish down there – mobbing a yew berry when it plops in, scattering as a finger of cloud darkens overhead. But the gate which cuts me off is still ramshackle, slumped in its frame so the double doors are squeezed together and could never open, even without the chain and padlock.

My mother's grave is here beside me, to the left. I used to imagine her smiling at me from her dark pit; I could see her yellow hair spread out, so her white face looked like a swift's egg on a cushion of moss. Now she has been dead so long, I see nothing. An empty hole in the earth, going down for ever. It's the same when I read the headstone. These names are not her names. They are envelope names, names on hospital lists. Along the shoulder of the stone, there's a ridge of black-and-white birdshit, where the churchyard sparrows perch and look over her.

The graves behind my mother, close to the wall, belong to my grandfather and my great-grandparents. This was their place, but they were always restless. Andrew and Jessie have a heavy-based cross which leans at a sad angle. My grandfather's is even wonkier, and the grass above him lumpy and rippled like the bed of an insomniac. I stand in front of each in turn. Blood of their blood. Flesh of their flesh. The little strips of lead, cut to fill up and blacken each letter of their names, are beginning to work loose.

I turn away from the graves thinking I must be late, but only a few minutes have gone by. So I take the car up the village street slowly, with time to kill. Here are the chimneys put up by the dead chimney-builder, their twisted brick columns like stiff smoke. Here are the two car-huddles I saw from the top road. Here is the village green – and in another half-mile, my father.

Before that, I come to my childhood home – the house where he lived for twenty years, and left only when my mother died. A line of trees protects it from the road: larch and ash, with a couple of Scots pines by the gate. When we first arrived, the house was living through its last days as the village rectory and the rector was still installed, waiting for the builders to finish his new place next to the church. He was sick, trembling on a chaise-longue in front of a fire, and his illness had worked its way everywhere. A lawn mower leaked oil in a corner of the sitting room. The apple store stank in an upstairs bedroom. There was a puzzle of bicycle parts rusting in a bath.

By the time my mother had her accident, the house had been tamed and was ours – the way we liked it. Then she was taken away, and everything changed. When the ambulance started bringing her back for an hour or two on Sundays – this was years later – the house became a nursing home until she was driven back to the hospital again.

The tree-barricade ends at the gate, and the house stands plain for a moment. A white box, its black windows giving nothing away. I blink, wondering what will come back to me, and see a winter Sunday like today, with flat cloud. It was late morning. The ambulance had just arrived at the front door, and we were carrying my mother into the house on her stretcher-trolley, taking things carefully because the rector was waiting for us indoors. He was going to perform the service called 'The Laying On of Hands'.

It was only a blessing, my father had said, but as we stood in a circle round the stretcher, blessing never seemed to happen. The rector was brusque, as though he suspected we might suddenly interrupt him. Was it because he knew how out of place he looked, his vestments giving a whiff of mothballs as he leant in to my mother? Was that why he pushed his voice beyond its usual singsong, insisting she open herself to receive God's love? It was frightening. My mother couldn't respond, her body rigid under its green rug, and her bulbous, marble-smooth hands huddled together in her lap. I concentrated instead on the fire burbling in the grate behind her; on the ordinary light slanting across her blanket. When my father cleared his throat, I thought he was going to speak up and end the embarrassment. But no, he settled himself again with his head bowed and his hands clasped, while the rector bent forward even more heavily, and the fire sank back, and the clock in the passage outside struck three, which was wrong, because we'd forgotten to wind it, and my mother kept looking up, her eyes full of tears now, fixing on the rector's face, on my father's, on mine, and the house spun away from us, melting into a wilderness of light.

*

Here is my father's cottage at last: a yellow-painted gable, and the small conservatory where he likes to sit and smoke and stare into space. I dwell on the few hundred yards of lane which still separate us – the gravel, and the black tar winking between. I take in the ditches on either side – grass-filled, shallow, more like drains than ditches – which lost their hedges years ago. I follow the wind, as it prances across the winter wheat that slopes down to the Blackwater, shying at nothing, then running straight, then pausing in a dusty circle, then sprinting. I see all this, but I am looking through it, into the world beyond. The air hurtles and charges, raising my father on the day we drove to the village the first time, when he turned in the car and said: this is where we live now. It lifts the yew tree out of the ground in its dark walk, and flinches in the echo of its catastrophe. It stretches out my mother. It presses forward the hearse which carried her coffin along this same lane, with the rest of us following behind in our own car, making conversation about the weather, the chimneys, the view down to the river, while at house after house people came to their front doors and watched us pass, one or two crossing themselves, their hands moving slowly over their hearts but ending with a flourish, waving us on.

SPURN POINT
A Drive

Spurn Point. I-Don't-Need-You Point. Don't-Come-Near-Me Point. Rejection Point. Everything about the name says stay away. But stare at it on the map: thirty miles east of Hull, dangling from the north shore of the Humber, it hangs between land and water, rock and sand. It looks like bait for the gaping river-fish, and would be the perfect place to feel lonely.

Hull itself is a bad place to feel lonely. I went to work there in 1976, ploughing up my old life while trying to plant a new one. Everything that should have been easy turned out to be difficult. I felt browbeaten and bloody-minded.

I began exploring on foot, looking for Larkin's 'grain-scattered streets' and 'barge-crowded water'. At first all I could see were 'flat-faced trolleys' and 'grim head-scarved wives'. Then I discovered the Old Town squeezed between Holy Trinity and the River Hull: the abandoned main street with its wooden cobbles and empty cathedral-warehouses; the Transport Museum with its dusty trams; the chunky mansion and the Slavery Museum where William Wilberforce lived; the humpbacked metal bridge which lifted to let tall masts through. When I had taken them all in, I slipped down to the Hull itself and saw the dredgers grinding heavily together, their blistered carcasses basking in Sunday silence.

Then I stood where the Hull flows into the Humber. Hilarious. In mid-river, an out-of-place pleasure boat was struggling inland, engine whining as it took on a strong head-wind. It was getting nowhere. In fact, it was going backwards. A man wearing a black sou'wester came on deck and glared at me. I looked away.

A mile distant, the far shore of the Humber was misty. This meant I had to imagine the ferry setting out from its rickety pier opposite at New Holland. Downstream, and more definitely, I made out the oil refinery at Immingham: silver pipes slinking in and out of each other, and slim chimneys with their madcap flames. It looked cheerful – like a child's drawing of what an oil refinery should be like. Somewhere beyond it, where the North Sea began, was Spurn Point.

I'd read about Spurn years before, in a book which said it was a peninsula, two miles long, separating sea water from river water at the mouth of the Humber. The book called it 'the oddest place in England', but I wasn't sure. I'd been brought up in East Anglia, and once or twice had been taken to Orford near Aldeburgh, on the Suffolk coast. I'd stood with my back to Orford Castle and looked across the River Alde to Orford Ness. A ragged sleeve of stones; shingle-humps; a weird huddle of pagoda-buildings. Surely that was 'the oddest place'?

I bought a car during my first summer in Hull, and made for Spurn as soon as I could. The drive was more like a sea journey than a land journey. I cut through the centre of the city, skirted the edge of the Old Town, then headed east along the dead-straight Holderness Road. Holderness is flat. Flat as standing water. Flat as a lake in a park. I sailed into it easily – past the raw terraces, and the prison with its blushing red wall, past the high-rise blocks. Away to my right, the Humber sometimes bulged towards me, sometimes swerved away, hidden beyond a skyline of stick-insect cranes and dock offices.

Then a roundabout, and everything changed: the sun came out, and the river swelled into view. I wound down my window and holiday mud smell enveloped me. Immediately, I wanted to let myself laze and slip out of focus – but the road wouldn't let me. It began weaving from left to right. Surely it could go straight in such level country? Of course it couldn't. The land on every side was private property. I was here on sufferance, picking my way between farms which had drawn up their boundaries centuries ago, crazy as the division of Africa. Just when I felt ready for a clear run, when my sails filled, a fence reared in front of me, forcing me to slow down and turn aside. At one point I stopped and got out, climbing a gate to take it all in: fields of ripe wheat as far as the horizon, stirring into water crests and troughs; scattered farm-houses bobbing in the heat haze. No living person in sight.

I drove on and reached Winestead, where Andrew Marvell was born and baptized. I couldn't tell whether his house was still standing, and the church was locked. At Patrington I stopped again. The church is known as the 'Queen of Holderness', and for the past several miles its spire had drawn my car forward like a magnet – a beautiful, slim, greenish magnet, shot through with ornamental air-holes. But when I pushed open the damp west door, and listened as the clock wheezed and struck midday, I felt the air close in front of my face: I wasn't welcome here. So I turned quickly and set off again, feeling I might be waking from a dream. The road had coiled back on itself and ran straight, leading me into a different kind of flatness, hunched and wind-whipped. The fields were smaller, the dark earth scored with scratches of sand. Hedges were scrawny, worked tightly into each other. There were no tall trees, only a few thorns with their arms flung up in horror.

Then the road lost confidence, narrowed, and gave out altogether. I was on a pitted cement track, with grass raised in a hackle down the middle. A pill-box squinted at me from a sandbank. A sentry-box appeared, and a barbed-wire fence. Had I taken a wrong turning somewhere, and reached some kind of military camp? No, it was all right. This was just junk left over from the war. Somebody leant towards me wearing a badge which said Yorkshire Wildlife Trust: he demanded money, then nodded me ahead. I did as I was told, and that was it; I clambered out of the car and started walking.

Half an hour later I was still walking – a high dune-wall on one side, dotted with clumps of marram and prickly bushes; on the other, a gradually widening pool. It was a backwater of the Humber, coated with yellow scum. I put my head down, and re-ran the history of the place. On the map, Spurn looks natural: a peninsula dragged down into the Humber by North Sea waves raking along the East Coast. And for centuries it was natural, creeping slowly west as the waves tore sand from its seaward side, tumbled it round the end of the Point – the Head – and dumped it along the landward, river side. Then people started interfering. In the seventeenth century, when the main business of Hull was whaling, barges collected boulders from the seashore of Spurn and ferried them back to Hull for ships to use as ballast at the start of their journeys. When these ships reached their fishing grounds, and started loading up with whale meat, the sailors chucked the ballast overboard. A large part of Spurn is sprinkled across the bed of the Atlantic.

After a couple of centuries, the Point's boulder-barricade was threadbare, with the sea threatening to break through. So in the early nineteenth century, they built groynes stretching into the sea to deflect the waves; artificial sand dunes; shingle dumps and chalk walls. This changed everything. A place that had survived by moving became a place that lived by staying still.

A hundred and fifty years later, the defences began to fail. I saw this myself, tramping into the wind. I came to a huge hole in the dune wall, and found the cement road torn up in front of me where the sea had charged through: bewildering scrape-marks and tearings. Just-inaudible groans and sighs. It was easy to imagine the next few years. The Head would become an island; the spindly Point would dawdle off into the North Sea and vanish.

When I reached the first lighthouse, three-quarters of the way to the Head, there was still the same scrubby dune wall on one hand, and the expanding backwater on the other. But nothing felt safe any more. Spurn was giving up. The whole planet was about to jink sideways, and leave me milling in thin air.

I took myself to the very end, beyond the second lighthouse and the lifeboat station, to the crown of the Head. The wind blew so strongly my eyes ran, and I kept staggering to hold my balance. Away to the left, remote yet overwhelmingly close, colossal ships rose and fell in big grey waves: rusty-nosed tankers, container ships, hefty fishing boats, all waiting for the tide to change so they could come in to dock. On my right, the enormously wide river – its muscles and sinews trying to stay still but failing, tussling into little peaks, then shuddering into oily hollows. Slap in front of me, where the sea and river met, angry breakers made a clear fault-line, clashing then backing off, quarrelling then making up. They looked like the beginnings of a mouth which might suddenly open and swallow all the waters of the earth.

I shielded my face and stared inland. That grim smudge must be Hull. None of it had anything to do with me now – not Hull, not anywhere. The sheer white sea-light and smothering wind cast me out of myself. I should have felt despair, but I felt nothing. A pure no thing. It was the space where madness might begin, but I clung to it. Then I shut my eyes, bowed my head towards the lifeboat station, and began the journey back.

NORMANDY
An Anniversary

FRIDAY, 4 JUNE 2004

'Of course we're going to leave on time. We're army.' It's early morning, and my father, stepmother and I have parked in a farmyard deep in the Essex countryside, where they live and he was brought up. Sixty years ago, my father was with the Essex Yeomanry, preparing for the invasion of Normandy. Now we're going back with a dozen veterans of the landings, and twenty or so other Yeomen. There they are now, milling round the bus in the silvery hedge-light. Grey heads, walking sticks tapping the wet lane, sloped shoulders.

Like everyone born shortly after 1945, I saw the war flickering at the edge of my childhood. My father stayed in the Territorials, my TV screen was filled with soldiers, and so was my weekly comic. For all that, the fighting felt remote – all the more so because my father very rarely talked about it. I used to think this was his modesty. Now I realize there was another reason. He didn't want the shadow of what he'd been through to fall across my own life. I'm grateful to him for this, but I also wanted to know his story. Today I'm going to hear it at last.

He tried to enlist in 1939, eventually joined the Essex Yeomanry in 1941, and by the spring of 1944 was stationed at Bewley, outside Southampton. He was twenty-three. 'We were confined to camp,' he tells me as we wind round the M25 towards Dover. 'So we knew something was about to happen. Terrible, but exciting too. We'd never seen action and we were ready. It was a bore, though, being cooped up waiting, and some of us couldn't stand it. They nipped out. Faces were seen at Southampton Races.'

In the small hours of 5 June 1944, my father's landing-craft,

15

loaded with self-propelled guns, Bren-carriers and men, set off into the Channel. 'But the weather was impossible – everyone being sick, the sky black as sin, and this awful pitching.' An hour or two later they were back in harbour, astonished that no German planes had seen the false start. Twenty-four hours later they went again. Did he think he was going to die? 'There wasn't much time to think, so I couldn't tell whether I felt lucky or unlucky. We started shelling, you see; we were busy. There was this clock-thing which combined the distance ahead with everything else we needed to know. We were firing on the defences, over the heads of the Dorsets and Hampshires, supporting them. The trick was for me to shout "Fire" when the boat wasn't on the crest of a wave and pointing at the sky, or in a trough and pointing at the sea-bed. When we got to the beach, I thought as senior officer aboard I should be first off, so I climbed into the leading vehicle, which wasn't my own, as soon as the front splashed down. But the boat got stuck on a metal spike, so my carrier filled up with water and stalled. Everything in it floated back to England while I swam ashore. The others got off OK and I found my own vehicle pretty soon, where my batman gave me a change of clothes. If I was going to get killed, I wanted to be wearing dry trousers.'

My father says all this very quietly. He was at Le Hamel, just outside the village of Asnelles, mortar and shell-fire hammering down. Ahead of him, a gently rising beach strewn with wounded men, bodies, burning equipment. 'The beach was a traffic jam, that was the problem. There was a pill-box off to the right where we were meant to be going, and that held us up until one of our sergeants, Palmer, was ordered forward to take it out. A huge great concrete blockhouse with a .88 inside, not like one of those piddly things you see on the English coast; it had already hit six tanks. Palmer got it with his second shot. Just popped the shell in through the letterbox. Then we were off.'

Five hours later we've reached our digs in Bayeux. At supper someone mentions the poet Keith Douglas – this man knew another soldier who'd been at Christ's Hospital School with Douglas, and played in the same rugby team. I've been thinking about

Douglas – about the tough, excellent poems he wrote during the North Africa campaign in 1941–43 ('The Behaviour of Fish in an Egyptian Tea Garden', 'Cairo Jag', 'Desert Flowers'), about his brilliantly hard-edged account of tank warfare, *Alamein to Zem Zem* (1946), and about him leaving Egypt to land in Normandy with the Sherwood Rangers only yards away from my father. I first read him at school, coming off the back of the First World War poets, magnetized by his difference from them. Wilfred Owen meets his enemy face to face in 'Strange Meeting'; Siegfried Sassoon stands beside a corpse with 'ungainly huddled' legs in 'The Dug-Out', Isaac Rosenberg confronts 'a queer sardonic rat' in 'Break of Day in the Trenches'. But Douglas is removed by temperament and machinery to a vital distance, his enemy appearing in 'a dial of glass'. This is partly what makes him feel so modern – fascinated by 'this gentle/obsolescent breed of heroes' fighting alongside him, and detached from them:

> To stand here in the wings of Europe
> Disheartened, I have come away
> From the sick land where in the sun lay
> The gentle slow-eyed murderers
> Of themselves, exquisites under a curse;
> Here to exercise my depleted fury.

SATURDAY, 5 JUNE 2004

It's the little things – the details that official ceremonies ignore, and the hand of history brushes over. 'You've heard about the cattle, have you?' asks one of the Yeomen. 'Dead cattle everywhere after we landed, all with their legs sticking up, stinking to high heaven. It wasn't only the shelling, though. No one was there to milk them, and they died. Nobody thinks to tell you that, do they? Not about the civilians either. Sometimes they were just lying dead on the road and we had to go straight over them.' But my father is anxious to get off the beach at Asnelles, and tells me he moved on through

Arromanche without much trouble, and kept going for the whole of day two.

Everything changed when they reached the open, rolling country we now come to. As dawn broke, the Yeomanry came under fire from two Panzer divisions concealed in a wood on top of a hill my father knew as .103. Our bus lumbers down a track between high hedges, which shrivel suddenly to give a spectacular view. There is the wood on the left, stirring quietly in the hot sunlight. And there on the right is a small sea of bean-plants where my father aimed his gun. He is sitting beside me looking slowly round him, not speaking – but one of his companions, Tony Richardson, has got the microphone. 'This was pretty rough,' he says. 'This was our initiation.' The grey heads are nodding and murmuring in front of me, and one of them recalls that the remains of a Yeoman were recently turned up by a farmer hereabouts. They could tell his regiment from his cap badge, and knew he was a gunner because they found a protractor among the bones. Following my father's gaze, I see an isolated barn as trouble, a church tower as an observation post, hedges as cover.

Sunday, 6 June 2004

None of the Yeomen mentions the war in Iraq. They don't want to talk about it, and if I drag the subject into view, they're quick to defend the soldiers. Yet they don't like the idea of 'world leaders' using their invasion of Nazi-occupied France as a way of justifying this new conflict. They wanted to defeat Hitler, and never thought of themselves as the instruments of politicians. More as decent sorts, doing a decent thing, linked by a decent sort of patriotism. If people call them 'heroes' they demur: this isn't the sort of language they use. Hearing them joking on the bus, it's easy to image what English soldiers were like sixty years ago – or at the battlefields of the Somme, or at Crécy, or at Agincourt for that matter, all of which we drove past on our way down. Blaming their superiors for cock-ups, looking out for one another, living on jokes and ironies. They have the same spirit that Edward Thomas wrote about in 1915 and 1916:

Time swims before me, making as a day
A thousand years, while the broad ploughland oak
Roars mill-like and men strike and bear the stroke
Of war as ever, audacious or resigned,
And God still sits aloft in the array
That we have wrought him, stone-deaf and stone-blind.

The Commemoration Service at the Bayeux cemetery crystal-lizes all this. When we've already stood in the battering heat for two hours, we're told President Chirac will be arriving late, and a scorn-ful cheer rises. The Yeomen say these big services mean less to them than the smaller-scale things, like the one we travel to next by the blockhouse at Asnelles – the one destroyed by Palmer's tank. The village is crammed, hundreds of veterans weaving among tourists, locals, well-wishers, with modern landing-craft lying offshore, and warships flashing in the lavender distance. As we gather round the Yeomanry memorial for speeches and wreath-laying, someone murmurs 'another corner of a foreign field', casting his eyes round the circle of bowed heads. A few hundred yards behind me, the beach where my father landed is buried under an enormous crowd, churning between beach cafés and the retreating tide.

MONDAY, 7 JUNE 2004

The morning after the night before; it might be an anti-climax. But as we bus off under another cloudless sky, past workmen disman-tling stands, there's a mounting excitement. Without the crowds we can see the land for what it was, and feel the pressure of the past more strongly. At Asnelles now the beach is deserted except for a gaggle of children racing sand-yachts. I stroll beyond them towards the place where my father waded ashore, and turn round to see him standing outside the blockhouse. His white hair gleams like metal. Above the memorial, on the gun-slit, there's a fragment smashed out of the concrete where Palmer's first shell bounced off. I pick up a smooth stone from the sand, put it in my pocket, then look up again to see my father disappearing round the back of the blockhouse, where the Germans who survived the explosion staggered out with their uniforms on fire. As I set off to find him, a young woman trots past me on a pony, then breaks into a gallop.

The two time-schemes in my head are distinct now: the hot holiday present and the suffering past. We turn inland, following the route of my father's advance, then stop at the cemetery at Tilly-sur-Seulles to visit the graves of some Yeomen. I slip off to stand at the grave of Douglas, who was killed near here on 9 June. He was a year older than my father. Someone has propped a single large poppy against the headstone, and the card reads 'Vergissmein-nicht' ('Forget-me-not') – the title of one of his best poems, and the only word of German I've seen or heard since we arrived. It's a poem that lingers over the details of decay, though Douglas was killed by a shell-burst which left no visible mark on his body:

> But she would weep to see today
> How on his skin the swart flies move;
> The dust upon the paper eye
> And the burst stomach like a cave.
>
> For here the lover and killer are mingled
> Who had one body and one heart.
> And death who had the soldier singled
> Has done the lover mortal hurt.

What would Douglas have written, had he lived? How would his Normandy poems have affected our sense of the war? His North African work has an exceptional pragmatism. 'There were several of them scattered about,' he says in *Alamein to Zem Zem*, coming across the bodies of some Libyan troops, 'their clothes seeming to have wrapped themselves round the places where arms, legs, or even heads should have been, as though with an instinct for decency. I have noticed this before in photographs of people killed by explosive.' That's the authentic, cool Douglas note, in his poems as well as his prose.

The bus rumbles on, through Aunay-sur-Odon and up the long wooded slope of Mont Piçon, the 'Normandy Alp', from where we can look clear back to the sea. Winding off the mountain, we pause at an innocent-looking jink in a lane. This is where Vere Brook, the second-in-command of the Yeomanry, was killed by a Panzer as he drove forward in his half-track to make a recce. Charles Raymond was alongside him in a jeep, and is with us now. He stands between the hedge and a buckled, buttercup field, with the sun roaring down on his bare head, banging his leg where a bullet went through his thigh. 'There used to be a ditch here. I lay in that until a Typhoon appeared and took out the Germans. Then I hopped back to our boys.' He laughs. 'Three miles. I don't know how I did it.'

TUESDAY, 8 JUNE 2004

Sixty years ago, Douglas had one day left to live. Three years earlier he had asked people to 'Simplify me when I'm dead', and wondered whether they would 'see if I seem/substance or nothing: of the world/deserving mention or charitable oblivion'. He has his answer now.

On the road back to Calais everyone is silent, locking away their memories. By the time we've crossed the Seine they're chatting again, but not about the war any more. 'Look at that!' A huge lorry carrying tree trunks. 'Did you get that?' A sweet-scented cloud billowing behind a tractor cutting hay. I sit across the aisle from my father and his wife, listening to them doing the crossword. After a while I start writing.

Sailing to Italy
A Diary

1

When John Keats first coughed blood, on 3 February 1820, he said to his friend Charles Brown: 'I know the colour of that blood. It is arterial blood. That drop of blood is my death warrant. I must die.' Through the following spring, he was nursed at home in Hampstead, and occasionally in London. His doctors bled him and starved him; his condition deteriorated steadily. By the late summer, it was decided that he should go to Rome, where the climate might do him some good. It was a desperate remedy.

He sailed for Naples from Tower Bridge on 17 September, taking his friend the painter Joseph Severn as a companion. Their boat was the Maria Crowther, a 127-ton, twin-masted, square-rigged brigantine. It had six crew and two other passengers – a Mrs Pigeon and a Miss Cotterell. Miss Cotterell was also consumptive, and joined them at Gravesend on 18 September.

By six in the evening, I've already packed. The children help me. Bag for the ship, bag for ashore. 'Sea-bag, land-bag, sea-bag, land-bag.'

An April sunset – drizzling, and only three days to May Day. Sparrows are fidgeting in the beech tree below my bedroom window. A thrush sings, its voice like loose change flung onto the ground. Beyond it: traffic, a police siren, one boy shouting and another calling back. I feel like a child myself, undefended.

First thing next morning, to St Katharine's Basin, by Tower Bridge. The cab driver wants to know why.

'I'm sailing to Italy.'

'Sailing to Italy?'

Salt Water (Faber and Faber, 1997)

I nod.

'Ever sailed before?'

'Only in the bath.'

I first see *Excelsior* from across the Basin – up to now, it's been photographs. Click: the slim black-painted hull. Click: the two paler masts. Now here they are in fact, but much smaller than I thought. More precarious and antiquated.

The moment I step on deck it's all right. Beautiful elaborate rigging. Big brown sails, all furled. Blue and red paint round the base of the tiller, on the capstan, on hinges. The ensign is tangled round a mast, and the deck worn pale with feet and sun and scrubbing brushes – the nail-heads and board-joints plugged with pitch. I pace from end to end. Eighty feet. That's the same size as the *Maria Crowther*, though this is a fishing smack, not a brig.

I doodle round, meeting the crew. Stewart White, the skipper: a huge man, fifties, with a fringe of thick grey hair. He was brought up in Sizewell on the Suffolk coast, where his father worked as a cowman on the cliffs overlooking the sea. Before the power station was built. 'We went there because my brother had asthma and our doctor told him to run wild and free.' He snaps his fingers. 'My brother was better in a year.'

Paul Collins, mate: younger, moustache, ear-ring, tattoo of the ship on his right forearm.

Bill Ewan, bosun: red-bearded, pipe-smoking, Scottish. The only crew member who's not an East Anglian.

John Cooper, bosun's mate: a thick-set vole.

Clinton Hall, watchleader: smiling, weather-beaten, veiny face.

Claire Walker, second watchleader: round glasses, soft voice, smoking roll-ups. She seems unlike the others, more reserved.

Liz Blake, cook: skirling laugh, fluorescent leggings. The others all wear jeans and brown smocks.

Paul takes me below to store my stuff. I have a forward cabin to myself – the top bunk full of life-belts, me below. There's a cupboard in one wall but it's packed with food. I can stand upright, and turn round without touching the sides. My bunk is like a coffin, rough planks making the wall I'll sleep beside, and long enough for me to stretch out straight. Just.

Then Paul takes me through the rest of the ship. First the galley: a stove and sink in one corner, a central table with folding leaves, a row of paperbacks, six bunks let into two walls. There's also a clock, a barometer, and a copy of the *Psalms* and *New Testament* in a wooden mount inscribed 'Think on These Things'. Next, a heavy iron door to a corridor which leads past the skipper's cabin. The engine room and the chart room. I glimpse a radio, a telephone, dials, blank screens. After these, the crew's quarters in the horseshoe stern – dark dull wood, small empty fireplace, six more bunks.

Climbing back on deck through the aft-hatch ('Mind your head'), Paul tells me the ship was originally a trawler, built in Lowestoft in 1921, then rebuilt between 1985 and 1988. Once there were hundreds like her. Now she's the only one left. 'Back in the eighties there were dozens lost in a single night. There's a song about it. Stewart'll sing it to you.' He means the 1880s.

When I'm above ground again, the deck feels larger – spacious, for all the coils of rope, the hatches and winches and rings, the main boom and the mizzen I have to keep ducking. Yet even there the crew are always in each other's way. The simplest movement means elaborate courtesy and planning. 'No, after you.'

There's a slow fidgety potter and the dock-bridges lift in the sunlight; the ship feels like a race-horse waiting for the start. Shining harness and strength held back. Then we're off.

With the engine pushing us downstream, and the current pressing us inland, we hover in the broad middle of the river. Sunlight and cold wind. Dazzle. My chest tightens as the crew begin hoisting the sails, releasing a slick of rainwater at the final stretch. The tackle leaves snaky wet-prints on the deck.

I sit in the stern. Stewart takes a hefty rope and ties the brass throat of the tiller first from one side, then the other, keeping us steady. A man waving on the dockside by the Basin entrance is immediately tiny.

The tide turns and we pick up speed. To left and right are more-or-less familiar things. Butler's Wharf; the churches and restaurants I know; the Embankment walks and restored streets: modern

'Cup of tea, I think,' says Paul.

We blunder on towards Brighton.

*

The wind chafes and frets, puddling rain off my oilskins, gluing me onto the ship and demanding I understand what all this equipment does. The detail is bewildering: the two masts with their ropes branching like a half-open, wind-stripped umbrella. The tackle worn smooth and gleaming. The sails with their neat holes for reefing and binding. It is a complete world, packed and self-sufficient.

But all afternoon, as the weather lifts and Brighton fades behind us, I look more and more towards the open sea. There are no details out there, just openness.

After supper the wind dies altogether. A beautiful, calm, back-lit evening, with silver mist coming on. I unwind my fishing lines from the stern and let myself drift away.

20 September: The Maria Crowther is off Brighton. A calm sea, but wind from the south-west indicates a storm approaching. It reaches them in mid-afternoon, blowing full in their faces. The ship begins to leak, Keats's cabin is flooded, and the Captain veers round and runs twenty miles back the way they have come, to Dungeness.

May Day. When I come on deck, Stewart says we're in Haslar, round the harbour from Portsmouth. I've never heard of Haslar. It's a marina – a jigsaw of different whitenesses. White veil of cloud overhead, very high and thin. White light on the water. White gin-palaces tethered in line beside us, deserted and dead-still in the early heat.

'You'll be safe here,' Stewart says, meaning on the ship, not in the harbour. 'There's no storm that can sink her. Rocks, that's another thing. But not weather.'

Has he ever been in danger?

'I fell overboard a couple of times. Both times I was fishing. It was off Lowestoft. I just went to pull in my nets, slipped, and over

I went. You wouldn't believe how fast boats go, even when they're not moving.' He rubs his face. 'I'm strong enough, but that boat . . . I kicked my boots off, I can tell you, and when I caught up, all I could do was cling on. Just hang there. I knew I had one chance to get back on board, you see. But I did it. Here I am.'

And the other time?

'The other time I got caught in the nets, that's what saved me.' He rubs his face again. 'I hate the taste of water.'

By mid-morning, there's not a cloud and the sun beating down. Mediterranean heat. We're waiting for provisions but they don't come, and won't come till afternoon. In ordinary life, so much empty time would seem enormous. Here it doesn't matter. The things that seem like events – making coffee, eating lunch – are all over in a moment. But the things that seem like nothing take hours, and fill up the day. Watching the shore complicate as the heat builds (there's a submarine dangling in mid-air outside the museum in the harbour). Trying to work out which rope, tied to which block, works which sail.

I drifted out yesterday. Now I am further off still. Gently rocking. The rigging creaking whenever the wake of a passing boat shifts us. It's the sound of something gradually tightening round my head, intense but painless, putting me to sleep.

21 September: Keats is off Dungeness, becalmed. He goes ashore, walking on the shingle beach, then returns to the Maria Crowther in the evening. He is weak and irritable, resenting the sickly Miss Cotterell.

We sail from Haslar at 10 – the gin palaces squeaking as we disturb them – and pass HMS *Warrior* on the opposite shore, its huge masts rigged like pylons.

It's another baking day, we're all in T-shirts and barefoot, and the crew are tetchy. They want real weather and something to do. 'This is just yachting,' one of them says.

Even so, the ship still feels higgledy-piggledy. Walking to the bow means first seeing who wants to come aft, then dashing from tiller to hatch-top to capstan, remembering not to trip over that rope, this hook, that iron bar, screwed to the deck ('It's not an iron bar – it's a horse,' says Stewart. 'A horse.')

And going below decks is the same. It means calling, checking, calling again. I am a child, finding easy things difficult, learning what is ordinary.

Except nothing stays ordinary. Within half an hour the land behind us is drowned in a mist – the pretty cupola of Portsmouth Cathedral is the last thing to disappear. Then the Isle of Wight begins to emerge alongside us: caravans outside Cowes; what looks like a fortified hotel at Yarmouth; scruffy woods coming down to the shore where a woman is walking her dog.

We have to dock at Yarmouth tonight – I want to spend tomorrow on the island – but the afternoon is ours.

So along the coast we go, tacking in a dozy zigzag, as close as we dare to Hurst Castle in mid-channel. There's a skyline of crumbling yellow stone, but the gun emplacements look as functional as garage doors. Seagulls float in and out of their darkness. A cormorant stands bolt upright on the rocks below: an exclamation mark.

There's no wind but the tide takes us, and as we pass the castle it floats off like a transfer in its watery sky-bowl. I think: that's it for today, we'll turn back in a moment. But the Needles appear, I'd forgotten about them. The smooth green ramp of the island raises its launching pad, bristling and climbing and keeping going – and then . . . Then nothing. No, not quite nothing. Three more stuttering chalk footprints. And then nothing, this time spreading all the way to the horizon.

The lighthouse isn't working yet, it just stands there looking like a toy in the evening light. All the same, we use it as a marker and start back to Yarmouth. While we do this, as though someone has thrown a switch, the tide turns and a wonderful wide O of water appears beside us, ringed by turbulent waves as the currents clash.

22–27 September. The Maria Crowther flounders slowly along the south coast, passing Brighton for the second time.

*

Keats came to the Isle of Wight twice: I want to see his places. But leaving *Excelsior* where we anchored last night, and driving from Yarmouth to Shanklin Chine in the south-east, I feel him slipping away from me – the solid ground swaying if I were still at sea, the whole island barred and bolted. Tightly bound parcels of grazing. Villages hunched over themselves. Kitschy gift-shops selling little framed postcard-poems: 'To a Grandmother'; 'To a Pussy' (rhymes with 'fussy'). When I am on the ship, nowhere, I am close to him without thinking about him. Here he can't keep his place.

Not even in the Chine. 'The wondrous chine', he called it, 'a very great lion', but in his day it had already been stared into stiffness. 'I wish I had as many guineas as there have been spy glasses in it', he said. There's the same long-falling, thin waterfall he would have seen, the same overarching trees, the same drowsy pigeon notes. Did their ancestors watch him here, making the steep climb? It's beautiful, but nothing gives him away.

And again at Carisbrooke, where an ant-army of schoolchildren is on a school trip. I stroll along the castle wall above the village where he stayed. A man in shorts is nailing up bunting outside a pub to celebrate VE Day. A shop window is a kaleidoscope of Union Jacks.

As we sail back past Hurst Castle and the Needles, the sun sets in a brilliant orange sludge and the moon zings up immediately. It's only a slim crescent, but makes a wide stripe on the water.

Bournemouth slides away, a cheerful Lucozade colour.

During supper Paul tells me about a storm he once sailed through off Denmark. Coming on deck he saw a vast wave behind them – overwhelmingly high – but it squeezed underneath and *Excelsior* surfed down its face like a dolphin. He makes a wobbling gesture with one hand, going 'Whoosh': 'Three-hundred-ton wave. If that lot had landed on us we'd have gone down.'

I fall asleep thinking about Keats missing Fanny Brawne, then about him missing his family. His brother George who married and went to America. His sister incarcerated with a guardian. Their dead brother Tom. There's a story of Keats playing cricket

once and getting a black eye; perhaps the children sometimes
played cricket together in the early days? All the boys, anyway.

It's 1812, and their parents are both dead.
The Keats brothers are playing cricket: George bowling,
John at the crease, Tom (who will be the first to die)
at mid-off with the sun in his eyes, seeing stars.

George runs in, it's short, John takes a heave,
and as luck would have it connects very sweetly,
so the ball (which for some reason is white)
travels in a steadily rising line and straight

through Tom's outstretched fingers, leaving a faint
sensation of burning, gathering speed as it goes,
lifting clear over a line of skinny poplars
which have their hair on end and mark the boundary

not just of the pitch but of the countryside itself,
dividing it from London, where the boys once lived,
and over which now the cricket ball is still
carrying and brightly visible – a pure white dot

glowing and dropping a few flakes of fire
onto the roofs, graveyards and gardens below,
which means anyone there who might suddenly glance up
would surely say: God! A new star! Or maybe a planet?

Up at dawn the next morning to see Lulworth Cove. It's lunar grey
in the early mist. On one bulbous hill, caravans flash their chain-
mail. In the cove itself there's a black fuzz of trees and a fishing
boat riding at anchor. I think about what I know: of Hardy, of the
tourists, of the army here (our chart warns us they sometimes fire
out to sea). But none of these things connects with the place now.
It is only itself – the darkening green hollows slipping into each
other; the deserted shore turning over its stones; the sea slithering
through cold holes in the chalk.

'Seen enough?' says Stewart, flapping his arms to keep warm. 'All right, then?'

The crew reset the sails and as we slide west towards Weymouth the mist burns away. All along the coast, sea-shapes repeat the wave-patterns of the cliffs.

Last night, at supper in the galley, we heard Stewart on deck playing his squeeze-box and singing. When I ask him about it now he gives an embarrassed laugh. 'Well, I sing in the pubs round Suffolk, you know,' he says, 'when I'm not doing this.' He pats the tiller, 'I've got hundreds of songs – folk songs, that is. They don't mean so much until you've been to sea. I mean: they're all true. You can learn things from them. I don't read poetry but I reckon they're poetry.' He opens and shuts his hands as if he's playing. Enormous splayed hands. His big head with its monkish fringe of hair.

It's hotter than ever today, freakishly hot. In the afternoon I lie on deck and topple into and out of sleep: the ship rocking forward, wind running down the sails in useless ripples, the engine puttering. Everything we pass on shore, the villages on tiptoe at the cliff edge, the smooth fields where cattle keep their heads down – all these things begin and end in the same instant.

With Stewart again. 'And I'll tell you another thing. See this?' This means the radar, which stands in the hatch in front of the tiller. Liquid crystals flicker at the foot of the screen, telling us the depth of the water we're sailing through, and bands of blue, red and yellow confirm it, and show whether the sea-bed is soft or rocky. 'I can tune it to show fish,' Stewart says. 'See?' Immediately, a rag of red bursts into the blue. Mackerel bunching together, then away in a fraying comet's tail. 'What do you think? Better put out your lines. You never know.'

Another furious, squashy sunset – rotting crimson and purple fruit – then darkness at one bound.

*

By morning we're off Teignmouth and have to stoodge around waiting for high water so we can enter the harbour. Russet cliffs tumbling into choppy waves. The town is another model village from this distance: Lego houses, a church, the Ness curling round to shelter the docks. I catch a lineful of mackerel and we have them for breakfast, rolled in oats.

When Keats nursed his brother Tom here in 1818 it rained almost continuously. He called it 'a splashy, rainy, misty, snowy, foggy, haily, floody, muddy, slipshod country'. Today it's cloudless, and when I go ashore to visit the place he stayed, everyone's in shirt-sleeves and dark glasses.

There's no trace of him in his house: new windows, the façade re-covered, his room a plain cube filled with Indian rugs and statues. When I get back to the ship I'm ready to leave at once, but we can't. High tide is at 10 tomorrow; we'll have to wait.

I lie in my cabin, trying to think what it will mean to lose sight of land. The photograph of a cruise ship comes into my head, and streamers flung down by the passengers to people waving them off on the quay. When the steamers break, the journey begins. It's like that. All week the coastline has been like a long ribbon held in my hand – a ribbon tied at its far, invisible end to London and everyday things, but all the time tightening and wearing out, humming with tension.

Tomorrow I shall simply let go.

*

What's the date today? 6 May 1995, says Stewart, counting on his thick fingers. It doesn't seem to mean anything but I repeat it. 6 May. The day I leave England.

I've taken my place in the stern by 9.30, watching the crew set to work. Hauling ropes. Unfurling sails. People are calling out to us from the harbour wall – voices I don't know. As we leave the entrance to the harbour, a family clambers into a blow-up dinghy and races out to circle us, red-faced and laughing. We wave down to them solemnly.

Solemnly. The mood is already different, even though we're still close to the shore. More serious. Suppressed excitement and anxiety.

The harbour master at Teignmouth has given Stewart two brill which he fillets on a hatch-lid, then sluices with sea water. He talks about the local council elections last Thursday. 'I don't care what colour people vote. Red, blue, yellow. I just want people to speak their minds.'

A huge murky jellyfish slides past – the phallic dome and unfinished-looking rest of it. And another cormorant, the sunlight so bright on its beak, it looks as though it's carrying a fish.

Then I start fishing myself. Twenty-four mackerel in an hour. Moon-coloured bellies, jet heads, the iridescent green-blue on the top of the body. The efficiency of their design!

In the early evening, at Start Point, we leave the land behind. A mist wraps it first, cloaking a school of small sailing boats. Then a lighthouse starts, the juddering flash seeming to throw the whole head of land out to sea. One moment when I look back, the hills are still there, half lit. When I look again, only a second later, they've gone.

Now the entire world is the boat – nothing else – creaking forward so slowly we might actually be standing still.

Three gulls have found a shoal of fish, plunging and popping up gobbling. Liz the cook throws out some peelings and more gulls arrive, circling the rubbish, swooping to collect a piece, climbing, and dropping it when they discover it's disgusting.

Supper and in my cabin by 9.30. When I spin my radio dial, all the voices that reach me sound frantic. Then I lie in the dark, asking myself questions. For instance: what colour are the sails exactly? Red? Brown? Blood? Liver? Tan? Tan. But something to do with fire as well, like the line of flame at the edge of a piece of burning paper. I roll this round my mind and it takes me back to my last birthday, then forward to now again.

> The air on my birthday weighed much more,
> even bringing me down to my knees once,
> so the blank sheet I should have been writing on
> flipped out of my hand into the fire and caught.
>
> I felt my ghost beginning to take shape inside me –

a shrug through my whole body, a mirror-flash –
and its spongy eyes swivelling round to discover
the low-ceilinged room where it will one day live.

The flames curled through the white in a steady line,
driving before them a narrow brown band
which was no longer paper and not yet fire
but the in-between where things give up or start.

*

My first morning with no sight of land.

A pigeon has joined us – a battered-looking racer with one pale-green ring round its leg and one turquoise. Clinton gives it some water and bread, but the others say they're going to eat it. The pigeon puffs out its breast feathers, cocks its head, and inspects them with a glittering eye. Maybe it only speaks French, someone suggests. The pigeon stamps in its water bowl, then wanders around the deck shitting.

Somebody says: the wonderful thing about sailing is you never know what's going to happen next. For most of today, nothing happens next. The pigeon attempts a few departures, circles the ship, and returns. The conversations on deck also circle and return. At 10.30 there's an astonishing CRACK out of the blue. Concorde breaking the sound barrier; we see its vapour trail curving away west.

We've planned to make a hundred miles a day, and when I ask Stewart how we're doing, he tells me the engine broke last night. He seems puzzled but not worried. 'Never mind. We'll fix it.' Various members of the crew disappear at intervals into the engine room; there's the sound of tinkering; then they emerge, shrugging. Paul holds a bit of the engine and rubs it with a towel. 'We've got a week,' Stewart says. 'Time to build a new engine if need be.' With what, I wonder.

Standing in the bow, I watch a rib of dark something slipping towards us. Weed? Debris? It's a stick, shaped like a longbow, turning gently over and over in the swell so it's not like a stick any more, but a bobbin. A bobbin bob-bob-bobbin' along. Occasionally cuttlefish scoot past – miniature deserted surf-boards.

The line of the horizon hardens, and people say this means lower air pressure and rain. There's no sign of it. After lunch I fall asleep, and wake to find one mackerel has attached itself to my line. I fish in earnest for a while, but there's nothing doing.

Still drowsy by evening, when I realize I've got a sore throat. Mysteriously, it goes after a couple of hours, and I talk to Liz on deck, watching a fog creep up behind us. One minute there's sun and warmth, the next wetness, semi-darkness, the sea gun-metal with no depth. Stewart appears with a foghorn – a big brown box like an old-fashioned projector. When he winds the handle it gives an alarmed moaning. I think of the bottle-top lowings I heard off the Isle of Wight – and beyond them of lying in bed in Hull nearly twenty years ago, hearing the buoys on the River Humber.

I roll into bed full of the sadness of that time, and try to banish it by listening to the radio again. Chirac is the new President of France. The Queen has opened the VE Day celebrations. These pieces of news reach me like reports from Mars.

The sea's much rougher tonight, and my sleeping-bag is made of slippy stuff which means I slither around with every roll and dip. It's easiest to lie on my back, but when I've done this for an hour, I turn onto my right and wedge against the side-board of my bunk. My head still sways with the swell – as if it's separate from the rest of me. Then over onto my back again.

Suddenly there's a clinking and a mad whipping sound on deck, which gives me a spurt of panic. After that, quiet again: the sense of rushing forward, of plunging speed, but I know it's not fast really. I try not to think about how much black water there is beneath me, how far we are from land, but Ruth comes into my mind, and my grandmother, both drowned. Falling asleep, I suppose I wouldn't make any effort to escape, if water burst down the hatches.

28 September: Still no favourable wind. The Maria Crowther puts in at Portsmouth for 24 hours. Keats goes ashore and visits his friends John and Laetitia Snook, at Bedhampton, near Chichester. He hears that Charles Brown is visiting near by, but doesn't have time to meet him and returns to the Maria Crowther the following day.

'Well, you're in it now,' says Stewart when I come on deck. He means the Bay of Biscay – and it's only two days since we left Devon. I look around as if I expected to see a sign. The sky has lifted, but not much. The swell is a large sullen shrug, each wave carrying us several feet forward even though the following wave tries to suck us back. And the deck lies at a steep angle, with sudden twisting lurches. Now and then, without warning, breakers crash over the sides and wither through the bilges.

John comes to talk. He tells me he's fifty-nine, and this is his last deep-sea voyage. He has a wife and two children near Norwich, in a house he bought twenty-odd years ago with money earned in Australia. He says he likes books about hoboes, especially W. H. Davies. His wide impatient face. 'Are you enjoying it?' he asks. 'It's no good thinking of home – there's nothing you can do about it, or it about you. You just have to sit here and watch it all slip past.'

The foghorn has disappeared from deck, and the pigeon. I wonder who killed it.

At breakfast, Paul starts talking about the war in Bosnia. 'If there is a God, I think he's Jehovah, making us suffer unto the sixth and seventh generation.' He has a way of looking down and away when he's saying something important, stroking the inside of his left arm with his right hand. 'Sometimes I don't think we deserve to survive, we species known as Man.' His hair flops round his face and he lunges forward to fork down bacon and slippery fried egg.

A tanker inches across the horizon, heading back to England. Our wake, which yesterday looked like the track of a steam iron through clothes, is now a quick turbulent trace stippled with foam.

Where is Keats in all this? I can't go back home and find him, full of news. But I can look at the sea and imagine what it made him feel. Emptiness. The wide wilderness of water. Monotony of the waves. These are all things which stop time, and turn each different moment into the same moment, each hour into one that could equally well be the hour before or the hour after. And simultane-

37

ously: the knowledge of moving forward. The flotsam drifting past. The knots of weed. A plank from a broken crate. All these say: the future is waiting, landfall is waiting.

Noon. We've made eighty-six miles in the last fourteen hours but the wind is building now, and colder, which means we may make up some time. All the same, it's fickle and fluky: the ship judders, sprinting for a moment then stalled, the sails whipped full then hanging slack again. It's queasy-making, stupefying. Nobody comes on deck except the watch, who take it in half-hour turns to work the tiller. Every few minutes they inspect the compass, housed in the hatch in front of them at knee height, then adjust the tiller and sit down on the rope which holds it, keeping the course steady.

By mid-afternoon we've reached the Continental shelf, where the sea bed dives from eighty-odd metres down to four miles. If it were earlier in the year we'd see whales here, feeding on the plankton which teems upwards as the cold deep meets the warmer current. I hang over the black water – darkness packed solid beneath me. Nothingness. Then I look up. White horses shamble past aimlessly. A red-and-black tanker, going three times our speed. A gannet cresting the swell, then flipping airborne, scrutinizing us, before it planes away into the distance.

Do the crew love being at sea so much because their lives on land are disappointing? They never talk about home, or, if they do, speak stiltedly. Stewart says, 'Oh well; I live in Lowestoft. I just don't . . . I can't see the sea from my house.'

I stand with my back to the main mast, looking straight ahead, and find myself thinking of Soho. Now is about the time I might be going out to supper. Bustle and bright windows. Stepping off the pavement into the road because there are so many people. Blares of music. Chewing-gum. Glossy heaps of bin-bags. Not long before Keats's day, these streets were still open fields and huntsmen coursing hares. I don't want to be there, I want to be here. But I miss it.

In a level meadow
skirting the city

the huntsman hollas
So-ho! So-ho!

Streets step forward
to stamp out the grazing,

clouds sink down
weeping brick dust and slate,

and a madcap hare
bolts from the blue

to end his days
in a print under tissue,

a zigzag of milk
dribbled in coffee,

the terrified eye
of a dragon from China,

the brindled bush
some prick works through

with his mouth half asleep
and the girl's too:

Sooo-hooo! Sooo-hooo!

In my bunk by 9. Still vaguely light, but no more point in the day. Last night as soon as darkness fell there were streaks of phosphorescence in the water, and spangling stars on deck – the plankton fretted into brilliant life. Tonight we're too far from land, and there's none.

I turn the dial on my radio once again, running through all the stations, trying all the frequencies. I get a snatch of French, of Spanish, a buzzy riff of rock-'n'-roll. Otherwise just the rush of empty space, and the slap-dribble-slap of waves against my cabin wall.

29 September: The Maria Crowther sails from Portsmouth, past Yarmouth on the Isle of Wight, past the Needles, and along the Dorset coast towards Lulworth.

I forgot to say: last night I helped set a larger jib. Taking down the old one was like felling a tree: a soft crash and the sky suddenly empty. The new sail seemed comforting as soon as we had it up – shelter as well as energy.

This morning the wind has worked round to the east and we've changed tack. Still cold, still grey without rain, the ship sailing more evenly. All the same, it could be yesterday. Or the day before.

Paul hung a bucket over the side to sluice down the deck, and brought up a crab, pale green, which lay on its back wriggling, then got booted over the side. What did it think had happened? A glimpse of the afterlife.

Long, blank morning, which suddenly concentrates at midday. The wind drops, the sun bursts out, and we hit a big shoal of mackerel. Twenty in half an hour, some around two pounds. I stop when there's enough for supper and, as I'm cleaning them over the side, a French turbo-prop, checking on fishing quotas, drones very low over us from the west. We can see the pilot in his cockpit – bareheaded, moustached, and grinning. Everyone waves and bellows as he drenches us with his racket. When the plane disappears into the pale south, there's an awkward silence, as though we're embarrassed to have shown ourselves pleased to see a new face.

In the afternoon I start reading *Don Juan*. Keats read Books 1 and 2 on his voyage, protesting that Byron made gay things solemn and solemn things gay. The poem is fitted to annoy him. Its mockery of hoping that posterity will bring what life denies. Its laughter at lovesick youths who fill landscapes with gods and goddesses.

I carry on reading for hours, sitting on the lifeboat-case astern, my feet on the tiller-shaft where it sinks through a hole into the sea. The water here is swimming-pool clear, catching the light off the keel, which is ochre.

Occasional conversations. With Bill, who worked on an oil rig off the Faroes for a while, made enough money to buy a six-bedroom house, then gave up. 'There were ninety-odd people on that rig and only two I'd want to have a drink with ashore. You might think I'm a bit rough, but you should see them.' He lights his pipe with the blowtorch he's using to melt pitch. Bits of his beard catch fire and he pats himself out.

At some stage it occurs to me that I've never been so bored in my life. But I don't want to be anywhere else. My boredom isn't pain; it's like a trance. Sometimes I feel as though I've been taken out of myself and am floating round the ship like Ariel. At others, as though my brain were lying on a wooden slab and shallow water sloshing over it, wearing me down to a sliver. My fishing line droops off the stern, and when I tweak and release it I think I'm fishing for minutes. I never catch one.

'Bloody Odin has let us down,' says Stewart, heaving into his orange jacket – 'Port of Felixstowe' fading across the back, kapok leaking from one elbow.

Supper at 6.30. It's a relief to have something to do, but the meal passes in near silence and by 7 it's over. Stewart produces his squeeze-box and sings 'Fiddler's Green'. The squeeze-box has silver filigree work at either end and tiny keys. It's almost impossible for his big fingers to hit only one note at a time. Even the jolly songs sound melancholy, fading into vacancy.

To bed but no sleep. The near-calm means the mainsail makes a new whining creak, very loud.

30 September: Still calm. Keats goes ashore at intervals: Studland, Holworth, Lulworth. He writes to Charles Brown about Fanny Brawne, the woman he loves and has left behind in Hampstead.

'The thought of leaving Miss Brawne is beyond everything horrible – the sense of darkness coming over me – I eternally see her figure eternally vanishing. Some of the phrases she was in the habit of using during my nursing at Wentworth Place ring in my ears – Is there another life? Shall I awake and find all this a dream? There must be – we cannot be created for this sort of suffering.'

Eventually, in the early morning, I fall asleep for a few hours, then wake up bleary and irritable. My shoulder aches, my hair is filthy and itchy. We've spent part of the night going backwards, and even though there's some wind now, it's only inching us forward. The crew seem adamant the engine can't be mended, though won't say what's wrong with it. 'You'll just have to chew fat.' A gannet drifts past, then climbs and dives. It looks almost as big as yesterday's aeroplane.

Paul throws some money into the waves. 'That's for Neptune. I reckon there must be a fortune down there.' All that happens is two more tankers appear. Behind them, bulbous rain clouds drag along the horizon, keeping pace with us. A rag of lavatory paper, tied to the rigging to show the direction of the wind, flutters its white flag. Jesus God, it's still only 10.30.

Just before lunch Paul notices one of the fishing lines is heavy in the water and starts hauling it in. It's a shark – a young one – silvery on top like a jet fighter as it lashes towards us through the water, meek white underneath when it rolls over. We winch it on board, still writhing and toiling, giving off a faint smell of ammonia.

There's great jostling and jockeying as everyone crowds round, tries not to get flailed, snaps photographs. The wide mirthless mouth, dragged open by the hook, looks senile. Liz sticks her head out of the fore-hatch and says she won't cook it. Paul puts on a pair of thick gloves and seizes it by the tail; the hook falls out of its mouth. 'It's a thresher,' says Stewart, pointing to the long tail fin.

As Paul lowers it back overboard, I glance beyond him into the flat sea and a whale appears, a hundred yards off the stern. The immense oily back, the spout exploding upwards from the blowhole with a world-weary moan. When it subsides, it leaves a circle of dead calm. Somebody shouts 'There she blows!' – the phrase children use as a joke and now is nothing but the truth. Paul drops the shark back into the water, where it lies still and stunned for a second, then whiplashes its whole body and melts into the blue.

For the rest of the afternoon we are completely becalmed. Big drizzly clouds lumber alongside and one drifts directly overhead, paints the deck dark brown, then abandons us to weak sunlight again. Everyone is quiet and hypnotized. Towards dusk, Stewart tells me he once sailed up from Corunna through these waters in a tanker. A hurricane overtook them, stripping all the new paint off their ship, mangling ladders, dropping them in such deep hollows they couldn't see the horizon. Near by were some small French fishing boats 'just bobbing up and down like corks. I could see the old boys leaning on the rails with their arms folded, staring at us. Just bobbing up and down like corks.'

When supper is over, Paul calls us up on deck. A school of dolphins is overtaking to port. They're too far away to see clearly, and we can't hear them, but they're still magical – the bodies pulled taut, the mute white splash as they dive, the zest and delight. We whistle and bang the side of the ship to call them closer but they ignore us, leaping in and out of their own world.

At midnight a dappling sound against the side of my cabin wakes me. We're moving. Then at 3.50 a tremendous rattling and creaking and the wind leaps up, as though someone has started an engine. The ship jumps forward in long even bounds, heaving me from side to side in my bunk as we begin to make real headway. There's some energetic pumping from the heads as the watch changes, and excitement running through all the silent bunks. My head is filled with expectation, though expectation of what, I'm not sure. Movement for its own sake.

1 October: The wind veers slowly round to north-east, and the Maria Crowther gradually loses sight of land. As the cliffs of Dorset fade, Severn finds Keats on deck, poring over the sonnet 'Bright Star'. Mistakenly, he thinks Keats has just written it; in fact he finished it several months before, and has now only transcribed it. 'Pillowed upon my fair love's ripening breast . . . So live for ever – or else swoon to death.'

Sleep from 6 to 8, then on deck. A battlefield. Everything drenched, the watch in padded boilersuits and hats with flaps over their ears. Rain clouds massing on all sides, with hot sunshine squirting in between. After an hour or so, a squall catches us, and sends the bowsprit daggering into deep waves as we drive ahead. We winch in the bowsprit a little – there's some danger it might snap – and a tremendous wave leaps over the bows, saturating us all and knocking Claire off her feet. She slithers across the deck like someone riding down a snow-hill on a tray, and crashes into the side. She's all right. Another huge wave, this one filling our mouths, ears, pockets. We reel back to the stern like drunks, and take shelter behind a flap of canvas by the tiller. But the rain still finds us, stinging, making us shout when we speak at all. Stewart says the crew think he should take in the topsail, it puts so much weight on the mast. But there's no need. 'It's a good stick,' he says. I squint up at the top. The weathervane looks jammed, it's so steady.

After three-quarters of an hour the rain goes, and there's a moment of calm. The ship flops sickeningly. A gaggle of seagulls performs a flypast.

I scramble down to the chart room. By the end of yesterday we were sixty miles off the Spanish coast – too far east. With last night's and today's wind we are sailing north-west – going backwards, in fact, so we can get clear of Cape Finisterre.

Come midday, we've travelled far enough, and turn south again. Stewart thinks we should make Gibraltar within a week. I want to ask him what day we'll arrive, then realize it doesn't matter. I don't care. We must be coming near to the middle of May now, but that doesn't matter either.

By mid-afternoon we're as far south as we were this time yesterday, but forty miles further west. More sodden clouds surround us. These look angrier than any we've seen before, and by evening the wind is strong. A storm is coming. After days of praying for wind, the thing itself is daunting. Skies going black, rigging beginning to whine, everyone shrugging into oilskins, tying ropes round their waists to lash themselves onto the ship.

It reaches us at sunset: gigantic swell and waves the size of houses, their tops whipped into foam and spuming over the bows. The bowsprit lunges into the water, vanishing altogether, then slicing up through collapsing white. The decks flood and empty, flood and empty, but the sea never gives up. It wants to smother us completely, charging towards us from all sides. It never occurs to me that we might sink. In fact it makes me want more – more rage, more danger. I want it to turn me inside-out, and at one point, when no one is looking, I untie myself from the rigging and move towards the bow, fastening myself on again where the waves will break over me more easily.

I cling there for an hour, scoured and hammered, then suddenly can't deal with it any more. So I crawl down to my cabin, strip off my oilskins and stretch out. But there's no chance of sleep. Sleep isn't what I want. I want something definite and final. What I get is a whole new orchestra of creaks and moans, and something rapping against the cabin wall with sharp irregular clunks. I wedge a pillow against the wall by my head, another by my hips, and the angle of our sailing keeps me pressed there.

Around midnight, there's a burst of shouting. Perhaps this is what I'm waiting for. Perhaps this is it.

It is. Even in the darkness, I can feel the ship poised on the crest of a mountainous wave – then just a wind-filled silence. We've taken off! We're flying! The whole length of the ship has launched clear of the sea and is ploughing through thin air. Only one thing can happen next, so I shut my eyes tight. Two. Three. Four. There's a shattering crash and roll, and a human groan runs through the entire length of the hull. It's the sound of supplication, but it won't do any good. The same thing is going to happen again. We take off, we lurch through space, we plummet down into a trough. I press my pillow over my head, as if I'm trying to suffocate myself, and can't tell how long I hold it there.

When I lift it away I can hear shouting again, and the grind of the capstan winding in a sail. The water beside me is making its two sounds, the close-up gurgle and the further roaring rush. I get up and duck into the galley without knowing why. Liz is there, leaning against the table, staring at a crossword torn from a two-week-old paper. The table bucks and slides beneath our hands as we stumble through a few clues together. Current account: fifteen letters. Electricity bill. Water leaks onto our heads through the deck. Sticky brown water, stained with pitch.

2 October: Favourable winds. The Maria Crowther is now out of sight of land, driving steadily south.

Early next morning. The corridor outside my cabin is flooded – water rocking fiercely over a sail that's been flung down in the night. I squint up through the hatch. The sky is thunderous, and enormous iron waves are crashing over the prow. Saturation. It's impossible to make myself heard, so I just stand there, my head poking out, listening to the kettle in the galley below me, slopping its water onto the hot-plate with a soothing sssh, ssssh, sssh.

I don't want to miss anything, so duck back to my cabin, climb into my oilskins, then scuttle aft and tie myself back onto the rigging. The gale has blown all night – mostly force 9, now falling to 8. A container ship is smashing north, close to us, and Paul is hoisting the ensign. Water parted from the sea, as Keats said in his storm.

For the next hour we cling tight. Someone is being sick in the bow, gripping the ropes as if crucified. Stewart, at the tiller, decides there's too much sail up, and gives orders I can barely hear. The crew, tangling with the blocks and tackle on deck, repeatedly vanish as walls of water shatter over them. Paul climbs barefoot into a fold of the mainsail, threading a rope to reef it, and swings there like a child in a papoose. As the mast dips it takes him out over the sea, then hoists him upright again. He keeps shouting to Stewart. He's loving it.

At ten the skies abruptly turn blue and the gale blows itself out. Nobody says anything. Is that all? Will it come back? For the next two hours we bowl along rapidly, the shadow of our sails casting over and away, the sunlight shielded, then released. Most of us barely slept last night, but we all stay on deck. The scrubbed sea. The bow-wave creaming. Clinton ties the tiller into position and sits on the rope as though it were a hammock. He knows the storm's over and has decided to be cheerful. 'Did you see Paul up there?' he asks, swinging his legs. 'Think of all those poor buggers at home now, in their offices. Burrr!'

Around lunchtime another smaller school of dolphins sweeps

close to the boat on the port side, but they show no interest in us and silently disappear. On the stern, at exactly the same time, there's an empty yellow life-jacket. 'Nobody in it,' says Stewart quietly. The rest of the crew look away. A little later, we hear an urgent voice bursting onto the radio – a boat calling Finisterre. 'Charlie Alpha Foxtrot. Charlie Alpha Foxtrot.' Finisterre answers. 'Medico, medico,' says the voice, but we can't hear why. The voice breaks up and there's nothing else.

At sunset, the sea and sky steadier, a big wind still following. Fifteen or twenty more dolphins bomb towards us through the swell. Pale wriggling bellies and sleek backs just visible inside their cliff of water, then leaping and diving as they reach the trough. They shoal round the prow, slinking over and under each other, up to and away from the ship, making excited high-pitched whinnies. We think they're here for our sake: the candid roll to show their neutral undersides; the intimate blowholes as they surface; the mouths carved in a cartoon smile. But of course they are pleasing themselves, not us. We mean nothing to them, and when they have played long enough they shear away. We go to supper in silence.

Before bed we hang the topsail, unreef the mainsail and mizzen. With eight of us, it takes an hour of hard work. The ship settles easily when this is done, the sea subsiding and sweeping us forward. In the last twenty-four hours we've made a hundred and thirty miles. More than twice what we managed in Biscay.

The wind sat in the north-east all night and now there's a spectacular dawn, the sun straining and blobbing in purple clouds, then hesitating, hesitating, before erupting into triumphant blue.

At nine, when it's already warm, there's a weather report of a gale in south Finisterre. Paul's heard it, and we question him in succession, each wanting him to say something new. Will there be any wind for us? Will we get where we want to be? He tells us everything will be all right, but we don't believe him. Anyway, we're hardly in Finisterre now. We're in Trafalgar.

Trafalgar. On land, history leaves its scar however we plough up battlefields, tear down buildings, spread new estates and factories. Out here it leaves no mark; it just survives in the names. The

Solent, where people watched the Spanish Armada blow past, then waited for Napoleon, and Hitler. Corunna, which we passed the day before yesterday. Cape St Vincent and Trafalgar which are to come. Their names roll through my head and I see ripped sails, cracked masts, blazing rigging – but none of it for long. In a moment I'm watching the waves again. The one to come like the one gone by. Always new but always the same.

By midday there's no wind at all, just low, flat, grey, unbroken cloud.

Something inside me gives way, and I slump at my place in the stern all afternoon, watching the wind run its hand listlessly down the sails. This is not boredom like before. This is real nothing, which gouges a hole in my skull and drags out my eyes on stalks to stare into it: failure; despair; disgust curdling into rage. When one of the crew comes up to me I look straight through him. Then he belches vilely and grins: 'Wind.' I want to stick a marlin spike into his chest and throw him to the shark which has just idled past, its fin slick and alert.

No change at 6.30, when a face looks out of a hatch and calls 'Supper'. It's the last thing I want. I just need today over and done with. 'Come on. Supper.' I force myself down into the galley. Each plate is piled enormously. The stove puffs and simmers in its corner.

Then back to the stern again, watching our wake form and scribble itself out, form and scribble itself out. At home, days can be steered round, or drunk into oblivion. This one has had to be endured. Two hours until it's worth even trying to sleep, and the prospect of the same thing tomorrow. Please God make the wind blow.

15 October: The Maria Crowther is caught in a severe storm as she reaches the Bay of Biscay. The passengers are all ill and take to their bunks once again.

Something is slinking against my cabin wall. Something I knew perfectly well, but which after a day's silence already seems strange.

Water, of course. Water purling past me. We're moving again: the tackle clunking as we change direction; the boom giving its tiny squeak as the mainsail fills.

I angle myself across the bunk to match the angle of the ship. As the slow hours ripple past, their minutes break into half-minutes, their half-minutes into seconds. And as each fragment snaps off and falls away, a wave breaks in its wake. Not a wave fribbling against the hull, but a wave inside my head. I am being cleaned out; rubbed away. I fall asleep towards dawn, diluted into the nothing around me.

Climbing on deck at eight: a row of glum faces. The wind has shifted to the south and all night we've sailed due east, making no progress down our course.

I stand next to Stewart at the tiller, expecting disappointment to crash down on me, squaring my shoulders to take its load. But whatever happened last night is still working. It doesn't matter any more that we can't meet deadlines. What matters is being here, seeing things I'll never see again.

Paul organizes a deck-scrub, more to rally people than anything, and as I duck forward to collect my broom, I look directly ahead. There's misty drizzle, and a tight yellow amphitheatre of sun.

Land.

A ridge of hills, jumbled pink and white houses. The sun fades and the scene with it, but inside half an hour the whole coast is back again. A town straight ahead, docks to the left.

We crowd into the bows, clumped together like people in a photograph. This should be marvellous, I tell myself, and hold my breath waiting for it to strike. The docks grow clearer: the insect-cranes and the ziggurat-containers. And the shore – a bow of white sand, with a fairground just beyond the ridge of dunes. There's a big top, the sloping roof striped pink and cream. The Ferris wheel hangs at a standstill.

'What do you think was the first thing Mrs da Gama said to Vasco when he came back?' I ask no one in particular.

'Christ, you smell,' says Stewart. 'That's what my wife always says to me.'

Everyone laughs, but it's a thin, melancholy sound, and I turn away down the deck. I don't want to see this place. It's too soon. I don't want to leave the ship either. Not this ship and not these people.

'What land is it?' I hear somebody asking.

'Oporto,' comes the answer.

'Foreign land,' says Stewart.

16 October: Today, and for the next two weeks, the Maria Crowther sails steadily south, stalling briefly in a calm off Cape St Vincent, at the southern tip of Portugal, and heaving to shortly afterwards when challenged by a man-o'-war. Keats's health improves as he approaches Gibraltar, but when he enters the Mediterranean he haemorrhages badly, and the last week before they reach Naples is hard going.

Yesterday there was a decision to take. We need water and provisions. Should we put in at Oporto, or head south for Lisbon, a hundred miles away? It seemed best to keep going, which meant Lisbon.

All last afternoon, and all night, we tacked along the Portuguese coast. Around dawn, there's the dismal clank of the anchor going down. We've stopped. For what feels like the millionth time, I squeeze out of the hatch on deck and squinny round. We're off a bare beach, a beach identical to the one we saw yesterday, only now there's a black jetty away to the right, and different dock cranes faintly visible beyond it.

Stewart calls us round the tiller. He says we've made only forty miles since Oporto and this means Lisbon is impossible. We need the provisions too badly. We have to turn back. 'How can we do that?' someone asks, and we all stare at the sky as if we didn't know what was there. Emptiness is there. Clouds like the smoke from wet sticks. The reflection of charcoal waves. We are completely becalmed.

As heat concentrates over the land, a feeble wind gathers, and by early afternoon we've started to tack north up the coast again. I doze in the lifeboat, clasping my hands behind my head. The sun comes out, the long beach unwinds, the hills gather and step out of their mist. That's our destination ahead – where those chimneys are billowing – but we never get any closer. I curl down into my nest and think I could stay like this for ever, living this in-between life.

*

It seems years since someone said: you never know what's going to happen next at sea. We expected to drift back along the coast, no trouble, but a strong south-westerly arrived in the early hours, and by dawn we're churning off Oporto in North Sea weather. There's cold, driving rain. The clouds are so low they even cover the tops of cranes in the port.

At ten, Stewart gets word that he can enter the harbour. Has he let them know we don't have an engine? He once told me, a long time ago, that ships like *Excelsior* never sink, they go down only when they hit something. This is a difficult entrance: a gigantic grey-stone pier to the left, a snub smaller one to the right, and the strong cross wind.

The crew stand at their stations by the rigging, waiting for orders, but Stewart keeps his eyes on the two piers. Then he angles the ship as if she were a dart, one massive hand gripping the throat of the tiller.

'Everybody ready? Here we go.'

It's finished almost before it starts, leaving me no time to feel anything. We whisk over the struggling waves, the sheltering walls loom round us, and the crew collapse the sails in a crashing flurry, both booms thumping down like wreckage. 'Drop the hook!' Stewart shouts. 'Drop it now!' The anchor chain makes its scrabbling rush and we stop dead, the ship groaning as we slew round to starboard. Paul cheers, standing among the heaped-up sails like someone who's killed a dragon. 'You won't often see sailing like that,' he says, grinning at me. Bill shouts, 'Tobacco!'

The first thing is simply to look around. It's a dismal place. Through the rain: green and white containers; a tanker with a lopsided lifeboat dangling astern; the concrete wall of the harbour daubed with the names of absent ships; fishing boats trailing clouds of seagulls.

A giant digger is filling a Russian tanker with gravel; every few minutes there's a clattering roar as another load tips in.

For the first time since leaving London, I feel sick. If we're going to get off here, I want to do it immediately. But we need someone to tow us ashore; without our engine, we're stranded.

A life-size plastic arm, torn from a doll, twists past us. The fingers have hooked a tuft of black weed.

After five hours, an enormous tug throbs alongside and throws two ropes astern, one big orange tie at the front. It's like watching TV – vivid but nothing to do with me. The trim fellow at the helm with his tartan shirt and metal-frame specs: he looks like a bank clerk. The brutal prow rears to show 'Monte Xisto' in big white letters.

Something goes wrong. The tug's too powerful to tow us safely, and as the fore-rope takes the strain, it wrenches the stanchion away from *Excelsior*'s hull. A splintering crack echoes across deck, and one of the crew gives a scream, as though they've seen a person injured. After all we've done, all the bludgeonings and becalmings, it's a machine that hurts us.

I don't want to see any more, and go down to my cabin. When everything's quiet again, when I've heard us thump against the harbour wall, I come back on deck and head straight for the ladder ashore. This moment should be extraordinary, I know that, but all I want to do is get it over with.

Each rung of the ladder is covered with sewage-stinking mud. It's revolting but I keep going, not caring, and claw forwards for a few yards on my hands and knees when I reach the top. Then I stand foolishly, trying to wipe the wet goo off one hand with my other wet hand, and begin staggering as the ground heaves beneath me.

I'm in a timber yard. Whole, colossal tree trunks are stacked ahead of me, yellow numbers scrawled on their bark, and a bulldozer is lumbering towards them like a dinosaur going into battle. I step backwards and lose my footing in the pulpy mud. I don't understand. Surely I shouldn't be here? It's not safe. I scuttle back down the ladder again and onto the boat.

Stewart is running his hand over the stanchion, where the tug wrecked it. 'It'll mend.' He walks to the stern with his head down and I follow. What we have to say is so obvious, neither of us wants to start talking. We just sit there side by side, the harbour wall steaming and reeking beside us. When I look back, there's only a patch of scummy black water, washing against breeze blocks. A dead puppy is wedged there, fawn belly bloated, stiff legs skyward.

I climb the iron ladder again, the earth still wobbly, and set off across the timber yard, looking for a bar.

*

Early next morning the provisions arrive. Then another tug, a smaller one, blathers towards us and by nine we're in open sea again. There's a steady wind from the north, polishing and clearing the sky. The long white curve of the shore is flung out beside us, straight and simple as an arm on a bed. Bill is standing by the broken stanchion, scraping mud off the rail.

I know what he's thinking, what all the crew are thinking. It doesn't matter any more how late we are. It doesn't matter how many storms have shaken us and how many calms marooned us: we've suffered all these things and survived.

I settle into the stern, where I have sat for a thousand miles, and stare straight ahead. Everything will be all right now. In a week we'll be passing Gibraltar – Keats said it glowed in the water 'like a topaz'. Then, in another week, Naples. The wind presses evenly against my back and the waves in front of us open and close like a million eyes blinking. Yes, everything will be all right now. I have seen what there is to see; the journey is already beginning to end.

I look into our wake once more, shielding my eyes. There is John Keats, signalling to me from two hundred years away. He is writing something down, throwing it forward for me to catch, and I will read it. Now he is speaking; I can see his wide mouth moving. But the wind and waves drown what he says, and his voice never reaches me. I guess. I imagine. I suppose. Possibly. Probably. Perhaps.

The breeze shifts but we still creak forwards, leaving him further and further behind.

2

Naples harbour. Naples. I wait for the exhilaration to strike me, but all that comes is a kind of creeping carefulness. I am bothered by what date it is, and can't decide. Late May. That will have to do.

We sail slowly into the dead centre of the bay: moist, mid-afternoon sunlight and listless air. Sloppy waves. After the open sea, the water seems to have no depth or secret life. Yet there's a fishing boat by the harbour wall, and two men feeding a golden net off the stern. They must be expecting something. And there are boys on top of the harbour wall, too, flicking out lines with long rods.

An argument is yammering in the back of my head. One voice tells me that everything I've seen at sea matters more than anything I'll see on land. The other voice says the land-world is the real world; I must find my happiness there or not at all. I feel detached from them both, letting the argument roll on.

But this is Naples, I tell myself again; this is where you wanted to be. Look at it!

I stretch my eyes wide. To my left, the jam-packed harbour of Santa Lucia. Straight ahead – a squat honey-coloured castle on its promontory. The *Maria Crowther* would have moored here, in that same shadow. I stare at the cannon-scarred walls, willing something to come clear. To my right, Vesuvius above the suburbs. The slate-thin cloud, tilting on the summit, dissolves as I watch. There's the ruined mouth of the crater, dipping on one side and brimming with black mist.

I look and look, but still feel nothing. My eyes fidget and swivel away to the green smudge of coast slicing down past Pompeii to Sorrento. All out of sight.

21 October: The Maria Crowther reaches Naples but is detained in quarantine for ten days. Keats is exhausted and ill; he writes to Charles Brown telling him that during this time, 'My health suffered more from bad air and a stifled cabin than it had done the whole voyage.'

For the first time in weeks, a day split into differences.

In the morning, to Pompeii; then back to Naples, to the Guanti Nuovi district, where Keats stayed for a few days before travelling to Rome – his house was destroyed when the area was developed in the 1960s. A gaggle of children watch me, soon bored but thinking they'll miss something if they go. And a crowd of adults, gathered outside a vegetable shop. A melon-faced fellow who carries crutches and sits on a crate. A sleek younger man – his son? He looks like an aubergine. Another: a warty lemon. A woman with hair like a dead lettuce. Her friend has a vest like a string bag. They're a complete set in Italian Happy Families. The Fruit-and-Vegetable Family.

Doodling through the streets, I have to nip on and off the pavement as mopeds rev behind me, ducking to miss awnings and washing.

Back to the bay in the afternoon, then the cloisters of San Girolomini. By now there's a strong sun carving shadows on the walls, splintering through the glossy leaves of lemon and orange trees. Half-a-dozen moggies follow, keeping to the shade. One gives a wheezing hiccup with every breath, and clenches its eyes shut in pain. Everything else feels padded, protected.

24 October: Keats writes to Fanny's mother in Hampstead: 'If I were well enough there is enough in this Port of Naples to fill a quire of paper – but it looks like a dream – every man who can row his boat and walk and talk seems a different being from myself – I do not feel in the world. O what an account I could give you of the Bay of Naples if I could once more feel myself a Citizen of this world.'

What does it mean to say goodbye to the ship? To a thing? I walk slowly from prow to stern, studying the rigging, the deckboards, the capstan as though I'd never seen them before. Ropes with their blackened sections where the crew wiped their hands clean.

Hatches scored with brushmarks. Blocks worn smooth and gleaming.

The crew stand in an awkward circle and we shake hands. When I reach Stewart we both take a step forward as though about to embrace, then change our minds. He's wearing his orange 'Port of Felixstowe' jacket. He looks exhausted. We bang each other on the arm – *bouf* – and turn apart. A moment later, from the far side of the harbour, I look back and see him hesitating on deck. If I called out he would hear me, but I don't know what to say. I stretch both arms above my head and wave for a long time. He does the same.

*

We take the road to Rome, the same Keats took, and stop at Solfatara.

I've heard about this place. It's an offshoot from Vesuvius, a sulphur field where they used to bring tubercular patients to breathe the stinking air and wallow in the sauna heat. It's supposed to look like Hell – in the old days, they reckoned the Elysian Fields were hereabouts, somewhere under these half-built houses and tatty hotels. The entrance to the Underworld was further off, nearer the volcano.

I pitch into the sun and stop short. Across a wide white disc of dry sulphur, the ground rises into a hill of steaming earth. Not just steaming. Actually smoking and bubbling, firing off steady jets of smoke, glopping and gurgling and shifting. I am shown through into a fenced-off section, following carefully in the steps of a gigantic black-bearded custodian. Vulcan. He shows me where I can walk safely, and where I will fall through.

I stand still and think about this. He's telling me: if I step off this path, I'll sink through the surface of the earth. I'm wearing thick shoes, but the heat comes through all the same, and the stench makes me dizzy.

I look down and suppose I'm about to imagine myself disappearing. In fact what I see is myself emerging. Head and shoulders bursting up through the red-hot crust, lava flaking off me like water. Then the rest of me comes clear, hands at my sides, straight as a missile, rising back onto the surface of the world.

All afternoon, we drive north past Monte Cassino and Sperlonga, through Terracina where Keats stayed, following the route of the Appian Way. In Terracina a fragment of the old road survives – ragged hunks of stone, desperately uneven. No wonder Severn walked for most of the journey, throwing flowers into the carriage where Keats lay exhausted.

They took a week; we reach Rome by eight. In the gaps between factories and villages, beyond advertisement hoardings and eucalyptus groves, the country flicks past in pieces: rush-dumps wagging along canals; a field of buffalo; a glimpse of coastline with its volcano-bobbles. At one point a flying-boat bumbles alongside, then curves out to sea.

I sit in the front of the bus drinking beer and thinking about my mother: her accident, the hospitals, her death. It takes more than two hours, and I am burying her as we reach the outskirts, my heart lifting at the wide streets and pine trees in the sinking sun.

I am coming back to life.

15 November–23 February 1821: Keats and Severn lodge in a house at the foot of the Spanish Steps. To start with, Keats is able to walk a little, and there are still hopes for his recovery. For the last six weeks of his life he is bed-bound, haemorrhaging badly, longing for death. 'Did you ever see anyone die?' he asks Severn at one point. 'Well then, I pity you.' Severn cooks for him, comforts him, nurses him. When the end approaches, Keats calls out to him, 'Severn – Severn lift me up for I am dying – I shall die easy – don't be frightened – thank God it has come.'

To Keats's house. After his death, all his furniture and movables were destroyed, as Italian law demanded. Later still, most of the rooms were altered, too. But his bedroom is the same: the room where he died.

It's early morning, and I climb towards him through a warm near-silence. The room is so small! Like a cabin, only taller. And the water crashing outside is so loud! I peer through the window.

There is the fountain in the square below – a sinking ship; the pale blue waves, jagged with reflections, skittering over the broken mast and sides. Wreckage and violent death. The end of the journey.

Here was his bed, along this right-hand wall; this was the glass he leant against, sickening, then lay down and looked through. The ceiling is the same, too: row after row after row of wide-eyed daisies. 'I can feel the daisies growing over me,' he told Severn. I stretch out on the floor and examine them, the coldness of the tiles seeping through my shirt and under my skin.

Then I kneel at the fireplace. This is what he must have seen, huddled in his bed. It's low and narrow – plain grey stone except for a frieze above the grate which shows two grimacing heads. The same head, larger, is in the centre. I bend closer. It's not a head but a devil's face, tongue stuck out hard, eyes stretching wide with anger and disgust.

Behind my back, Keats is emaciated. The light swells and fades as his days pass. The fountain throws its water-shadows across the ceiling. Voices rise and fall. The little cabin-room holds still for a while, then begins to shift forwards and slip-slide. Dissolving.

Here is his death-mask in a display cabinet. The life-mask beside it is fleshed out and eager, the wide top lip jutting over the lower, even under the weight of plaster. The death-mask is smaller. Nose beaky. Cheeks hollow. Hair brushed back so I can see how much had fallen out. Just a thin stripe in the centre of his forehead. A drained-out face, scooped and flayed.

The devil is still poking out his tongue. Water in the fountain is battering over the sides of the drowned ship.

6 February: Doctors perform an autopsy on Keats and discover that his lungs are almost completely destroyed. They are surprised that he has lived so long. He was twenty-five years old. Next day he is buried – outside the city walls and in darkness, as the Roman law required.

The bell clanks, the door in the gateway opens, and I turn left through the first jumbled part of the graveyard into the more spacious section where he lies. He's in the far corner, beyond those pine trees, where someone is taking flowers from a twist of paper and spreading them on the ground.

I keep walking. The pyramid of Cestius holds up its sightless triangular mirror. A heavy pine-cone unhinges and crashes to earth; there's an explosion of yellow sap. Cats appear everywhere, prowling through the strawberry-woven grass, slinking round the tombs.

The man leaving flowers vanishes and I keep walking. But I'm not getting anywhere. I can't compete with the backwards-rolling earth. It lifts me through the room where he died, past the sinking-ship fountain, over the jagged stones at Terracina, above the warren of Naples, and out into the bay.

I come to a standstill on deck, in the middle of nowhere, one hand holding the rigging, the other shading my face. There's no land, no gulls, no fish rising, nothing. Just the big greasy waves slithering forward, the thump and squelch of water against the prow. I remember that I have been more bored here than I thought possible. I have been half out of my mind. Now I can't feel any of these things. Now I am only and exactly where I want to be, wind and sunlight swarming over me.

Come back, is all I want to say. Come back and let me have it again. This time I will know what it means to feel happy.

Then I am standing behind him, resting both hands on the warm stone. The man who was laying flowers on the grave has reappeared. He has a wide-mouthed face and swept-back brown hair. I look straight into his eyes as he asks my name.

HAYDON BRIDGE
A Break-in

In September 1946, when he was twenty-four, Philip Larkin went
to work as sub-librarian at University College, Leicester. Within
three weeks he had met Monica Jones, a lecturer in the English
Department. After three years they became lovers. After another
six months Larkin left Leicester for the library at Queen's University, Belfast, where he stayed for five years, seeing Monica at intervals. In 1955 he was appointed Librarian at the University of Hull,
and remained there for the last thirty years of his life. During this
time he and Monica took annual holidays together, met at least
once a month, wrote to each other and/or spoke on the telephone
nearly every day. The relationship was in certain respects deeply
troubled (by jealousies, by distance), and in others very happy.
Monica was Larkin's steadfast companion and his soul-mate. He
dedicated *The Less Deceived* to her: it was the only collection of
poems he dedicated to anyone.

*

In September 1961 Monica bought a small house in Haydon Bridge
in Northumberland, on the main Newcastle–Carlisle road: her
family had originally come from that part of the world. She meant
it to be somewhere she could escape the worries of her private life
and her university work. Larkin was initially suspicious of the
house but soon admiring. He took holidays there, hunkered down
for weekends, always visited at New Year. When he wouldn't or
couldn't leave Hull, Monica was often in Haydon Bridge alone –
writing letters to Larkin, waiting for him to ring. The house was
their special place, their burrow.

In June 1983, when she was sixty-one, recently retired from
Leicester, and living in Haydon Bridge more or less full-time,

Monica developed shingles. Larkin, who was staying, took charge. He ferried her south to Hull and put her in hospital, where she lay half blinded for several days. Then he brought her back to his own house in Hull. She stayed ten months – until the following April – before returning to Haydon Bridge meaning to re-start her life. But she was still sick, and anyway Larkin missed her. Within a few days he came to collect her again. He helped her pack, then sat in the car while she checked for last things, drew the curtains, switched off the electricity at the meter, and locked the front door. Anxiously, he drove her back to Hull.

Larkin thought Monica was fatally ill. In fact, he was. Within a year he was in hospital for tests; on 2 December 1985 he died of cancer. Monica stayed in Hull – depressed, sick and exhausted. She wanted her own life back but couldn't reach it. She worried about her house in Haydon Bridge but was too ill to get herself there.

*

Early in 1986 Monica asked me to write Larkin's biography, and over the next few years we saw a great deal of each other. She sat in what had once been Larkin's chair, his tweed coat still slung over the arm. I sat on the sofa, his Rowlandson watercolour on the dark green wall behind me: cattle resting under an oak tree. Sometimes I formally interviewed her; sometimes we just chatted. Sometimes we looked at photographs of him or by him; sometimes we read his books. There was no hurry. She had known Larkin better than anyone. I had to ransack her memory.

Monica said nothing about the letters Larkin had written her. If I asked where they were she would shrug – lighting another cigarette, pouring another drink. Did this mean she didn't want me to see them? Or had they, like his diaries, been destroyed? She wasn't telling.

One day out of the blue she said most of the letters were in Haydon Bridge. Why didn't we drive up together to get them? It was a forlorn hope – she was too ill – yet she didn't want me to go without her. The house was theirs: a secret place, where she and

Larkin had lived to the exclusion of all others. Once the door was open, that life would be over.

*

Months passed. Monica grew more frail. Eventually she decided I would have to go without her, and I drove up with a friend from Hull, Marion Shaw, in the autumn of 1989. As far as I knew, no one had been into the house for five years.

We roller-coastered the wet road towards Hexham, then on. Rain was swirling in from the North Sea behind us. So much had fallen in recent weeks, the moors were yellow and sour-looking. As we ducked down into Haydon Bridge, streams bulged in the ditches beside us.

The house was smaller than I'd expected, and uglier. Packed into a tight row near the Old Bridge, on the main road, it had a jaded white front, a slate roof, plain modern windows and a front door which opened straight off the street. I got the key from a neighbour and opened up – but the door was stuck. Peering through the letterbox, I could see why. There was a mound of junk mail on the mat: offers of free film, estate agents' bumf, cards from taxi companies and window-cleaners.

I shoved the door violently and we were in. A tiny box of a hall; the sitting room to the left; stairs rising straight ahead. The stairs looked crazy. There was no carpet (just the pale section where a carpet had once been) and at the sides of each step – cans of food. One of these had leaked, oozing blood-coloured treacle into a puddle at my feet, I tried to wipe it up, scrape it up, somehow get rid of it, with a piece of junk mail. It was impossible. In the end I hid it beneath a few bright envelopes.

The smell seemed worse when I turned on the electricity. Sweet open-air dampness like a rotten log. There was noise too, noise I couldn't recognize. A roaring, but somehow subdued. When I turned into the sitting room I understood. Outside the window at the back, beyond a cramped yard and a towpath, was a gigantic river. The Tyne; invisible from the road. Within the first few seconds of looking, I saw a full-grown tree sweep past, then heard the trunk grinding against the bridge away to my left, out of sight.

The window was broken – a hole like a starburst and slivers of glass on the purple carpet.

We weren't the first people here for years, we were the second and third, at least the second and third. Drawers in a sideboard lolled open, empty; in the grate, jagged pieces of crockery poked out of a soot fall. And there were books all over the floor – books flung about for the hell of it – and a deep scar on the window-seat where something heavy had been manhandled into the yard then away along the towpath.

We tiptoed through the shambles, closing up, straightening, tidying, our hands immediately grey with dust. It was wet dust, sticking to us and clinging in our noses and lungs. Monica hadn't told me where I might find the letters, but it didn't matter. They were everywhere. In books, down the side of a chair, under a rug, on the window-seat. A few lay flat and saturated in the yard, scrabbled out when the last burglar left.

It was the same upstairs, though the dust seemed lighter there, maybe because the rain had eased off, and the sun was starting to break through. The river sounded quieter, too, and I could see a family on the opposite bank – a man, a woman and two children, walking a dog.

I went into the lumber room, into a jungle of clothes and hangers which had a small box at its heart, stuffed with letters.

Nothing in the bathroom.

In the smaller bedroom: under the window overlooking the river, a bed with letters inside and underneath it, and a cupboard crowded with damp dresses which tore when I touched them.

In the larger bedroom: more letters in books, an empty case of wine, an ironing board with a half-ironed dress draped across it.

When I got downstairs I was breathing in gulps, as if I'd been swimming.

We counted the letters into plastic bags. There were nearly two hundred of them. Then we went through the house again, found the last handful, turned off the electricity, locked up, returned the key to the neighbour, arranged for the window to be repaired, and climbed into the car. The sun had gone in; it was starting to rain again. Larkin had sat in the same place, gazing back at the little house, feeling anxious. I was exhilarated and ashamed.

*

I wasn't the last. A week or so after I'd taken the letters back to Monica, a van drew up outside the house in Haydon Bridge and two people got out, kicked open the front door and stole nearly everything inside. If the letters had still been there, they would have gone too. By the time this happened, I'd read them – and two hundred others, that Larkin had written to Monica in Leicester.

Painters

JACOB VAN RUISDAEL
True Understanding

We know precious little about Jacob van Ruisdael. He was born in Haarlem in 1628 or 1629, didn't travel much (his longest trip seems to have been to the eastern provinces of the Netherlands in the early 1650s), was living in Amsterdam by 1657, had one document-ed pupil (Meindert Hobbema), never married, cared for his rela-tives, occasionally suffered ill health, painted hard, sold decently but not spectacularly, and died aged fifty-three or fifty-four in 1682. He seems never to have kept a journal, and no letters or other personal documents have come down to us. Who taught him? Probably his frame-maker father and landscape-painter uncle. Who bought his paintings? In most cases we're not sure. What was he aiming to achieve? If he ever said, his words are lost.

All this helps to explain the approach Seymore Slive takes to Ruisdael in his catalogue to the show at the Royal Academy. Slive, who is Emeritus Professor of Fine Arts at Harvard, is expert at tracing the ownerships of paintings, at connecting them to recog-nizable geographies, at making connections between contempo-raries, and at tracking references over the centuries. He is also bracingly appreciative of Ruisdael's magnificent effects of depth and solidity, as well as his attention to things-in-themselves. But he is just as bold in his resistance to allegorical readings. Speaking of *The Great Oak*, in which a few animal bones are scattered at a crossroads, and *Landscape with a Pool and Figures*, in which more bones strew a path leading to a road, he says, 'There is no reason to call the bones . . . allegorical symbols, nor do I see the cross-roads in them as references to two ways of life.' Elsewhere he adds, 'An interpretation of Dutch landscape that admits one and only one reading impoverishes the subject. Additionally, it fails to take into account how skimpy and flimsy is our knowledge of the interpretation of Dutch artists. Broad generalizations based on it are correspondingly shaky.'

Given Slive's scholarship, and the fact-deficiency he keeps mentioning, it seems foolish to disagree: very few paintings by Ruisdael actually court an allegorical reading. There are those bones, of course, which can't help suggesting the transience of life, even without a skull amongst them. There is the owl, perched in a blasted oak and perhaps being mobbed by smaller birds in *Oak Tree and Dense Shrubbery at the Edge of a Pond*, which allude to the *vanitas* theme, or to *melancholia*, or to the myth of Athena, or simply to discord in the world at large. Most famously of all, there are the two masterworks *The Jewish Cemetery*, with its gloomy ruins and admonitory tombs, and *Windmill at Wijk*, where the massive building towers over a shoreline and surrounding houses: even Slive admits, 'It was not uncommon for analogies to be made between the natural forces that power what man has made and the divine spirit that gives him life.' Elsewhere, though, the landscapes, seascapes, townscapes and portraits of buildings come with no obvious pointers as to how we might interpret them. In this respect, as in the depth of his scholarship, Slive is reliably right.

It seems as though John Constable, one of Ruisdael's most appreciative admirers, would have approved. Constable conceded that *The Jewish Cemetery* (which interestingly he knew as *An Allegory of the Life of Man*) had a message to communicate, but felt this damaged the painting because sermonizing lay 'outside the reach of art', and was anyway unclear: 'There are ruins to indicate old age, a stream to signify the course of life, and rocks and precipices to shadow forth its dangers. But how are we to discover all this?' This appears to mean that Constable thought the painting 'failed' simply because it lacks what Slive calls 'an exegesis of [its] signification'. It also suggests that Constable felt landscapes were best able to deliver their meanings, strike their echoes, create their parallels, when the viewer's attention is drawn to physical realities.

In this respect, Constable is a wonderful guide to Ruisdael. He first came across him as an apprentice painter, studying and copying, and soon focused his praise on the purity of the older artist's vision. He felt that whereas several of Ruisdael's contemporaries made 'an incongruous mixture of Dutch and Italian taste, [and] produced a bastard style of landscape, destitute of the real excellence of either', the man himself was faithful to things as they actually appeared. 'I have a print hanging up in the room where I am now writing,' he once told his wife Maria, 'a view of the shore at Skeveling by Ruisdael, which gives me great pleasure. The waves are so well done that it is impossible to look at it without thinking on Bognor [which the Constables liked and knew well] and all that is dear to me.'

Constable is enjoying a sympathetic association here, but his further implication is crucial: it would not be possible without clear-seeing. Constable's brother Abram said, 'When I look at a mill painted by John, I see that it will *go round,* which is not always the case with those by other artists.' It was a smart remark, and takes us to the heart of Constable's genius, where accuracy and authenticity generate a mighty emotional strength. This is what so pleased him about Ruisdael: we can hear it in the remark to Maria, and even more clearly in his response to *Thatched-Roofed House with a Water Mill.* 'It haunts my mind and clings to my heart,' he told his friend Archdeacon Fisher, the very day he saw the painting, '– and has stood between me & you while I am now talking to you. It is a watermill, not unlike "Perne's Mill" – a man & boy are cutting rushes in the running stream (in the "*tail* water") – the whole so true clear & fresh – & as brisk as champagne – a shower has not long passed.'

The same sort of admiration fills Constable's great copy of Ruisdael's *Winter Landscape*, where it is once again fed by a family knowledge of mills and milling. 'The picture represents an approaching thaw,' Constable said. 'The ground is covered with snow and the trees are still white; but there are two windmills near the centre; the one has the sails furled, and is turned in the position from which the wind blew when the mill left off work; the other has the canvas on the poles, and is turned another way, which indicates a change in the wind. The clouds are opening in that direction, which appears by the glow in the sky to be the south (the sun's winter habitation in our hemisphere), and this change will produce a thaw before morning. The concurrence of these circumstances shows that Ruisdael *understood* what he was painting.'

Slive writes unsurprisingly well about Constable's insights, and his argument benefits from them. But if his pragmatism helps to settle the difficulty of how to look at a Ruisdael (relishing the minute botanical precision, the marvellous depiction of trees – especially oaks and beeches, the delicately cross-cutting waves in his marine paintings), it still leaves open the question of how to interpret what we see. For one thing, the clarity of his views rests on a paradox: yes, we can tell that creamy-flowered shrub in *Dunes by the Sea* is the wayfaring tree *viburnum lantana,* which even the great Linnaeus missed when he was botanizing in the vicinity; yes, we can identify the soil types, grasses, birds and so on – but what about the features of the landscape that Ruisdael invented? His friend – and presumably to some extent mentor – Allart van Everingden encouraged him to produce a number of Swedish scenes, which Ruisdael produced without ever leaving the Low Countries. His monumental painting of Bentheim Castle hoists the whole edifice onto a hill that did not in fact exist. Even the decay which appears genuine in *Two Water Mills and an Open Sluice* is introduced for effect.

The easiest way to solve this apparent conflict of interests is to say that both of them – the accuracy and the make-believe – exist to promote a higher artistic good. Ruisdael moved hills, distressed buildings, thickened woods, arranged clouds and altered watercourses because he wanted to create the best possible spatial relationships, the perfect interplay of foreground and distance, and the most telling ambivalence of light and shade. But does this mean we should look on the paintings as being most definitively about themselves? If we do that, the rewards are immense: these are very beautiful images, executed with an extraordinary mixture of skill and panache, fidelity and daring, respect for littleness and thrill at grandeur. Yet this does not account for the whole of our experience when looking at them, just as Slive's catalogue, for all its brilliant scholarship, seems a degree too lofty and chill compared to the pictures on display.

Actually loftiness isn't a bad word to use of Ruisdael. Not the loftiness of indifference, but the loftiness of a grand vision which combines magnificently with things at ground level, and thereby becomes not just approachable but admirable and warm. He is a painter in whom artifice and observation are inseparable, and while this means that we are always conscious of his works as compositions, it hardly prevents us from bringing our own associations and – through those associations – our own readings to bear on them. Just reminding ourselves of their recurring subjects proves the point. Ruisdael's paintings are obsessed by heroic trees (often showing signs of age and damage), deep and shadowy woods, water torrents in wild places, barely visited coasts, and colossal ruins. Where people appear at all (and by no means all the figures in these paintings are by Ruisdael himself), they are occasionally shown working (in the gorgeous group of paintings which show the Haarlem bleaching fields, for example), but much more often found travelling along lonely tracks or halting in sandy byways.

These are not pictures which wag their finger at us, and ask us to accept a single moral point of view. They are, however, paintings in which the observer feels the lot of human beings is to be isolated (even when working) and transitory. Where the cycles of nature offer the consolations of natural process without any more immediate and individual comfort. Where even the strongest have no proof against time (those crumbling castles). And where a spire or church tower might or might not be able to hold its own under enormous skies. In all these respects, the overwhelming mood of the paintings is melancholy – a melancholy that is at once braced and offset by a love of particulars, just as it was two centuries later in paintings by Constable. The balance of these things, and the aesthetic harmony it allows, is evident in virtually every picture in the Royal Academy show. To take just one example: *Cottage under Trees near a Grainfield* shows a thatched, red-brick building with smoke rising gently from the chimney, a woman at the door, and a couple resting in the shade. An image of contentment, in other words – but complicated by the massive oak leaning above them, and by the single cartwheel mouldering in the scrubby foreground. The image recalls the mixture of endurance and vulnerability, let alone some of the principles of design, in Constable's *A Cottage in a Cornfield* – and in doing so it anticipates Constable's great maxim: 'We see nothing till we truly understand it.' 'It', for both artists, means life and death, as well as paint and painting.

SAMUEL PALMER
Shadowlands

Samuel Palmer: Vision and Landscape is the first big Palmer show to be mounted in this country since 1926. That seems an amazingly long time ago, considering how often Palmer is invoked as the disciple of painters who rarely leave the headlines (Blake, in particular). It means we have got used to thinking about Palmer as a background figure – someone as shadowy as his best-known works, in which barely individuated figures trudge or traipse through crepuscular landscapes, and the moon (and sometimes even the sun) draws a sepia veil across hard details and recognizable features.

One of the great achievements of this marvellous exhibition is to prove that vagueness and suggestion are only half the story. By giving adequate wall space to sketchbook drawings and suchlike, the curator, William Vaughan, lets us appreciate how meticulously Palmer observed the world around him, differentiating tree types, bird types, stone types, actual constellations – rather than just 'stars'. And also how busily Palmer trained himself to do this in his early years (no doubt encouraged by his mentor and father-in-law, John Linnell). In a sketchbook study of 1819, for instance, we find him differentiating cloud varieties with the same hawk-eyed discrimination as Constable. In a tree study of 1824–25, the inscription, and mini-sketch of a line of trees in the corner, leave us in no doubt that the whole thing was based on direct observation.

But this same tree study also has a hard-profiling that suggests that while listening to Linnell, Palmer was also learning important lessons from Blake: from close scrutiny of his work, initially, then first hand when the two men became friends during the last three years of Blake's life. Although Palmer never went so far as Blake in promoting imagination over observation, and although he was a

Samuel Palmer: Vision and Landscape (British Museum, 2005)

much less radical thinker, he nevertheless discovered a great deal from the older artist about how to free the eye and the hand. Those definite outlines in the tree sketches are not the evidence of secure containment, but evidence of things struggling to escape – they are, so to speak, trees about to walk.

Palmer himself made a kind of escape when, with a small band of kindred spirits, he went to live in the deep-sided, shaggily wooded Kent village of Shoreham in 1826. It's important to set the move in context. Elsewhere in Europe during the post-Napoleonic period, a fair number of artistic communities were recoiling from problems associated with the Industrial Revolution, and immersing themselves in the rural past. (The most obvious model for Palmer's group, which he called 'the Ancients', was 'the Nazarenes' – an association of German artists who, as Vaughan reminds us, 'had achieved great success in Rome with their work and by the 1820s . . . were the talk of Europe'.) The reactionary aspect of the enterprise may have set Palmer at odds with Blake; the visionary element was highly sympathetic. Works produced during the Shoreham period have a tight grip on everything that is numinous in the land- and skyscapes he saw around him.

It's a paradox, of course: the numinous, almost by definition, is something we expect to defy exact transcription. But this is where Palmer's attention to detail comes into play, acting as a counterbalance to his interest in the ethereal. His early Constable-like skies, with their fine actualities, were replaced by a fabulous, billowing 'bright cloud'. His human figures, where they appear at all, are generic ploughmen or reapers or sowers. But they are set in a place that is recognizable and palpable. Although the scale is skewed (leaves are often wonderfully large and voluptuous), everything has a magnificent solidity, a compressed burliness, which keeps sentimentality at bay.

Cornfield by Moonlight, with the Evening Star, c.1830, is a good example. This little picture, once owned by Kenneth Clark and now in the British Museum, shows a shepherd and his dog slipping into a field of stooked corn, as the waxing sickle moon and evening star pulse in the sky overhead. A moon that size couldn't possibly shed such intense light; the star has the glare of a burning-up satellite. The actuality of the place is also questioned by the sense that it depicts an all-too-typical Virgilian scene. (Palmer loved Virgil: indeed, there is a compelling literary dimension to his work. Milton and Cowper haunt him. Wordsworth, interestingly, does not – even though the overlap between their interests and insights is so great. Maybe Palmer thought Wordsworth's landscapes were too dissimilar in purely physical terms?)

There's plenty of realism here too. Although the shepherd is kitted out with a staff and broad-brimmed hat, the angle of his walk has a touching humanity – at once tentative and magnetized by the scene ahead. The same is true of the dog, twisting round nervously in the gloom to check that his master is following. And differently true of the ink drawing in the foreground, where lines are heavily scored to the point of impatience.

For all this, we still have to accept that Palmer depends on shadows and shadiness for his best effects. In a late autobiographical letter, he gave some clues about the significance of this. When he was 'less than four years old' he says, and standing with his nurse, 'watching the shadows on the wall from branches of elm behind which the moon had risen, she transferred and fixed the fleeting image in my memory by repeating the couplet, "Vain man, the vision of a moment made,/Dream of a dream and shadow of a shade."' He goes on: 'I never forgot those shadows, and am often trying to paint them' – implying that their main 'meaning' for him has to do with transience, mortality, evanescence.

When we look at a characteristic Shoreham work such as *Cornfield by Moonlight*, we can see the implication carries a good deal of weight: the shepherd walking into the stook-maze might well be about to disappear for good. Yet the mood of the painting suggests otherwise. It isn't exactly a cheerful picture – it's too dark for that – but it does exude a sense of settledness (the harvest gathered in), even of contentment. In other words, Palmer's shadowlands are a place of lost content – lost in the sense that it is under threat from the modern age, and from the passage of time itself, but not in the sense that it is beyond the reach of the enlightened individual. It's the same message we find repeated in the majority of his other paintings from the valley. In the overarching blossom of *In a Shoreham Garden*, for example, or the deep valley of *Yellow Twilight*, or the famous *Magic Apple Tree*.

The title of this last example was given by Palmer's son A. H. Palmer, who after his father's death had such difficulties reporting on the activities of the Ancients. While admiring their achievement as painters, he was suspicious of their closeness to one another, and destroyed several notebooks from the Shoreham period least they gave the public an impression of suspicious intimacy. (Such a thing in fact seems highly unlikely.) He made a pretty disastrous call with the title of this picture, too. 'Magic' suggests something merely supernatural, whereas Palmer clearly intended to celebrate divine generosity and abundance. How could it be otherwise, when the heavily loaded tree is skewered by the spire of a church rising in the lower centre of the painting?

The closeness of the Ancients diminished with time, and Palmer finally left Shoreham in 1835. His departure marked the end of one of the most intense and productive episodes in Romantic art – but Palmer kept most of the results close by for the rest of his life. At the end (he lived to become a high Victorian, and died in 1881), he looked upon it almost as a portfolio of curiosities. For us, it is the main concentration of his genius. Which is not to say that Palmer goes off the boil as soon as he leaves Kent. Touring Wales and visiting Italy, establishing himself and his family in London, he certainly started to produce works of much less oddity, and greater commercial charm. It's really only towards the end of his life that the visionary gleam returns – and this time, it's for tragic reasons.

One of Palmer's children died in 1861 – a son, with whom he was evidently especially close – and the loss jolted him back towards greatness. He became as reclusive as he had been in Shoreham, and once again allowed things-in-themselves to combine with things-imagined. His two great late etchings *The Bellman* and *The Lonely Tower* are probably the best examples (the show as a whole proves what a vigorous and deep-biting engraver he was). Both are beautifully illuminated by Palmer's technique:

they have the same simmering shadows and sudden lights that we find in his best paintings. And both have a wonderful sense of depth: the bellman's steps downhill towards the village are like a slow bird-swoop into a nest. *The Lonely Tower* in particular has a terrible pathos. There is no direct reference to his dead son, but the tower stands over the village where he died, and the stars in the sky are in exactly the same configurations as at the time of his death. It is an image that grips us with the same quiet intensity as Constable's unspoken elegy for his wife, *Hadleigh Castle*.

Will this show, so long overdue, restore Palmer to the high place he deserves in the story of British art? Not all the work is of equal quality and interest (especially during the more conventional middle period), and most of the images are small, which might work against them here. But his originality, fascination, and integrity are all proof of greatness. So is the beauty of many of the pictures – not the beauty of an entirely other world, but beauty that connects a longing for transfiguration with a deep human involvement in the familiar details of ordinary life.

JOHN CONSTABLE
Another Word for Feeling

As John Constable reached the peak of his fame during the twentieth century, he suffered the fate common to many great artists: people stopped looking thoughtfully at his paintings and began simply to admire them. They were valued less for their restlessness and originality than for their capacity to seem fixed and inevitable – to distil a version of landscape and a vision of England that were safely predictable. Not surprisingly, this way of seeing soon turned into sentimentality: the prettification of his childhood haunts in the Stour Valley, and the translation of his most famous works into tea trays, drying-up cloths and biscuit-tin lids. As he was clasped to the national bosom, the living air was squeezed out of him.

Paradoxically, the embrace turned out to be a form of relinquishment: while the public merely doted on him, they ignored his reality. Equally paradoxically, there turned out to be a slow-burning benefit in this: the lack of proper engagement created a breathing space in which his work acquired a kind of distance and could once again be considered afresh.

Michael Rosenthal was among the first to take significant advantage: when he published his study of Constable in 1983 he offered a view of the paintings that replaced kitsch with clarity. Constable had strong reactionary instincts (he fiercely opposed the Reform Act), but he was not a stick-in-the-mud. He was vividly alert to the social forces that shaped his landscapes in the years before and after Waterloo, he was radical in many of his methods (painting oils *en plein air*) and he was fascinated by contemporary science – especially the science of weather. Most important of all, he was obsessed by the question of how to combine truth to nature with truth to deep feeling and what he called 'moral duty'.

In the twenty-odd years since Rosenthal's book appeared, its

The re-opening of the Painting Galleries at the Victoria and Albert Museum, 2003 message has been reinforced. For one thing, the post-devolution-ary debate about Englishness has encouraged critics to examine Constable's place in the national pantheon. For another, several important figurative painters have rallied to his cause. In an inter-view given to accompany the Constable show he chose for Paris in 2003, Lucian Freud spoke warmly about the 'mental freshness' of the Stour paintings, and extolled their tight geographical focus. 'My idea of travel is downward travel, really,' he said. 'Getting to know where you are better, and exploring feelings that you know more deeply. I always think that "knowing something by heart" gives you a depth of possibility that has more potential than seeing new sights, however marvellous and exciting they are.'

The Victoria and Albert Museum has always been a magnet for Constable's admirers, thanks to the magnificent collection left to it by his daughter, and the equally fine oils given by John Sheepshanks in the mid-twentieth century. For the past several years, most of these have been exhibited in the Henry Cole Wing, and although their impact was terrific, they were not shown to best advantage. The light was unsympathetic and the presentation cramped. Now, as a part of the V&A's ten-year Future Plan, they can be seen as they deserve, in the refurbished Paintings Galleries. It marks an important stage in the rescue of Constable from the strange public stasis in which he languished for so long.

The new galleries comprise five rooms, originally built in the 1860s and required to be 'light and airy'. They are both of these things, but they're also pulsingly intense, the walls painted in bold but sympathetic colours, and the collections mounted so as to cre-ate an appropriate sense of context. (The Academy Room, for instance, which contains the Sheepshanks bequest, is hung as the Royal Academy was in 1840, the pictures densely clustered on the walls.) Everything on show is tremendously enhanced by the new arrangement: it's at once gorgeous and intelligent, and allows us to make all manner of connections and distinctions.

Constable's *Cottage in a Cornfield* is just one of many paintings that prosper. With none of Constable's other works near by, it appears between a pair of works by his friend and biographer C. R.

Leslie, both of which show scenes from *The Winter's Tale* (*Autolycus* and *Florizel and Perdita*). These are capable high-Victorian productions, the figures dutiful and the interpretation pat. To turn from their predictabilities to Constable's brooding scene is not just to move from make-believe to real life, but to feel seized by something at once known and mysterious.

The slumped wings of the cottage's thatched roof, the corn lapping at the walls, the deep shadow of the middle ground (which almost obscures the figure of a donkey and gives the five-barred gate a threatening solidity): all these things mean that Constable's image of seclusion is charged with a sense of isolation – almost of neglect – and of inevitable process. The cottage appears to have grown out of the ground like a mushroom and, like a mushroom, seems bound to disappear with time.

A blend of faithful seeing and powerful feeling is the single most arresting thing about the core of the Constable collection – his daughter's bequest. This contains work found in his studio at the time of his death, the bulk of which is oil sketches (some of them free-standing studies, others some kind of preparation for later and more 'finished' pictures). Mark Evans, the curator of the re-opened V&A galleries, has decided that two of these – one showing Dedham Vale, the other Constable's father's house – are sufficiently complete to be presented as finished works, gold frames and all. The remainder (twenty-two of them) have been remounted more simply; showing the whole sheet wherever possible, so that we can see how wonkily shaped were some of the surfaces that Constable used. Such plainness and candour are greatly to the paintings' advantage: they allow us to remember that Constable thought of them as drafts, but also lets us see how excitingly worked and compact they are. Those who prefer Constable's sketches to his more polished things – the final versions of the 'six-footers' and suchlike – will feel vindicated by this approach. Every one of these paintings is exceptional. The *Study of the Trunk of an Elm Tree*, for instance (which Freud put at the start of his Paris show), is a little masterpiece of observation: the wrinkled elephant-hide of the bark, and the gradations of the falling shade, are marvellingly precise. Yet once again our looking cannot be separated from our feeling – not just the feeling of recognition, and of finding something familiar made strange and compelling, but the apprehension of an almost indefinable melancholy. Constable never raises his voice to tell us about passing time and the isolation of the individual, but these things are manifest everywhere in his work and are all the more plangent for his modesty.

Even where he is more explicit, we feel included rather than talked at. *Study of Tree Trunks* is a case in point. Here the 'moral duty' of the work is articulated by the figure of a woman standing at the edge of the trees' shade and seen oddly from above, as though Constable had done his painting while sitting in the branches. She is alone and pensive – maybe waiting for someone, or daydreaming – and the breeze distressing her clothes and hair makes her seem on the point of vanishing. But the painting silently asks us: what sort of vanishing? The vanishing of death? Or the vanishing of being subsumed – like the cottage in the cornfield – back into the landscape that is her own? Constable leaves it to us to decide.

It has always been accepted that Constable had his gloomy side. Compared with the sparkling and storm-tossed craft of his contemporary Turner, he was like one of his own lugubrious barges, especially after the death of his wife Maria in 1828. But this new presentation of the sketches makes us rethink the extent and function of his melancholy – and if the two tree-trunk paintings weren't enough to do this, there's always the great oil *Watermeadows near Salisbury*, which appears in the adjacent room of the gallery among the Sheepshanks collection.

Like others in this group, it has a much greater degree of finish than any of the works that were bequeathed by Constable's daughter. This does nothing to inhibit its mood. Taking a low-level stare over the river and fields close to the house of Constable's friend Fisher, it records a view in which the only living creature is a crow, flopped down and straggling in the grass, and painted so small it might almost be a drip of paint. The glassily flat river, the sedge withered from the banks, and the gnarled willows all amplify the bird's message. This is a landscape crammed with actualities, yet flattened by the feeling of things being posthumous. Life is here and beautiful, the painting says, but also in some sense over: it exists because of Constable, but also without him.

It's well known that in the last part of his life, following his move from Suffolk to London in 1820, Constable often made paintings of his birthplace that remembered things as they had been during his childhood. They have a deliberate element of nostalgia about them – nostalgia for a pre-Enclosure, pre-Reform England, as well as for a time of personal innocence and security. This helps to explain why so many of the paintings eventually became so popular: they offer an apparently authentic but in fact not quite real vision of a golden age. Their reactionary element is reassuring.

Maybe there are some paintings in which sentimentality becomes too dominant: *The Cornfield*, for instance. But there are dozens in which the sense of loss is rendered as a hard fact, and in such a way as to lift it from the description of a mood into a presentation of the whole human condition. Virtually every one of the Constables in the V&A makes this transition – not so that we leave the galleries feeling hammered by regretfulness, but so that we feel loss held in a proper balance with discovery and relish. They are some of the greatest landscapes ever painted, and have never looked better or more resonant than they do now.

J. M. W. TURNER
In Venice

Henry James, with a wonderful roll and relaxation, said that 'To spend one's mornings in still, productive analysis of the clustered shadows of the Basilica, one's afternoons anywhere in church or campo, on canal or lagoon, and one's evenings in starlight gossip at Florian's feeling the sea-breeze throb languidly between the two great pillars of the Piazzetta and over the low black domes of the church – this, I consider, is to be as happy as is consistent with the preservation of reason.' But James also, and not so relaxedly, said that Venice was 'the bugbear of literature'. Language blunders in the wake of its fluid and fleeing facts, or is too easily fixed on one of the innumerable paradoxes that are its special character and charm.

Painters might well say the same, but at least they can do without words. For painters the difficulties have more to do with the problem of precedent (though this is also a part of the writer's bugbear). How do you make art and the world new? How, in particular, do you deal with Turner, whose images of Venice are so intensely sympathetic to the place that they have come to seem integral to it? His melting domes and spires, his floating bridges, his low views and long shuddering reflections: all these feel definitive in their lack of definition.

Turner didn't have the same problem of dealing with himself, but his approaches to Venice were fraught with many of the same difficulties that strike painters today. For centuries, the city had been a supreme test and talisman of artistic endeavour. Fifty-odd years before Turner's arrival, Canaletto had produced a series of world-famous views that simply could not be ignored. They combined topographical, antiquarian and picturesque qualities to create a daunting sense of immaculacy – almost perhaps, of completion.

Turner in Venice (Tate Britain, 2003)

Turner was not easily deterred by precedent (in fact he was just as likely to be stirred by its challenge), but there were other good reasons why he waited until his mid-forties before making his first visit to Venice. The wars with France had effectively closed Europe to British travellers for most of the early part of the century – and besides, he was engrossed by compelling subjects close to home. He might have looked across the Channel and imagined Italy as his 'Terra Pictura, the land of all beauty', but he knew that English rain and swirling, misty English light were indispensable to his genius.

All this helps to explain why, when he eventually arrived in Venice in 1819, Turner did not immediately seem to make it one of his hallmark subjects. Even if he could deal with Canaletto (whom he included in his first oil painting of the city: Canaletto is shown implausibly working on a gilt-framed canvas, presenting a view that could not be seen from that particular angle), there were other bugbears to overcome. There was Shakespeare. There was Samuel Rogers, from whose poem 'Italy' he would later quote a few lines to accompany *Approach to Venice* (1844): 'The path lies o'er the sea invisible/And from the land we went/As to a floating city, steering in . . .' Most conspicuous of all was Byron. The Fourth Canto of 'Childe Harold's Pilgrimage' had appeared only a year before Turner arrived, and confirmed a popular idea of the city – oriental, mysterious, erotic, ravaged and nostalgic:

> She looks a sea Cybele, fresh from Ocean,
> Rising with her tiara of proud towers
> At airy distance, with majestic motion,
> A Ruler of the waters and their powers:
> And such she was; – her daughters had their dowers
> From spoils of nations, and the exhaustless East
> Poured in her lap all gems in sparkling showers.
> In purple was she robed, and of her feast
> Monarchs partook, and deemed their dignity increased.

Recent scholars have pointed out that Venice was not as put upon in the aftermath of the Napoleonic wars as has often been suggested. It had certainly suffered badly during the wars themselves, but with the restoration of Habsburg rule it enjoyed comparative prosperity. These facts, however, mattered less to Byron and his contemporaries than the city's reputation. As far as they were concerned, Venice was only just holding its head above water, and its beauties were made more precious by their vulnerability. Byron's friend John Hoppner said the city 'indeed appears to be at her last gasps, and if something is not done to relieve and support her, must be soon buried again in the marshes from which she originally sprang. Every trace of her former magnificence which still exists serves only to illustrate her present decay.'

Although Turner never met Byron in Venice (Byron was out of town), he absorbed the poet's sense of the city, stirring it in with similar impressions he gleaned from other writers. In this sense his views of Venice, no matter how revolutionary their technique, might be said to contain existing and often backward-looking texts – sometimes visibly (as with the Shakespearean subjects such as *Juliet and her Nurse*), more often implicitly. The city we see is at once contemporary and historical: recognizably early or mid-nineteenth century, but bright with antique costumes and strolling beauties. It is also exemplary, recalling fallen civilizations while warning about the fate of later empires, especially the British Empire. Like Venice, Britain was a seagoing power, dependent on trade. Might it not go the same way in time?

Wonder and warning, novelty and nostalgia: these were the elements of Turner's response to Venice. And when we combine them with the question of how to deal with bugbears, we can begin to understand why he might have been slow to make the most of the material he collected in 1819. Although he worked with his usual energy, finishing many important watercolours and filling about one hundred and sixty pages of his sketchbooks, it was not until his second visit in 1833 that he began to lay claim to Venice.

Paradoxically, it was the fact that the city had by then become an even more fashionable subject that quickened his approach. Encouraged by several new patrons and the commercial opportunities that presented themselves, Turner installed himself in the

Hotel Europa and set about discovering districts he had ignored fourteen years earlier. This time he worked harder still, completing nearly two hundred pages of sketches, including forty-odd very beautiful nocturnal studies on various types of off-white paper. When he got home again, he began the first of three large oils of Venetian subjects that he would exhibit at the next three Royal Academy annual shows.

Although a few critics raised their eyebrows at Turner's new commitment to a place so widely associated with other painters, these works were generally well received. His peers certainly thought the city allowed him to become more extraordinarily himself. 'He seems to paint with tinted steam', said Constable, brilliantly, 'so evanescent, and so airy.' In the work Turner produced during and after 1833, there is an even greater boldness in his treatment of transient yet elemental forces. Close up, the paintings look like atom-storms – frantic flights and concentrations of colour; at a distance, their governing forms begin to emerge, rarely clear, but precise in their imprecision.

Even though many of the subjects deriving from this second visit are out of the way, there is a tendency for the pictures to focus on traces of grandeur. When he returned for the last time, in 1840, he allowed a new kind of intimacy to emerge in even his most monumental images, and spent a good deal of time sketching apparently insignificant things – balconies and suchlike. These probably owe something to Byron (balconies being a site for assignations), yet they seem entirely fresh in terms of emotional response and technique. 'Atmosphere is my style,' Turner once said, and atmosphere in these late Venetian works is his subject too. It is thin and thick air that engrosses him as much as objects.

A mere three visits; only a few weeks spent in the city; hundreds of works ranging from hasty sketches to large-scale oils: the story of Turner's relationship with Venice is frankly extraordinary. Having resisted the city for so long, then been slow to capitalize on his first visit, he ended by making it a cornerstone of his achievement. Yet in a way this is not so much extraordinary as inevitable. Turner and Venice were made for one another. Contemplating and then remembering its decaying magnificence, the great master of dissolving forms found an ideal subject.

Pierre Bonnard
Adventures of the Optic Nerve

In 1985 I saw a small pencil drawing for sale in the window of a shop in Camden Passage, north London. It was a woman's face, eyes lowered, right hand raised half for support, half for shelter. The whole thing had a provisional air about it – it was a sketch, dashed off. I could imagine the artist quickly flipping over the page and beginning again. At the same time, I found it completely engrossing. The woman's face was indistinct but beautiful – and there was something beguiling about her averted look. Not only shy but mysterious. Possibly tired. Exhausted, even. Or ill. In the bottom right-hand corner was an elegant monogram: PB. Pierre Bonnard.

I'd first fallen in love with Bonnard's work about fifteen years earlier, when I went to live for a while in Paris during that painful-blissful time between leaving school and going to university. I knew very little about paintings except that I wanted to find out about them, and took myself off to galleries most days. At that time, the city's main Impressionist and post-Impressionist collections were hung in smaller locations than they are now. They didn't seem so obviously a part of the mass-culture industry. This often meant overcrowding, poor labelling, dodgy lighting. But there was a sense of closeness. I'd feel as if I'd made a special journey to a particular rendezvous. Perhaps this is why Bonnard so quickly meant so much to me. His paintings combined with the atmosphere to seem amazingly intimate. Those sunlit dining tables and curled-up pets. Those windows opening on to pulsatingly hot landscapes. That woman – always the same woman, apparently lying in her bath, bending over her bath, drying herself . . . They all conveyed strong feeling by speaking quietly. They made a virtue of hesitation and indeterminacy. They

Bonnard (Tate Britain, 1998)

were sumptuously alive but also introverted.

I can't remember the darker elements in the paintings bothering me in those days. I wasn't averse to feeling sad, but I wanted my sorrows presented more grandly. I needed to know what the matter was. Occasionally, when I returned to Bonnard after looking at works by his friend and contemporary Edouard Vuillard, and after thinking about Vuillard's great paintings of marriage-muddles and stymied families, I would think I was being simplistic. But never mind. When I eventually returned to England, I felt it was enough merely to have discovered Bonnard. I was wrong. According to most people I met, he was pretty minor really. The nudes, yes, they were good. But where was the inner conflict? And what was he doing painting like an Impressionist in the 1940s? Compared to what was happening in America . . .

The domination of European taste by Americans during the middle part of the twentieth century had created a consensus: Bonnard was a minor painter, not austere or astringent enough to be truly Modern, and too interested in the self and its illusions to be modernly True. I heard the objections and felt confused. If I'd been more clued up, I'd have been defiant. In 1966, three years before I'd been to Paris, the Royal Academy in London had mounted the largest ever Bonnard show, and had included a number of previously unknown nudes and self-portraits. These 'new' works had generated a great excitement in critics and other painters, and had begun to alter their impressions of Bonnard's achievement. Today, one only has to glance at two of our most famous English contemporaries, David Hockney and Howard Hodgkin, to see what has been taken from Bonnard's palette. His technical legacy is vital, too: the way flat surfaces in his work (tabletops, balconies) keep shifting and dwindling, sinking and rearing up on end. And that woman in the bath – Marthe, Bonnard's almost-lifelong companion. Obviously there were things to know about her which would complicate our sense of the pictures as oblique but heartfelt narratives.

As long as there is an argument about the role of subjectivity in painting, there will be people who decry Bonnard. But thirty-two years after that RA exhibition, the new show at the Tate can only raise his reputation still further. Selecting one hundred and twenty-odd works from the nearly two thousand that Bonnard left, it runs from the small intimiste works he produced in the 1880s and 1890s (he was born in 1867), through the nudes of the next two decades, on to the larger landscapes and interiors of the 1920s and 1930s, and climaxes in a number of great, late nudes and self-portraits.

'Painting', said Bonnard in 1914, is 'the transcription of the adventures of the optic nerve', and the sheer dash and delight in his work are always bewitching. But he is a plangent painter as well as a potent one. His eye for what is pent up in colour, and what is fraught in context, means that when we look at his work we feel caught in the act of discovering a troubling secret. This is what gives his best paintings their particular and intense charm: their mixture of nearly opposite sensations. Pleasure and doubt, giving and restraining, deliquescence and disturbance, are all bound together in his recurring images – especially his images of Marthe. 'Celui qui chante n'est pas toujours heureux,' Bonnard wrote in one of his notebooks. Quite so.

All this is much less charged in the early works – though they have their own tensions. Take *The Croquet Game* (1892). On the left of the painting, sheltered by Gauguin-esque greens and shadows, a foursome and their dog are playing. On the right, in the open but also in the background, a gaggle of pale girls is circling with an abandon that would have made Matisse lick his lips. It's an everyday, sun-blessed, easy-going scene, Japanese in treatment. Yet it's perplexing for all that. What is the relation between the two groups of people – let alone the people as individuals? Why is the croquet partner in the white coat and boater gazing away from the game with such a lurking expression? Why are the couple in dark clothes melting like Vuillard subjects into the surrounding foliage? There are no clear answers. The painting obviously has separation at its heart, as well as union. It is as interested in the perils of dissolution as the pleasures of dissolving.

Eight years later, in the early masterpiece *Man and Woman*

(1900), these ambiguities are much more obvious and more sombre. Once again, the canvas is effectively divided into two, this time by the big, slim, dark erection of a folded screen. To the right is Marthe, sitting naked on a bed with one leg drawn up. To the right is a standing male nude – presumably Bonnard himself – his genitals obscurely painted, the right side of his body and his whole right arm pressed out of the picture. The atmosphere, apparently, is one of post-coital tenderness. But every sign of ease – the nakedness, the two cats on the bed, the rumpled linen – is countered and checked by something opposite. The man is edged aside. The woman is self-absorbed. The screen is divisive. As the elements in the painting negotiate with each other, they create an extraordinary drama – making it at once sexy and severe, loving and lonely.

These paradoxes have a characteristic effect. Warmly as the paintings draw us in, they also hold us at a distance. We are made to ponder as much as we are made to feel. Bonnard often intensifies this by including himself in the pictures, reminding us that we are dealing with an artefact not a slice of life. ('Let it be felt', he once said, 'that the painter was there.') In *Man and Woman*, he appears as the looming lover, at once satisfied and marginalized. In other pictures we see him sneaking onto the edge of the canvas (his leg in the *Large Blue Nude* of 1924, most of his blue-dressing-gowned body and his palette in *The Bathroom* of 1934–40).

And when we get to the end, and see the man himself again, face to face, in the late self-portraits? It is not the main purpose of these amazingly candid and modest works to teach lessons about the unreliability of the visible world. They are about age, and human change. The wispily bearded young student of the 1889 self-portrait has become a bald, slight and bashful figure with his hands raised (*Self-Portrait, c.* 1938–40). He's probably squeezing out a tube of paint; but then again, he might be raising his fists to defend himself. It's a deeply touching image, so vulnerable it's almost pathetic.

This takes us back to Marthe again, and the late bathroom scenes which are the triumph of Bonnard's career. In these, the ambiguities which fill his other works are tightened to a new pitch.

Take the *Nude in the Bath* (1936), one of the greatest of them all: the bathroom itself is a gorgeous box of colours – the tiles reflecting blues, umbers, yellows, purples and pinks; the chequered floor is transformed to a haze of brilliant dots; the bath is a lovely disc of flowing light in which the eternally young body of Marthe floats with blissful unselfconsciousness. Everything speaks of pleasure, closeness, trust, warmth.

But look again. Marthe's face is a smudgy dumpling; her identity blurred. Her long soak might be a melting, a leaving of the world. As elsewhere, and with great delicacy, the painting leaves these thoughts hanging in the sun-filled air. They are never urgent or articulate enough to dim the painting with anything like a mood of depression. But they insist on the possibility of sadness. Sadness which, when we turn to Bonnard's biography, we find spelt out, in Marthe's lifelong health worries and obsessive self-cleansing. She would eventually die, in 1942, five years before Bonnard, of tubercular laryngitis. Sarah Whitfield, the curator of the Tate show, tells us that a hydropathic regime was frequently prescribed for this illness.

Which is not to say these bathroom scenes are 'really' portraits of a patient. One of Bonnard's greatest gifts is his ability to make very personal subjects seem open and available, without in any way violating their intimacy. This is partly why his genius has finally earned the reputation it deserves. His best paintings fuse the conflicting elements of his life (his life with Marthe) into images which combine painterly beauty with psychological truth. And they encompass the big themes we expect to find in great art by proving over and over again their love for the familiar. The corner of a table. A dining room in the country. A young woman washing.

Or a young woman looking down, shielding her face. A young woman in a small drawing, in a shop in Camden Passage, and me reflected in its glass, gazing and gazing, feeling poor. Though I bought it, of course.

Howard Hodgkin
Emotional Situations

Recommending the 1994 Bonnard show at the Hayward, Howard Hodgkin said that to possess one of the paintings would be like owning a piece 'of life itself'. It's easy to see why he should think so. His own incandescently stabbing and swiping style has obvious affinities with the stippling and soaking we find in the Intimists in general and in Bonnard in particular. Like him, they appear to define a world in which form is at ease with the idea of formlessness, in which lack of definition is accompanied by a consoling sense of belonging, in which the big colours of abundance and contentment put everything else in the shade.

Yet the deeper we gaze into Bonnard, the more disturbing he looks. Those sultry gardens, for instance. They're not just drenching colour-cascades, where ordinary human anxieties are washed away. They're places where pathways squirm to escape into a world beyond, and cannot; where a stooping figure might be the gardener lost in shadow, but also might be someone whose identity has thinned. Each little Eden, each bower of bliss, is also a theatre where Bonnard produced dramas of confinement and lost identity.

It's the same, or similar, with the pictures of Marthe in her bathroom. These beautiful images, which in frame after frame show a girlish figure in a state of apparently perfect relaxation, are not only portraits of unselfconscious pleasure, but also of a determined – almost a demented – longing to be clean. There's biographical support for this troubling view. We know that Marthe was agoraphobic. We understand that she spent much of her life in the grip of health worries, obsessively washing herself, trying to purge some imagined taint.

Even if we didn't know this from the biographies, we'd be able to work it out from the paintings. Their cumulative effect is not only

Howard Hodgkin by Andrew Graham-Dixon (Thames and Hudson, 1994)

to make us marvel more and more delightedly at the effects of light playing through water and upon floor tiles, or to encourage us to smile more and more broadly at the comedy of the little dog on the floor, or to help us imagine more and more easily the warm wind stirring the colours as it sidles through an open window. As we do these things, we are also increasingly disconcerted by the way Marthe's obsessional pose seems to be wearing her out. In the end she seems less an identifiable and ageing woman than a weirdly ageless slip of a thing: a girl-shadow, an ectoplasm, a sliver of pale soap.

So what does Hodgkin mean when he says that Bonnard captures 'life itself'? Not that the earlier painter's colours are merely life-enhancing, or that his scenes and narratives show a state of agreeable dissolution. Rather that Hodgkin's own paintings are places where we can follow a similar kind of argument between extrovert and introvert impulses, between contentment and confinement, between the pleasures of repetition and the desolation of obsession. For both painters, 'life itself' means seeing with unusual clarity, and registering with unusually strong feeling, the ways in which pleasure and pain, satisfaction and satiety, are actually tangled up with each other, and do not exist separately.

In his public remarks, Hodgkin has always been reluctant to admit what these pleasures and pains might be. His paintings he says, keeping everything vague, are 'representational pictures of emotional situations'. They show 'the evasiveness of reality'. They hanker after 'the glancing, slightly dematerialized quality that one does actually see' in reality. Andrew Graham-Dixon, in his book on the painter, interprets all these statements in broadly technical terms. He develops Hodgkin's suggestion that abstract and representational art are not necessarily opposed, and speaks about the form of the paintings as a kind of 'anti-realism' in which nothing is specific, all memory is incoherent, and circumstances matter more than specific places and people. 'I would like to paint pictures where people didn't care what anything was', Hodgkin has said, 'because they were so enveloped in them.' And again: 'There are many aspects of the subjects which I paint pictures about that would lose their meanings if they were too specifically represented, and that's why I am forced into metaphor . . . I'm forced into the use of metaphors because, if you particularize too much, especially about private emotions, they would remain in the painting.'

In the most general and commonsensical way, all such remarks open a gap between life and art – and Graham-Dixon wisely avoids any crude biographical readings. Yet the way he develops Hodgkin's *obiter dicta* leads him to interpret the paintings according to surprisingly strict modernist principles, and these look pretty dusty beside the glowing images they are meant to describe. Especially when he makes out – which he often does – that the main business of the paintings is to refer to themselves. In 'Passion and Jealousy', typically, we hear very little about passion and jealousy, and a good deal about how 'Hodgkin's multiple omissions are also ways of modestly admitting defeat, of saying how much is beyond the capacity of any work of art to include'.

When Susan Sontag criticized critics in her famous essay 'Against Interpretation' (1964), she concentrated her attack on those who strain to 'find the maximum amount of content in a work of art'. Thirty years on, Graham-Dixon honourably respects Sontag's honourable opinion. It means that his text is never less than tactful, and can be revealingly straightforward (in his two chapters on Hodgkin and Indian art, for instance). Its lack of analytic intent produces problems, all the same. It makes Hodgkin's works seem merely ends in themselves. It catches their delicate technique, but misses their circumstantial toughness.

Twenty years ago, Bruce Chatwin briefly managed to do both. Writing about Hodgkin's *Bombay Sunset*, he said it was painted 'in the colours of mud, blood and bile' – implying that it was possible to attach clear-cut emotional values to the paintings' colours, and to analyse their impact by speaking precisely about their moods. Graham-Dixon realizes that he is dealing with work of exceptional emotional power, but he won't risk discussing its particular context or significance. He concedes that 'There are a lot of pictures about fucking', and even 'several pictures about not fucking'. He also admits that 'much of the work' is filled with 'melancholy'. Yet he doesn't make nearly enough of these things, or allow us to feel directly their delight, or their frustration, or the bleakness which mingles with their beauty.

To say it again: Graham-Dixon has Hodgkin's own pronouncements to justify his restraint, but those who want to read the work more candidly, more *à la* Chatwin, could equally well enlist the artist's support. They might dwell, for instance, on the phrase Hodgkin used twice in his public 1988 conversation with David Sylvester – 'the tumescence of colour' – and want to develop its narrative potential in a large number of the paintings. In *Counting the Days*, to give just one example, where a sexy gush of yellow, red and white is threatened by a blank black blob which first snubs it, then wobbles off into an alluring but empty blue.

This painting alone is enough to remind us that Hodgkin benefits from a hands-on, delving kind of criticism. But it shows something else, too. The titles of his paintings (about which Graham-Dixon says virtually nothing) cleverly release and restrain our interpretations. It's well known that the only surviving example of Hodgkin's juvenilia is *Memoirs* (1949), painted when the artist was just seventeen. It shows a bald, thick-lipped and tightly dressed man staring at a woman on a sofa; the woman's head is, so to speak, out of the frame, and her alarmingly spiky hands (one suffocation-blue and flaunting a huge hard ring) accentuate yet protect her groin. The man, chin on palm, has a look which Graham-Dixon calls 'eagle-eyed'. Lascivious yet contemptuous would be a more extended way of putting it.

The title *Memoirs* draws our attention to the gap between the man's perception of the woman, and to the interval separating the work from its inspiration. Yet for all this precocious distancing, *Memoirs* summarizes a nexus of feelings that has remained remarkably steady, and exceptionally urgent, throughout Hodgkin's work. His titles have constantly alerted us to this turbulent centre of his imagination, hinting at stories of sexual pursuit and possession (*Waking up in Naples*), migrainous depressions and disappointments (*Snapshot*), and scorched escapes into other geographical and emotional climates (*Indian Sky*). Taken together, these and many other related paintings reveal an intensity in Hodgkin that Graham-Dixon only wants to suggest. Their 'life itself' is a dodgem-ride between extreme moods – a ride made all the more disturbing for its being rigorously hemmed in, passionately argued round. Brilliant reds buck and cavort unexpectedly; rainy greens sweep in out of nowhere and refresh; sudden blacks insult and smother. It's a world where desire remains perpetually innocent and vulnerable, where excitement is both necessary and threatening, and where longing competes – sometimes exuberantly, sometimes stubbornly – with despair.

No one should want to give a narrowly biographical account of these works – which, once they gain the courage of their convictions by the late 1970s, consistently achieve a lush magnificence that is both technically very impressive and emotionally very involving. At the same time, though, everyone should realize that their titles state openly what the paintings themselves achieve more complicatedly. They tell the direction of a story, but also welcome us into a narrative. They perplex us, but also make us feel at home. They are, if the word can be made to sound serious enough, flirtatious.

So, crucially, are other elements of his work. His portraits, for one thing, where the titles (*Mr and Mrs E. J. P.*) and treatments (*Keith and Kathy Sachs*), half reveal and half conceal the identity of the sitters. His frames, for another thing, which are invariably painted so as to become a part of the subject, and thereby render it open-ended yet contained. As we set these and all such dualities side by side, we develop an image of Hodgkin that is deeply Keatsian. Like Keats's poems, Hodgkin's paintings assemble all the elements of a circumstance or a personality, and allow them to co-exist. To prefer one point of view over another, they say, would be to run the risk of distortion. To privilege certain aspects would be to deny others.

For such an artist, not making up one's mind is a sign of strength, and showing the beauty of diversity is a way of recording the truth of humanity. Given this, it's inevitable that Hodgkin's remarks about his own work should insist on 'evasiveness' and 'truancy', and appropriate that they should mention 'metaphors' and 'emotional situations'. But this doesn't mean we have to be coy about the paintings' subjects, or their daring. As we see their necessary distances and separations, we nevertheless feel their broken narratives, their depressions and tumescences, their bleak moons and smiling bays for what they are: not just cunningly abstracted and generalized, but demandingly actual and intimate.

AN IMAGINARY LIFE

EDWARD THOMAS
An Imaginary Life

Edward Thomas chose to be a writer because it offered him certain kinds of freedom, but spent the first part of his writing life complaining that he was 'destined to reflect many characters and to be none'. Between 1897, when he published his first prose book at the age of nineteen, and the outbreak of the First World War sixteen years later, he produced thirty volumes of topography, biography and belles-lettres, compiled more than a dozen editions and anthologies, and produced over a million and a half words of review. Although this work made him conspicuous in the Edwardian literary scene, he was haunted by a sense of failure. He was incapable of finding the form in which he could do himself justice; every new venture left him feeling blocked, shackled, disappointed.

The difficulties were echoed in Thomas's private life. He married his wife Helen Noble in 1899 when he was twenty-one, had three children in short order, and spent a great deal of his home-time veering between dependency and resentment. He also had long periods alone – sometimes in London scouting for literary work, more often tramping the countryside to collect material for his books and end the 'sort of conspiracy going on [in my head] which leaves me only a joint tenancy and a perpetual scare of the other tenant and wonder what he will do'.

At his best the young Thomas was a scrupulous self-doubter; at his worst he was excessively self-mortifying. As a result, the story of his first thirty-five-odd years seems at once dizzyingly busy (all that work) and stiflingly uneventful (all those choked ambitions). It is much more nearly a story of failure than success. One or two of his books are entirely fresh and heartfelt (*The South Country*, for example, and *In Pursuit of Spring*); several contain passages of fine writing; the majority are blighted by haste or padding. Much the same can be said of his marriage. Parts were settled and contented, others frustrated and angry. On at least one occasion, when he was overwhelmed by professional and personal worries at the same time, he contemplated suicide. 'It is', he wrote in his diary on 9 October 1907, 'dislike of the effort to kill myself and fear that I would not carry it through if I half did it that keeps me alive. Only that.'

It took a stronger personality than his own, and an irresistible event, to set Thomas on a new road. In October 1913 he met Robert Frost, who had been living throughout England for the previous year. Frost bombarded Thomas with sympathetic verse-theories about 'the sound of sense', boosted his self-confidence, and soon succeeded where others had failed in persuading him to leave 'his old nest of prose' and start writing poems instead. 'When it came to beginning I slipped into it naturally,' Thomas said, remembering Keats's opinion that poetry should come as naturally as leaves to a tree. In the next two years he wrote almost one hundred and forty poems, often plundering his previous prose books and recasting their best passages.

Frost was a driving force for Thomas, but his influence was confirmed by the war. As its shadows closed round Thomas through the spring of 1914, they concentrated his mind by focusing his feelings for England, which had always been his subject as well as his home, and by forcing him to take decisions. Frost was about to return to America and wanted Thomas to go with him. Thomas was tempted, but conscious that he had other and more fundamental commitments. At the age of thirty-six there was no strong pressure on him to enlist, but in August 1915 he finally made up his mind. He abandoned the idea of visiting America, and joined the Artists' Rifles. When his friend Eleanor Farjeon asked him why, he scooped up a handful of earth and said, 'For this.' It was a confident gesture, but ambiguous – patriotic and also deathly. At this time the average life expectancy for a British officer in the trenches was one month.

Thomas spent a year and a half in training camps then sailed to

France at the beginning of 1917. A few weeks after he arrived in the trenches *An Annual of New Poetry* was published, containing eighteen of his poems under the pseudonym Edward Eastaway. This confirmed his sense of a new purpose in his life, but he knew that life itself was more precarious than ever before. On Easter Day, on the eve of the battle of Arras, he wrote in his diary:

A bright warm Easter day but Achincourt shelled at 12.39 and then at 2.15 so that we all retired to [the] cellar [of the billet]. I had to go over to battery at 3 for a practice barrage, skirting the danger zone, but we were twice interrupted. A 5.9 fell 2 yards from me as I stood by the f/c post. One burst down the back of the office and a piece of dust scratched my neck.

Dud shells were not uncommon in the trenches, but this failure seemed like a sign to Thomas. When his Commanding Officer, Major Lushington, teased him about his narrow escape, then asked, 'Whose turn is it for O[bservation] P[ost] tomorrow?', Thomas said it was his. Another officer chipped in that 'a fellow who was as lucky as he was would be safe wherever he went'.

The following morning, Easter Monday, 9 April, Thomas arrived at the Beaurains OP before first light. The artillery barrage began as the sun rose, with Thomas reporting back to the gunners on a field telephone, and sheltering in a crater from incoming fire. At 7.36 a shell landed near by, just as he was standing to fill his clay pipe. The blast poured over him, squeezing his heart and wrinkling the diary – and a letter from Helen – that he had tucked into his pocket before setting out. As he staggered backwards, a piece of shrapnel skimmed towards him, missing his chest but lacerating his left arm between the wrist and elbow. He collapsed into the shell-hole unconscious. Stretcher-bearers recovered him that evening. He later wrote of the 'strange, almost mystical swaying between earth and heaven' he had endured in the shell-hole, and of the 'bafflement' he felt the following day, when he woke after surgery in the field hospital to find that his left arm had been amputated below the elbow.

Helen's relief that Thomas's life had been spared overwhelmed all her other feelings. For the remainder of the war – which held most futures in suspension – they were happier than at any time in their marriage. As they took short walks together, gardened together, read to the children together, Thomas had no choice but to accept Helen's help, and she felt that by taking complete charge of her husband's life she was at last 'being of some use'.

There was another reason for the change in Thomas. Before leaving for France he had arranged for the publication of his first collection of poems to appear under his own name. When the book came out in mid-1917, dedicated to Frost, its reception helped to convince Thomas that he had indeed 'risen from the ashes' of himself. He told Frost, 'My critics, I admit, have given me more satisfaction than I expected and I dare say deserve. They at least will be content if I persevere.' Frost's own reaction to the book was predictably enthusiastic ('it is good with a whole lifetime of goodness distilled'), yet flecked with a trace of possessiveness. Reminding Thomas of his own more dramatic achievements in the monologues of *North of Boston*, he ended by urging Thomas to 'flex that strong right hand of yours to unroll the larger canvases you are equipped to paint'. Thomas took the advice without a murmur, apparently unaware of Frost's controlling instincts.

While Thomas was still training to be a soldier he had often felt unlike himself. 'Is peace going to awaken me as it will so many from a drugged sleep?' he had written to Frost from Hare Hall Camp, in Essex, late in 1915; 'Am I indulging in the pleasure of someone else?' But when the Armistice was signed in 1918 he found it was impossible to turn back into the person he had once been. The pain and inconvenience of his arm meant that long 'tramps' were now beyond him, which in turn meant that a major part of his writing, and of his income, was also taken away. Besides, the market for books like *The South Country* had shrunk. As England struggled to put the war behind it, and moved towards the Jazz Age, Thomas's kind of prose seemed suddenly quaint and out of date. In the summer of 1919 he wrote to his friend Gordon Bottomley, admitting that the 'strange holiday' he had enjoyed since returning from France could not last much longer. 'If I met the old ET on the road today,' he said, 'I could not fall in with him and talk in the familiar way. If I am to continue, it must be thanks to some desperate remedy. Which remedy I have yet to discover, though the siren songs from North of Boston are ringing in my ears.'

When Thomas considered Frost's repeated invitations to visit New England, he was determined to look on America not merely as a refuge but as a land of opportunity. He was used to new beginnings, but what he called 'my American experiment' was a more drastic step than any he had taken before the war. All the same, he persuaded himself that his decision was as 'natural' as his 'slip' into poetry: he sailed from Liverpool to Boston in February 1920, expecting not just a warm welcome but a continuing shared journey of discovery. He was right to feel confident. Frost greeted him as 'a lost brother', and for the first few weeks was always willing to give help and advice. But as the thrill of novelty wore off, tensions began to emerge. It was almost exactly five years since Thomas and Frost had last met, and although they had corresponded busily, neither was quite prepared for the changes they found in each other. As far as Frost was concerned, Thomas was still the tentative almost-poet he had first encountered in 1913; Thomas, for his part, still thought of Frost as a foreigner who needed his social and literary help. In fact Thomas was more decided than before, and Frost a great deal more bullish. *A Boy's Will* and *North of Boston* had been successfully published in America in 1915, and when *Mountain Interval* followed in 1916 Frost was generally recognized to be one of the leading poets of his generation – much in demand as a teacher and well-paid reader of his poems. In his first letter home to Eleanor Farjeon, written a month after his arrival in America, Thomas said: 'Robert surprises me by seeming a little larger in himself than I remembered, and a little more determined to make my life a part of his own. Am I to be the lady chapel and he the cathedral?'

Thomas had arranged to travel ahead of Helen and the children, who arrived in Boston four months after him in June 1920. Frost was in the process of leaving a farm in Franconia, New Hampshire (because the 'winter killed apple trees', he said to his English friend Jack Haines), and was settling with his family 'a hundred miles further south and out of the higher peaks' in South Shaftesbury, Vermont. He suggested that Thomas make his home in the farm at Franconia, and arranged for him to teach literature for a few hours a week at the local school. In addition Thomas was expected 'to keep an English weather eye' on Franconia, for which he would be excused paying rent.

Neither Frost nor Thomas wanted to admit that things were uneasy between them. Frost frequently stayed at Franconia, walking with his friend through the surrounding orchards, and talking late into the evenings on the veranda. There were, however, two clouds on the horizon that neither man could ignore. One was the reserve that Thomas felt in Frost's response to his recent poems. As Thomas absorbed the New England landscape, he continued to adapt the strict naturalism of his early pieces. But while Frost chose to embed his own darker thoughts in expansive monologues, or in shorter poems which seldom strayed from smooth-flowing iambic pentameters, Thomas wrote nervously, even sketchily, winnowing from his lines the last traces of nineteenth-century poeticism, and producing a series of tense, terse lyrics which often convey a sense of fragmentation.

In this respect, and also because they include shockingly matter-of-fact memories of the war, these poems break Thomas's last remaining ties with the Georgians, and affiliate themselves to the experiments launched in the late 1910s by Ezra Pound and T. S. Eliot. When Thomas had reviewed Pound's *Personae* in London he had first been enthusiastic, then recanted. Now he seemed to be changing his mind again – not by launching after Pound into obscurity, but by harnessing the distraught spirit of modernism to the traditions of time-honoured pastoral. Frost would later say, 'I like to read Eliot because it is fun seeing the way he does things, but I am always glad it is his way and not mine'; when Thomas read *The Waste Land* soon after it appeared in 1922, he wrote to Eleanor Farjeon:

I am left stumbling, of course, in my stretch after some of the allusions and so on. But the whole of it, the *feel* of it, is something I recognize and think I have always known. This is no small achievement for something so obviously new, and I would rather greet it with open arms than go to the wall as a back-slider or any of the old brigade.

Although Frost doubted the direction his friend's work was taking, he now encouraged Thomas to publish a second collection of poems (it was three years since *Poems* had appeared). Thomas gave the idea serious thought, even going so far as to draw up a contents list, but in the end decided to wait. His reasons, given in a letter to Frost in June 1921, shed a bright light on the changes that he felt he was undergoing as a writer:

You are quite right that my readers, such as they are, may forget me if I do not publish. But when I review what I have done over the last years, I hesitate. I suspect a publisher would want to advertise me as 'a war poet' and I cannot feel happy with that pinned on my chest along with my medal and my empty sleeve. For one thing I was in France for so little time, I cannot feel I deserve the accolade. For another, my reflections on the war – though numerous enough – have never or rarely been about war and war alone. I am not Sassoon, and am glad to have been spared the reasons why I might be. For another, I have a sensation of moving between fixed points, and am disinclined, as a result, to report on my whereabouts since I do not entirely see them myself.

The second 'American problem', as Thomas called it, was more acute and more personal. Even though his marriage to Helen had often been turbulent, he had always remained faithful to her – and made a point of owning up to his few innocent 'infatuations'. When Frost's wife Elinor introduced Thomas to the daughter of her former school friend Betsy Bellingham, shortly after he had arrived in Franconia, he succumbed again.

Ruth Bellingham was eighteen – an eager, bright school graduate who lived with her parents near Thomas's farm. It is unlikely that she had any intention of doing more than capturing his attention – to start with, at least. But in the comparative isolation of Franconia, and with his self-esteem weakened by the lurking difficulties of his friendship with Frost, Thomas soon began to lose control of his feelings for Ruth. By May she was visiting him almost every day.

Most of the written evidence for their relationship comes from the reminiscences of Frost, and a single confessional letter Thomas wrote to Jack Haines in England. In this he admits to seeing Ruth regularly, describes her as 'my open-hearted New England admirer', and says, 'I would say I am in love with her, always supposing I have a heart capable of loving.' Frost later corroborated this. 'Edward', he told a mutual friend, 'became enamoured of a young lady at around this time, which all things considered was not to be wondered at. What was remarkable was how much it consumed him, and how the damage done by the thing became greater than the thing itself.' Frost meant that Thomas had not only hurt his marriage but their friendship. Even though he continued to make regular visits to Franconia, and had ample opportunity to walk and talk with Thomas, he resented not having the whole of his attention. This, combined with his hesitations about the divergence in their work, threw a shadow over their friendship.

The situation was even more difficult for Helen. When she arrived at Franconia with the children in late June, and was introduced by Thomas to Ruth, she saw at once that her dreams of a happy reunion had been dashed. Within a matter of days, she confronted her husband, who responded with his customarily awkward honesty but remained stubborn. He continued to see Ruth several times a week as the summer turned into autumn, and although Helen tried to accept her diminished role in things, she and Thomas knew a crisis was inevitable. It came in September, when she announced that 'living in this odd, lopsided triangle' was impossible, and told Ruth's parents that she wanted their daughter to stop seeing her husband. The Bellinghams, who had supposed

Ruth's visits to Thomas were innocent and merely friendly, were shocked, and immediately dispatched Ruth to stay with her aunt in Boston for an indefinite period.

In the weeks after Ruth's departure, when Helen expected that he would 'come back' to her, Thomas withdrew even further into himself. He stopped writing poems. He took little interest in the farm. Frost grew impatient with him (calling him 'a booby') and more than impatient with Helen. Helen herself became so wretched that by Christmas she accepted yet another change was necessary. She offered to return with the children to Steep, having lived in America for a mere eight months. Thomas stayed for another year – a year of little achievement and evident unhappiness. His main task before leaving Franconia was to repair his relationship ('mend his walls', as he later put it) with Frost and Helen. Over the next few months he came to feel that Frost was actually a part of the difficulties he now faced. There was no obvious anger between the two men, no showdown, but a strengthening sense in Thomas that his friend was partly responsible for the hiatus in his marriage.

By the following summer, Frost and Thomas were often meeting again, and 'getting on famously', as Thomas said to Helen. 'By which I mean he goes about it famously, and I in my less conspicuous way.' As this suggests, both men were working to keep up appearances, but knew the bloom had faded from their friendship; although they continued to defend each other in public, and professed how close they were and always had been, their unique connection had been broken. They would never again be 'elected friends'.

Helen was more forgiving. In a series of long letters written from Franconia during the summer and autumn of 1921, Thomas reassured her of his love without ever quite apologizing for his interlude with Ruth, or asking for forgiveness. Helen told Janet Hooton she was 'not alarmed' by this. 'I have known him too long, and too well, to expect him to creep back to me – it is not his way. If he comes at all it will be as a man who feels that he has made his own decisions, and not because he pities me or the children. For myself, I will be happy. My existence is like a shadow without him.'

Thomas turned back towards Helen with a characteristic slowness. She was as ready for him as her word. When he eventually packed up at Franconia, and sailed to Liverpool in the autumn of 1922, she stood on the quayside to meet him. By this time, after his many twistings and turnings, Thomas was indeed convinced that he had made a free choice. Helen later described how quickly they resumed their old routines – with Thomas soon producing enough reviews and other kinds of hack literary work to keep his family afloat. If either of them felt an irreparable harm had been done to their marriage, they never said so.

In the spring of 1923 Helen told Eleanor Farjeon that she felt she had Thomas 'back from the war a second time, to heal and help'. But it was Thomas himself who took the most decisive step towards recovery: he at last agreed with his publishers to put out his second collection of poems, *The Apple Orchard*. It appeared the same month as Frost's fourth volume, *New Hampshire*, but now the differences between the two poets were as striking as their similarities. Frost's book contains many of his best and best-loved poems. It celebrates eternal verities and natural rhythms in generally colloquial lines, perfecting the sagacious fireside manner which would soon make Frost the most popular poet of his day.

Thomas's book is much more agitated and highly strung. In the several poems which deal directly with the war ('The Fire Step', 'Larks by Night') he is never as graphic as Sassoon or Wilfred Owen, but certainly catches the same sort of pathos – the pathos of mangled pastoral – that appears in Isaac Rosenberg's `Dead Man's Dump'. Elsewhere in the volume, whether Thomas is writing about his farming experiences in New England or his knotted feelings for Ruth and Helen, he develops the painful candour which first appeared in his so-called 'household poems' of 1916, in which he had told Helen he would give her 'myself . . . if I could find/Where it lay hidden and proved kind'. Invariably the poems are built on a smaller scale than Frost's, and they lack the grandeur of his confidence. The compensation is a thrilling sense of particularity – they seem written with no barrier or defence between the poet and his subject. Not surprisingly, many of the book's reviewers commented that it bore distinct resemblances to Eliot's *The Waste Land,* which had appeared the previous year. As the *Chronicle* said: 'Mr Thomas's poems may not have the evident learning and cosmopolitan range of Mr Eliot's modern epic, but they arise from and inhabit the same darkness.'

Thomas's book did not earn him much money, but it did make his reputation as one of the foremost English poets of the 1920s – and brought him other kinds of reward as well. One he especially valued was a letter from Thomas Hardy inviting him to call on him at Max Gate. Thomas had always admired and often reviewed Hardy's work, and judging by his report to Frost of their first encounter, they hit it off at once. 'TH', Thomas told Frost, 'is like his own darkling thrush – a little, eager, piercing man singing beautifully among (or I should say against) the shadows. He gave me tea out of a brownish cup and we talked of you among other matters. He has asked me to visit him again, and I shall. His wife hovered as I was leaving; she has the air of wanting to fuss over him, but hardly seems to know him. He showed more affection to his dog; a curious business.'

Thomas met Hardy at least six more times during the next few years, and came to see him as a 'venerable, if not a candid friend'. They were never intimate (their correspondence was sparse, and always concerned with practical details of their meetings, rather than more personal things), but they evidently felt validated and encouraged by one another. Hardy admired the naturalism in Thomas – even borrowing from Thomas's poem 'Out in the Dark' for his own 'The Fallow Deer at the Lonely House' – and Thomas felt a deep kinship with the realism and plangency of Hardy's vision.

Hardy respected Thomas's melancholy; it echoed his own bleak view of the universe. But he had no way of knowing how large a step Thomas had taken into unhappiness since his return from Franconia. Thomas's other friends were able to make a better judgement. When he toiled up to London looking for review work, and arranged meetings with poet colleagues such as Harold Monro, Lascelles Abercrombie and Wilfred Gibson, or with fellow naturalists like G. A. B. Dewer and W. H. Hudson, he struck them as 'entirely drained' (in Hudson's phrase). There was none of the occasional pre-war wittiness or the settled equilibrium he had found before leaving for America. 'Truly I am concerned for him,' Monro wrote to Walter de la Mare; 'He comes among us like a ghost, as though this earth is no longer his natural habitation.'

We can see what Monro meant in photographs taken at the time. When Thomas had left for France in 1917 he already looked much older than his thirty-nine years – his face gaunt and his eyes hooded. Now, in his mid-forties, he could have passed for a man of sixty: his clean-shaven face tanned by the sun, but hollow and exhausted-looking; his hair thin; his shoulders stooped; his clothes hanging loosely from his thin frame. No doubt his amputation was partly to blame. No doubt, too, the anxieties of his mainly free-lance life had left their mark. But there are also signs of a more fundamental, clinical problem – a physical wasting and degeneration.

Helen was especially concerned. Knowing that before the war Thomas had often visited doctors to complain of stomach ailments, and had repeatedly put himself on particular vegetarian diets, tried to give up smoking, even consulted a friend and advocate of Jung's named Godwin Baynes, she now became convinced that her husband was suffering (as she said to Janet Hooton) 'more in body than in mind, or as much in both'. When she eventually persuaded Thomas to visit a specialist in London in the spring of 1926, she was dismayed but not surprised to hear that he had been diagnosed with cancer of the lower intestine. He was immediately admitted to hospital for an examination, and returned to Steep in the early summer.

By early autumn it was clear to everyone that Thomas was a dying man. Helen feared that his death-sentence would plunge him into solitary misery, but she soon found otherwise. He greeted the news of his illness with the same resolution that he had found as a soldier. Even though he no longer had the energy to walk more than two or three miles at a stretch, and handed over most of the garden chores to Helen, his appetite for writing was actually refreshed by his predicament. Following Frost's example, he ordered the local carpenter to build what he called his 'poet's tray' (a portable sloping desktop) and spent his mornings 'putting my life in order, or rather into a disorder that may be interesting to others'.

This 'disorder' consisted largely of poems. Those written before the battle of Arras had come in a flood: nearly a hundred and fifty in twenty-four months. Most of them had been shaped by his steady concentration on natural things, and on the imminent loss of those things. But the mood of his post-war work was not merely mournful, it was unflinchingly bleak. The seasons, the weather, the songs of birds: all proved that he still felt he was 'an old inhabitant of earth', but their signals were always interrupted by intimations of 'nothingness'. They brought him closer to the spirit of Eliot, and anticipate the severities of Samuel Beckett.

As a young man Thomas had often complained that his need to earn money (let alone his lack of self-confidence) had kept him from the work he most wanted to do. During his last two years he was at least spared this kind of anxiety. In the same way that he had campaigned in the early 1910s for W. H. Davies to be awarded a Civil List pension, now Davies and others including Hardy petitioned for him – with the result that for the first time in his life he felt (as he said with appropriately heavy irony) 'a free man although I am everywhere in chains'. Rather than spread himself across a number of different plans, he chose to concentrate on one in particular: the completion of the childhood autobiography he had begun many years earlier.

This memoir, which was not published until 1929, has been widely recognized as a classic – a book crammed with insights into the evolution of his writer's mind, and also a moving evocation of the England first threatened and then devastated by the war. It also contains a number of shrewd, sharply etched portraits of famous contemporaries (Frost, Hardy, W. H. Hudson, de la Mare et al.), one of which has a special value, since its subject was not well known at the time Thomas met him. This is the reminiscence of Wilfred Owen.

Owen was in the same regiment as Thomas – the Artists' Rifles – and in November 1916 had been stationed at Hare Hall Camp in Essex, where Thomas was teaching map-reading, field-sketching and the use of a compass and protractor. They only overlapped for a week, and neither had yet published the poems that would make their names. (Owen's poems were first collected, with an introduction by Sassoon, in 1920.) But Thomas was already known by name to Owen as the author of a short book on Keats, which had appeared earlier the same year.

On 16 November, the day after he arrived at Hare Hall, Owen introduced himself to Thomas. As Thomas remembered in his autobiography:

He came to me in the mess one evening as an acolyte, as though in writing about Keats I had gained some contact with the immortal spirit. A compact, berry-brown figure still somewhere between boyhood and manhood, very punctilious in his turn-out, with his belt, boots, etc., waxed to a high polish and his moustache very trim and perfect. I would like to say I felt immediately aware of his genius, but this would not be true. We spoke of Keats, of course, and also of other writers, but nothing he said about them was distinguished by a particular insight.

It was his enthusiasm which made him stand out. He talked of Keats as though he was an old acquaintance, with whom he had shared confidences. I shall not easily forget the sunset waning behind him as we sat in our hut, gilding his hair and the side of his face, with the chat and racket of the others continuing around us. He told me he was writing verses, and I confided that I was about the same business myself, and we agreed we should show one another some specimens. But amidst the excursions and alarms of those days, our exchange never took place. I saw him only once more and by chance, when we coincided at the crossing-point of two paths in the barracks. I was on my way to class, and he was off to some other business of his own – hurrying, cramming his cap upon his head. We saluted one another in a scrambling fashion, and smiled, but that was all. When I first read his poems after their publication, I cursed myself for not shaking his hand. Truly, I believe that he had held conversations with John Keats, and had discovered something of his true essence.

Thomas finished his autobiography in the late spring of 1928. His health, as though it had depended on the work, immediately deteriorated. Because he was no longer strong enough to visit London, friends came to him – usually finding him in a wicker chair on the back lawn of the cottage, facing the massive beech hanger which rises behind Steep towards the villages of Froxfield and Uffington (which he had mentioned in his early poems). Helen, who would later write an extended memoir of her life with Thomas, remembered that 'he would watch the trees in a wise silence, as though uncertain whether he expected them to come close and consume him, or himself to rise up and enter their shadows. It is strange to say, but Edwy was more content during those last days than at any previous time. He often told me sorrowfully that he was dying before his time (he was fifty), but also that he felt he had filled his time, not always with happiness, but with the search for happiness at least.'

In September 1928, after staying briefly in France, Frost and Elinor came to England. It was their first visit since 1915, and Frost was anxious to see old friends like Gibson, Abercrombie, F. S. Flint, Edward Garnett, and de la Mare, and also to call on the Poet Laureate, Robert Bridges, whom he had last seen in Michigan three years previously. The climax of Frost's tour was lunch at Steep – but it was not a success. Thomas was too ill to sit with his friend for more than an hour, and Frost could scarcely conceal his annoyance that Helen stayed with them throughout. 'O he was polite, all right,' Helen later wrote to Janet Hooton, 'but what is it to be polite at a time such as this? Edward never made a secret of how much he owed to Robert.'

Helen knew, but could not admit, there were too many ghosts in the cottage that day: the ghosts of Frost and Thomas as young men finding themselves and each other; the ghosts of the war that Thomas had fought and Frost had observed; the ghost of Ruth Bellingham; the ghosts of roads taken and not taken, which had led the two men in diverging directions. Thomas, however, was beyond making this the reason for anything so obvious as a falling-out; if he felt any unhappiness about this final meeting with his friend, it was absorbed into the larger miseries of his illness.

A week after Frost left England, Thomas took to his bed for the last time. He died in the early hours of 31 October – Keats's birthday – with Helen at his bedside; he was buried in the churchyard at Steep the following Saturday. It was a small gathering ('I wanted to keep him to myself a little longer,' Helen told Janet Hooton), but fraught with a sense of larger significance. The shade of Thomas Hardy, who had died the previous January, was represented by a wreath from his widow, Florence. Frost also sent a wreath; the card was inscribed with nothing more than the two words of his name.

Three months later Helen organized a Service of Thanksgiving in the same church: it was filled to overflowing with friends from the village, London writers, and the whole large network of Thomas's literary acquaintances (including the sickly Gordon Bottomley). De la Mare, who had known Thomas since the mid-1900s, gave the address. Thomas, he said, had 'straddled two worlds and made a bridge between them'. He meant that by surviving the war, and continuing to write poems which were predominantly pastoral, Thomas had conserved what we now know as 'the English line' – the tradition and style which the modernists and the war had threatened to shatter. There is a large element of truth in this, but it makes Thomas sound as though he never developed far from his Georgian roots, and that his poems were essentially of a piece with the work that de la Mare and his contemporaries continued to produce into the middle of the twentieth century. In fact, when Thomas's *Collected Poems* (running to just over three hundred pages) was published in 1930, it was his departures rather than his preservations which caught the attention of reviewers, and which have proved the basis of his present-day reputation. In

1914 he had written to Frost, 'I want to begin over again . . . and wring all the necks of my rhetoric – the geese'. By the time he came back from America in 1923 he had no more necks to wring: his language was as plain as familiar speech, but compressed and nervous to a degree which marks a distinct break with his Georgian origins. He had, in fact, become an English modernist, whose late poems, despite their surface-simplicity and lack of private jokery, have more in common with W. H. Auden (whose adult career began in 1927) than with his eulogist de la Mare. If Thomas had been killed rather than mutilated on Easter Monday 1917 he would have left behind one hundred and forty-odd poems – enough to prove that he was the best of the Georgians, and to influence successive generations of English poets. But this influence would have polarized a debate between the 'English line' and the modernists – to make the former seem inflexibly cautious traditionalists, and the latter like the standard-bearers for everything radical, forward-looking and progressive. (It is, for instance, easy to imagine a poet like Philip Larkin feeling the modernists were antagonistic to his own poetic beliefs.)

As it is, Thomas's work during the post-war years makes such a stand-off unnecessary. Past and future meet in his work, just as peace and war, England and America, health and illness, love and solitude meet in his life. Thomas once called his younger self 'a superfluous man', borrowing Chekhov's phrase; in his autobiography (and thinking not only of his amputated arm) he referred to his middle-aged self as 'a patched-up man'. The difference between these two descriptions accurately suggests that by the end of his life he had found ways of reconciling the tensions which formed his character. 'My two roads', he went on, with an affectionate nod to Frost, 'have become one road – the chalky dust-path of my growing-up, and the hard metalled track of my later time. If they had stayed separate, would they have led me to different destinations? I cannot tell. The best a man can know is that he is easy in the place where he finds himself. I am easy where I am, even knowing that I cannot remain.'

POETS

JOHN DONNE

1 A Melancholy Lover

The picture of John Donne 'in the pose of a melancholy lover', which was bought by the National Portrait Gallery in the summer of 2006, has fixed a particular image of the poet in the public mind. It shows him soulful and amorous (the folded arms and sensual mouth), theatrical (the wide-brimmed black hat), dressy (the lacy collar and furred cuff), and enigmatic (the deep background shadows). An inscription bowed into a semi-circle round the top of the portrait reworks a phrase from a Latin psalm which can be translated as 'O Lady lighten our darkness'. Does this mean the picture was originally intended for a lover, or is it a kind of prayer to the Virgin Mary, and therefore also a reference to Donne's Catholic background? We can't be sure. Like so much else about Donne, the inscription is ambiguous – as much a fusion of 'contraries' as the man himself.

Books which emphasize the conflicts in Donne are hardly rarities. Paradoxes haunt the previously standard *Life* (published by R. C. Bald in 1970), and the best critical studies (including John Carey's landmark *Life, Mind, and Art*, 1981). But no biographer has taken more trouble than John Stubbs to put them in a post-Reformation context, and to examine their causes and their effects. His evocation is at once highly readable – because it's dashing as well as detailed – and sombre: although the poems may sometimes be playful, they arose from circumstances which were often frustrating and difficult. By giving these problems due weight, Stubbs manages to make Donne seem recognisable and sympathetic, and also the breathing inhabitant of a world which has long since disappeared.

John Donne: The Reformed Soul, by John Stubbs (Viking, 2006)

Donne was born in 1572, the son of Catholic parents who understood that if they wanted to get on in the world they would have to play down or actually disguise their faith. As it turned out, his father didn't have much time to make his mark: he died when Donne was four. (It's tempting, though, to think his trade influenced Donne in deep and subtle ways. He was an ironmonger: images of hammering, beating and forging occur throughout his son's poems, and the gradual move from a secular to a religious life might also be said to represent a larger sort of re-shaping.) His mother was a different matter. Long-lived and devout, she helped to form Donne's career both by reminding him of first principles, and by proving how dangerous they could be. Her faith required her to spend much of her life outside England.

Donne and his younger brother Henry got used to treading carefully from the start. They were educated first at Hart Hall in Oxford, where they hurried to finish their studies before turning sixteen, at which age anyone wishing to take a degree had to swear an Oath of Loyalty to the Reformed, Protestant Church. Then they went to Cambridge (probably: the record of Donne's early life is pretty vague), where they were able to continue working – though still cautiously. Catholics were generally treated as outsiders at best, and at worst – and the worst happened to several members of Donne's family – they were harried, tortured and put to death. Two years after Donne became a student at Thavies Inn in 1591, his brother Henry was visited by some of Topcliffe's Papist-hunters; they discovered he was sheltering William Harrington, a young Yorkshireman who had trained as a seminarian priest in Europe. Harrington was brutally mutilated, then executed, and Henry dispatched to Newgate. As Stubbs says, incarceration in the plague-filled gaol 'was all but a death sentence': he lasted only a little while.

We don't know the degree of Donne's original devotion to Catholicism, and therefore can only guess what it cost him to suppress his faith. But we can easily see the effects in the poems he began writing during this time. The tension of their arguments, their interest in reconciling opposites, and their compacted logic may be aimed largely at affairs of the heart, but they are matters of the mind as well, and as such reflect the larger picture of Donne's circumstances. To stand apart cleverly putting down women may have been a (sometimes misogynistic) way of asserting independence and superiority; the same things are also a sign of exclusion and anxiety – characteristics which are often missed by critics who highlight the poems' wittiness.

Even though Stubbs doesn't say enough about the extraordinary range and modernity of Donne's language, or its supple braininess, he's very good at showing its social and personal implications. He's excellent, too, at picking his way through the complicated evidence for Donne's movements in this pioneering part of his life. Footloose in London, seeking to live openly as a literary gent even if he could not do the same as a Catholic, he did his best to find patrons at court and elsewhere – signing up for military adventures with Raleigh which indicated, among other things, his willingness to oppose Catholic Spain. Eventually, in 1598, he was taken on as a secretary to Sir Thomas Egerton, the Lord Keeper of the Seal and senior judge at the Court of Chancery. Apparently the difficulties of his background were behind him, and his career about to take off.

But then Donne got snared in problems of his own making. He fell in love with Egerton's niece Ann, and married her. Ann's father was outraged (he'd wanted his daughter to make a much nobler and richer catch), and Egerton sacked Donne, who fled to a house in Pyrford, near Woking, owned by Ann's cousin, where the sense of exile that had always haunted him became a cold reality. The happiness of the marriage offered some comfort, of course, but as for making money and advancing himself – that now seemed impossible. He travelled a bit (to Paris and Italy for no very obvious reasons); he wrote; he studied law; he helped raise a family – but gradually he slipped into a mood of redundancy. He was 'John Donne undone', and knew that everyone in power, including the new King James, saw him in the same light. 'His Majestie remembered me, by the worst part of my historie,' he complained.

By moving to Mitcham on the River Wandle, and renting lodgings in London, Donne showed that he was still looking to regain something like his old position. But Stubbs paints a grim picture of his efforts during the first part of the new century. Desperate for preferment, he made connections where he could (including important friendships with the Countess of Bedford and Magdalen Herbert), he produced defences of the King like a 'masterful groveller', and he even considered offers to enter the priesthood – something his secular interests, and his widely known early reputation as a man-about-town – made problematic, to say the least.

Yet it was the Church that came to his rescue. Jack Donne became Dr Donne, the Dean of St Paul's. The transformation seemed improbable to many at the time. Stubbs, however, persuades us that it had an impressive logic. Even while he was still a student and wrestling with his Catholic inheritance, Donne had always wanted 'to discover for himself which form of Christianity was the right one'. The record of the 'Holy Sonnets', several of which were written before he took Holy Orders, suggests that his smart thinking actually deepened his convictions, rather than complicating or thwarting them.

This isn't to say Donne's character became any less dependent on paradox in the last part of his life. With his wife dead and his surviving children often demanding his attention, with his mind set on questions of faith but also filled with the business of a large and difficult job, with memories of his past 'sinfulness' informing his ideas about true religion, he contained in himself the same mass of opposites that made his sermons so exceptional. Twisting and turning, hammering and pounding, delving and delighting, they range widely in order to describe a centre – a vision of a common 'mutuall cause', and the need for 'equilibrium' in both Church and State. At their deepest level of argument, they are intent on condemning 'extremity'. In their language and performance they are often themselves extreme – splendidly theatrical, and still speaking to us directly across the centuries. Just like the portrait of the melancholy lover, in fact, though embodying a broader wisdom. And proving that although Donne lived a life of extraordinary variety, and was tugged in a multitude of opposite directions, he was 'entire of [him]self', as well as 'a part of the main'.

2 *Devotions Upon Emergent Occasions* and *Death's Duel*

John Donne's genius thrived on contradiction, and *Devotions Upon Emergent Occasions* is one of his most paradoxical works. It concentrates on death while celebrating life; it is sombre but not sad; it is egotistical but alarmed by isolation. *Death's Duel*, its independent pendant, is similarly crosshatched. It finds its energy in exhaustion and its spiritual hope in bodily defeat.

Death's Duel was the last sermon preached by Donne – on Friday, 25 February 1631, a little under ten years after he had been installed as the Dean of St Paul's Cathedral in London, and a little over a month before he died, aged fifty-nine. According to his biographer Izaak Walton, it was an extraordinary performance, even by Donne's standards: 'To the amazement of some beholders, he presented himself not to preach mortification by a living voice, but mortality by a decayed body, and a dying face.'

Evidently Donne's congregation was transfixed by his farewell, but his air of finality was not without precedent. In 1623, eight years before he ascended his pulpit for the last time, Donne had already appeared in his *Devotions* as a man waiting at death's door. Not slumped before it, spent and frightened, but rapping on the timber with his remaining strength.

Here is what happened. The early part of 1623 had been crammed – as had every year since Donne's election as Dean – with Cathedral business, associated legal business, and family business: Donne's wife, Ann, had died giving birth to a stillborn child in 1617; he had been left to supervise the upbringing of their seven surviving children. On 21 October 1623, he arranged a dinner for Edward Alleyn, at which Alleyn confirmed that he wanted to marry Donne's oldest daughter, Constance, then aged twenty-one. (Alleyn, 1566–1626, was an interesting catch. He had begun working as an actor with the Lord Admiral's Men during the 1590s and took the leading role in several new plays by Marlowe and Shakespeare. In 1613 he had moved to Dulwich, where he built the College of God's Gift.) Donne was in good health when the wedding plans were made. At the end of the following month, however, he

Devotions Upon Emergent Occasions and Death's Duel (Vintage, New York, 1999)

was struck down by the 'relapsing fever' then sweeping through London. He immediately brought forward the date of the wedding, which took place on 3 December.

Relapsing fever was so called because even when the initial danger was passed – the first week was critical – there was a strong likelihood of the patient succumbing suddenly during convalescence. Donne seems to have been over the worst by 6 December, but he was still feeble two months later. As late as February 1624 he described himself as being 'barred of my ordinary diet, which is Reading'.

The fact that Donne managed to plan, write, and publish his *Devotions* during this extremely difficult time is remarkable. Or rather it shows – and not for the only time in his life – that when most gravely threatened he was also compelled to produce his most defiantly lively writing. He began taking notes for the book as soon as the first wave of his illness had broken, organized its intricate structure at a feverish pace, and completed it during his recovery (which fortunately did not include any 'relapses'). He described the process in a letter to his friend Sir Robert Ker:

> Though I have left my bed, I have not left my bedside; I sit there still, and as a Prisoner discharged, sits at the Prison door, to beg Fees, so I sit here, to gather crumbs. I have used this leisure, to put the meditations [I] had in my sickness, into some such order, as may minister some holy delight. They arise to so many sheets (perchance 20.) as that without staying for that furniture of an Epistle, That my Friends importun'd me to Print them, I importune my Friends to receive them Printed.

These friends, and the official licenser, had first seen the completed *Devotions* at the very beginning of 1624, before the manuscript was entered in the Stationers Register on 9 January. They had 'received it printed' by 1 February. In other words, the book was not only written very fast but brought into the world very quickly, which suggests that it was intended to strike readers as being immediate and personal.

The reality is more complicated. In certain respects Donne was indeed concerned to create a palpable here-and-now. He describes the course of his illness in some detail, shows himself disordered and distressed during the first few days of his suffering, reflects on the treatment he received from his doctors (among them Simeon Foxe, the youngest son of John Foxe, author of *The Book of Martyrs*, who would also treat him at the end of his life), and provides enough anecdotal detail to prove his serious and particular case. Moreover, his language is always frankly intense: 'Whether it be Thy will to continue me long thus,' he says at one point, with a typically warm sense of actuality, 'or to dismiss me by death, be pleased to afford me the helps fit for both conditions, either for my weak stay here, or my final transmigration from hence.'

In other respects *Devotions* stands at a distance from its audience. This has less to do with period features of the writing, which can seem remote from modern usage, than with the very ingenuities that make the writing so arresting. We feel, as we often feel reading Donne's poems, that the emotional weight matters less than intellectual fireworks. Critics who believe there is something inherently disparaging about this separation often seek to heal it by saying, with T. S. Eliot, that thought was an experience for Donne. His brainwaves were in their way as charged and self-defining as the heartbeats of the Romantics. But this argument, while properly characterizing much of what is vital in his work, risks misrepresenting our experience as readers. *Devotions*, like all his greatest writing, is a performance, which means it holds us at arm's length. To put it another way: Donne's sickbed is a stage, and we admire the patient as if we were looking at him across footlights.

The structure of the book makes this certain. The twenty-three sections that follow 'The Stations of the Sickness' are each divided into three parts: 'Meditations Upon our Humane Condition', 'Expostulations, and Debatements with God', and 'Prayers, upon several occasions, to Him'. Although these sections are respectful toward their narrative of crisis and recovery, they read more like a set of daring intellectual adventures than a series of meditations on steady subjects. Their tight, recurring patterns, their relentless inquiry, and their discursive dazzle combine to generate a sense of detachment in their speaker.

Within the tight world of each little trinity, Donne makes raids on ideas of the Holy Trinity – wondering why an all-powerful God permits disease in the first place, pointing out how disease antici-pates death ('a sickbed is a grave'), calculating how we celebrate the 'blessed dependency' between God and ourselves, and remind-ing us how this 'spotted' life is a preparation for its immaculate sequel. The great achievement of the structure is to allow these thoughts their element of linear progress while creating the impression of a mind rattling around in a wheel. A point in his ill-ness begets a certain idea; this certain idea begets other ideas; these are differently examined in the three approaches that constitute each section; then the process starts all over again. No permanent resting places. But always the surrounding certainty of God's love, and of death. 'I need go no farther than myself,' Donne says; 'for a long time I was not able to rise; at last I must be raised by others; and now I am up, I am ready to sink lower than before.'

There is another constant, besides love and death. Sin. Human wickedness in general, and his own sin in particular. Although Donne never makes a detailed reference to his career as a young man – his life as a love poet and raffish European – he glances at it frequently and always in dismay. 'If I confess to Thee the sins of my youth,' he says in the tenth prayer, 'wilt Thou ask me if I know what those sins were? I know them not so well as to name them all, nor am I sure to live hours enough to name them all.' Elsewhere he refers to his 'sinful memory' with a feeling of disgust – with so much disgust, in fact, that he appears positively enthralled by his corruption. Why? Because although Donne's sins are burdensome to him, they are enabling. They are the means by which he defines his humanity and are therefore also the proof of his need for God.

In this sense Donne interprets his illness as a mixed blessing. On one hand it is a massive, consuming emblem of his fallen state. On the other it represents a step along the road to salvation, which can be fully achieved only by death. More than ten years before he produced the *Devotions*, in *Biathanatos* (first published in 1646), Donne had written a notorious defence of suicide. Now he is excited by the thought that self-murder might not be necessary ('I do nothing upon myself, and yet am mine own executioner'). The first prayer in the *Devotions* moderately asks God to 'enable me by thy grace to look forward to mine end'; later he reassures us, 'I fear not the hastening of my death'; later again his voice melts: 'Death is in an old man's door, he appears and tells him so, and death is at a young man's back, and says nothing; age is a sickness, and youth is an ambush; and we need so many physicians as may make up a watch, and spy every inconvenience. There is scarce anything that hath not killed somebody; a hair, a feather hath done it; nay, that which is our best antidote against it hath done it; the best cordial hath been deadly poison.'

The note of acceptance here is unignorable. But if we tried to persuade ourselves that its calm music swells slowly and surely through the *Devotions*, we would imply that the book's contradictory elements were eventually resolved. They are not. However profoundly Donne accepts that 'the whole course of life is but an active death', and however eagerly he anticipates the prospect of his release, he is always buffeted by opposites. The self that longs to be transfigured is also the self that feels insulted by extinction, and clings to a dramatic identity in spite of itself. The sickroom might be a physical prison, but even here the mind is exhilaratingly nimble, adventurous and free. It is, he says, an 'inexplicable mystery': 'My thoughts reach all, comprehend I their creator am in a close prison, in a sickbed, anywhere, and any one of my creatures, my thoughts, is with the sun, and beyond the sun, overtakes the sun, and overgoes the sun in one pace, one step, everywhere.'

Donne knows that his self-delighting mind supports his spiritual effort: it prevents his faith from becoming complacent or merely passive. In some respects, though, it creates problems. The worst of them has to do with the question of how his self connects with the world around him. The *Devotions* are preoccupied by solitude: not the bliss of solitude, but the threat of solitude. As a young poet, as a priest, and as a preacher, Donne spent his life producing words that were determined to reflect and engage with society at large. Illness threatens this relationship. 'Solitude is a torment which is not threatened in hell itself,' he says, and again: 'How little and how impotent a piece of the world is any man alone?' Eventually Donne consoles himself by declaring that individuals are never truly isolated:

No man is an island, entire of itself; every man is a piece of the continent, a part of the main. If a clod be washed away by the sea, Europe is the less, as well as if a promontory were, as well as if a manor of thy friend's or of thine own were: any man's death diminishes me, because I am involved in mankind, and therefore never send to know for whom the bell tolls; it tolls for thee.

'Because I am involved in mankind.' The imagery of this famous passage dramatizes what is at stake, as do the other language patterns that bind together the *Devotions*. At regular intervals, for instance, the alarming disorder of illness is rendered as a conflict between rival kingdoms. So many glimpses of insurrection and war are flashed before us that our sense of the individual gradually expands to fill the space normally reserved for a country. That is to say: the self is not a timorous and quailing thing, trembling before its creator and insisting on its own littleness. It is a dynamic and heroic thing – as intrepid in its way as its alter ego the explorer-lover – and always looking for new ways to increase its reach. At the same time, Donne is always on the look-out for new ways to define the limits of the self, as we can see by registering another significant language pattern. Donne's poems are famously fascinated by things being stretched or extended (compasses, 'gold to airy thinness beat'); his *Devotions* are strewn with images of impermanence. In both cases the effect is to convey a sense of volatility – of a speaker who is at once freed and troubled by living between worlds. Wax ('These heats, O Lord, which Thou hast brought upon this body, are but Thy chafing of the wax, that thou might'st seal me to Thee'); a river (which in its course describes 'the precipitation of man's body to dissolution'): these and other images in the *Devotions* ensure that our pleasure in the artfulness of Donne's mind is always accompanied by sympathy for his plight. They mean that while we relish the text he produced, we realize that he was himself a body turning into a text. Illness writes on his body ('I have cut up mine own anatomy, – dissected myself, and they are gone to read upon me') but also makes him legible as God's creation: 'These spots are but the letters in which thou has written thine own name and conveyed thyself to me.'

It is the persistence and complexity of these paradoxes that make the *Devotions* such a consoling work. The same applies to *Death's Duel*, though the mood here is more uniformly dark: it is a black mind-labyrinth lit by lightning flashes, echoing with the clatter of mental swordplay. Coincidentally, Donne's daughter Constance was once again a part of the background story. In the summer of 1630, he went to stay with Constance and her second husband at Aldeborough Hatch in Essex, and while there he fell ill, probably with gastric cancer. On 13 December he made his will, and when he returned to London in late January 1631, his friends were shocked to see how wasted he had become. Not that this prevented him from preparing *Death's Duel* minutely, writing it out in full before committing it to memory, perhaps because he knew it would be printed after his death.

Like the *Devotions*, *Death's Duel* has a tightly organized, well-founded structure (the sermon actually begins by saying, 'Buildings stand by the benefit of their foundations that sustain and support them'). Taking as his epigraph 'And unto God the Lord belong the issues of death (i.e. from death)' he wrings three meanings from the phrase: 'deliverance from death', 'the disposition and manner of our death', and 'a deliverance by death'.

The first third of the sermon is the longest, showing once again that Donne's mind was most urgently stimulated by the struggle between opposites. As he reminds his congregation that the fact of their mortality has been evident since birth, that their bodies have only one destination, and that their sinfulness accelerates the journey toward it, he adopts the same tactics as he did in the *Devotions*. He tries to meet death on equal terms by matching its force with his eloquence. Making his last hours his finest hours, he both prepares himself for God and reminds himself of what he is about to lose.

In the briefer second and third sections, Donne shifts his attention from ideas of deliverance to thoughts of judgement, and finally to the example of Christ's death: 'There now hangs that sacred body upon the cross, rebaptized in his own tears, and sweat, and embalmed in his own blood alive. Then are those bowels of compassion which are so conspicuous, so manifested, as that you may see them through his wounds. Then those glorious eyes grew faint in their sight, so as the sun, ashamed to survive them, departed with his light too.' These almost final words are among Donne's boldest: his congregation, staring at his hollowed face, hearing the rasp of his exhausted voice, realized – as Walton realized – that he was invoking the 'blessed dependency' not merely between his listeners and their God, but between himself and his suffering Christ. The sensational egotism of the comparison is the triumph of his compassion.

And also of his theatricality. In *Death's Duel*, as in the *Devotions*, we are engrossed by the evidence of an exceptional mind engaged in the act of thinking for itself – Donne's sentences change direction to accommodate ideas as they rush toward him, his lexicon riffles and even expands (he coins 'contignation' in the first paragraph) as he tries to find words for everything that is in his head. At the same time, he validates his thinking for others. Donne had been conspicuously slow to give up a secular existence and turn to the Church, and his decision was more obviously swayed by the King's intervention than by his own faith. But once he had embraced his new life, he retained and adapted the authorizing intelligence he had developed in his old one: an intelligence that dreads isolation, regrets corruption, and acknowledges mortality; that delights in audacious argument, in proud wit, in outrageous flights of fancy; that knows these things brand him as fallible but also understands how they honour common humanity.

The Romantic Sisterhood

1 Iron Hinges

It is a truth universally acknowledged that the achievements of the first-generation Romantic poets depended greatly on the women in their lives. Henry Crabb Robinson said of Wordsworth: 'If Providence had not blessed him with a wife, a sister, a wife's sister and a daughter . . . it is probable that many of his verses . . . would have been scattered to the winds.' (He might reasonably have added: 'or not have been written at all'.) Coleridge's daughter Sara echoed the thought. 'Never', she said, 'was a Poet so blessed before (as my father) in the ladies of his household.' In both remarks, we can hear a note which has reverberated down the years. Admiring but admonishing, proud but piqued, they link the two poets with all those other geniuses in history who have demanded more or less permanent coddling and obedience.

Kathleen Jones is the latest biographer, and will not be the last, to try and unravel the paradoxes. Beginning her story close to the end of the eighteenth century with the three Fricker sisters (one of whom married Robert Southey, another Coleridge), and then casting the net of her narrative to catch all the Lake poets before throwing it forward again to bring in their children, she works hard to discover abiding themes and recurring patterns. If much of the material in her book is well known, the arrangement usually makes it seem fresh – and it's delivered with a likeably urgent sympathy.

At least, it is when Jones is rescuing her women from obscurity, and exploring the difficulties of their lives. When she turns aside from these aims and starts openly chastising the men, it's hard not to feel put off, no matter how strongly we might share her view of

A Passionate Sisterhood by Kathleen Jones (Constable, 1997)

things. We are told, for instance, about the 'unforgivable' letter Coleridge writes to his wife Sarah, and about Wordsworth's 'deplorable act of cruelty' to his daughter Dora. These censorious outbursts cast a long shadow, making the book slightly monotonous. For all the fascination of its narratives, and in spite of the justice of its cause, the emphasis returns too routinely to the idea that its heroines are victims, and does not discuss often enough – or illuminatingly enough – their function as collaborators, contributors and originators.

Which is not to say that victimization was negligible within the families and in the world at large. From the moment Jones takes up her story of the three Fricker girls, we are forcibly reminded about the segregations and prejudices of the times. Because the sisters were good needlewomen, and lived briefly in Bath, they were linked with 'a profession with a dubious reputation'. By marrying as they did, Sarah and Edith – and Mary, who attached herself to the short-lived Robert Lovell – hoped to escape their background: Southey and Coleridge were radical idealists, planning their utopian Pantisocratic settlement on the banks of the Susquehanna. When the women agreed to go with them, they looked forward to a life based on a belief in 'the Fraternity of universal Nature', where their responsibilities as mothers would be bearable because, their husbands assured them, 'An infant is almost always sleeping.'

There was, of course, no journey to the Susquehanna, just a good deal of trekking from the West Country to London and back, and a simultaneous endorsement and explosion of their original loyalties when Wordsworth burst on the scene. This, in turn, brought more trekking – to the Lake District, which became home to most of the 'sisterhood' – and more faces: Sara Hutchinson, Wordsworth's sister Dorothy and (eventually) his wife Mary and daughter Dora. There are times when Jones struggles to keep such a large cast of characters all moving forward together, but if this means that the tone sometimes becomes perfunctory ('In June 1813 George Fricker arrived at Keswick in the last stages of tuberculosis'), it also allows us an appropriate sense of bustle and contradiction. Soon after they were formed, the ideals of Pantisocracy had been eroded by indecision, by poverty, and by the sheer grind of daily events.

This grind hurt the women more than the men. Reading their letters, which Jones quotes well, we can see it building through regular references to headaches, toothaches, and stomach aches, but over the years these comparatively minor ailments coalesced into something continuous and very grim. Take the Coleridge strand of the story. As Coleridge fell in love with Sara Hutchinson and became seriously addicted to opium, his wife bowed under the yoke of her disappointment: two of her four children died young, her dependence on the Southey household was accepted but felt as a failure, and her contribution to Coleridge's work was suppressed. (He revised a number of early poems to write her out of them.) It's no surprise to find that in middle life Sara invented a private 'nonsense' language, which entertained her family but was evidence of her instability and isolation.

Things were hardly less depressing for the Southey family, once they had settled at Greta Hall in the Lakes. Although Robert's wife Edith was generally regarded by his friends – women and men – as not giving him everything he wanted, Jones shows that she was entitled to a good deal of sympathy. Four of her eight children died young, and she eventually declined from fusspottery into 'settled melancholy', unable to tolerate strangers, and sometimes raving in a 'mania'. When she died, Southey quickly married again, only to lose his own wits soon afterwards. Jones reminds us that however richly he deserved the scorn which was poured on his work and his later politics, he died a pitiable man, surrounded by the ghosts of pitiable women.

The Wordsworth story is better known, and anyone telling it is likely to feel that the man himself was more directly responsible for the unhappiness around him than Southey ever was. Jones certainly thinks so, but while her indignation at his self-absorption feels justified, her treatment of other parts of his life is sketchy. She does not sufficiently develop the idea that in early adulthood, William's relationship with his sister Dorothy was profoundly enabling, as well as enabled. Dorothy was often co-opted as her brother's poetic eyes as well as ears. She was required to comfort and guide him through his love affair with Annette Vallon. She transcribed many of his greatest poems and inspired others. In return, she rejoiced in feeling the enormous electricity of his interest and love, wiring much of it into her daily life, and much into her marvellous journals. Did she really expect to control his marriage when it inevitably occurred? Jones is brisk but telling about the terrible decay – first physical, then mental – which it precipitated, and the photograph she gives of the final entries in Dorothy's last journal is desperately sad. Among the broken words we can see: 'Torments . . . dysmal gloom . . . no iron hinges.'

In her heyday with her brother, Dorothy wrote brilliantly, and lived on the brink of greatness. Because her fall into frailty took her further than anyone else in her circle, and meant leaving finer work behind, it dominates all the surrounding narratives. Yet thanks in part to their jostling closeness, and in part to Jones's diligent assembling and synthesizing, we can see what is typical in Dorothy's story, as well as what is exceptional. Like the women around her, she endured – and accepted – a heavy load of frustration before sinking into her final twilight. Unlike them, she briefly fulfilled her immortal longings.

2 How Deep a Blessing

A little over fifty years ago, the literary critic F. W. Bateson suggested that when William Wordsworth and his sister Dorothy were staying in Lower Saxony at the very end of the 1700s they realized they were falling in love with each other. Hence the strange passion of the Lucy poems, which were written at this time, the subsequent 'desperate remedy' of William's marriage to Mary Hutchinson, and Dorothy's slow self-sacrifice and eventual collapse into something like insanity. Bateson's comments had the effect of a hawk in a dovecote – surprisingly, given that the evidence to support them was so readily available; not surprisingly, since all the world loves a scandal. Since then Wordsworth's biographers have routinely

The Ballad of Dorothy Wordsworth, by Frances Wilson (Faber and Faber, 2008)

slowed down their march through his life to consider the question of his incest, generally agreeing that while there's no proof sexual acts took place, the relationship itself was (as Stephen Gill, for instance, says) 'unquestionably, profoundly sexual'.

Dorothy's account of her brother's wedding day, contained in one of her Grasmere Journals, comes as close as anything she wrote to making a confession – especially in a passage that was later heavily deleted (we don't know by whom). She had spent the previous night sleeping with the ring that William would later give to Mary on her own finger, then on the morning itself, before he went off to church without her, she 'gave him the wedding ring – and with how deep a blessing! I took it from my forefinger . . . he slipped it again onto my finger and blessed me fervently'. Or rather, this is what everyone once believed she did – thanks to Helen Darbishire, who used infra-red light to transcribe the first complete edition of the Journals in 1958. In the latest edition, produced by Pamela Woof in 2002, the fervent final few words turn out to be a misreading of 'as I blessed the ring softly'. This is clearly a much less sensational phrase, but the fundamental questions remain. What precisely was the nature of the relationship between William and Dorothy? What did they give one another in life, and what did they take away?

Frances Wilson, whose previous biography *The Courtesan's Revenge* has already shown her to be an exceptionally shrewd analyst of erotic complexities, is the ideal person to turn to for answers – and *The Ballad of Dorothy Wordsworth* doesn't disappoint. Realizing the stakes are high (the whole story could so easily shade off into vulgarity or silliness), she writes with a definite sense of astonishment, but controls it with calm scholarly interest, and a prevailing mood of humane tolerance. The combination is deeply attractive and original. Wilson says that her book tells 'the story of the four small notebooks' we know as the Grasmere Journals; actually it is a complete biography of Dorothy which concentrates on the 'threshold years' she spent with William between Christmas 1799 and October 1802, and is written in such a way as to seem entirely lucid and yet absolutely rapt – darting and discriminating, scrutinizing

137

and savouring, pondering and picking over, brooding and braving. It's a method that wouldn't work for every kind of biographical subject, but in this case it's brilliantly apt and sympathetic.

Wilson inevitably reappraises Dorothy as a human being, as well as re-evaluating her as a writer. Hitherto, there has been a tendency to praise her 'responsiveness' above everything: when Coleridge wrote that she was 'a perfect electrometer – it bends, protrudes, and draws in, at subtlest beauties and most recondite faults', he said what oft was thought but ne'er so well expressed. The emphasis catches something important about Dorothy: her sensitivity to atmospheres and landscapes was extraordinary, and so was her ability to tune into and combine with her brother's imagination – as we can see in the several instances where their writings echo one another. (The similarity between Wordsworth's poem 'A Night Piece' and Dorothy's Journal entry for 25 January 1798, where she describes how the night sky 'seemed to cleave asunder, and left [the moon] in the centre of a black-blue vault', is a good example.)

But while Wilson pays proper respect to this side of Dorothy's genius, she also strips away the layers of slightly sentimental approbation that it has licensed over the years, allowing her to seem as she was: elusive, as well as intimate. When we follow Dorothy from her early childhood (spent apart from her brothers), to the various halfway homes in Norfolk, Windsor and the West Country, then back to her full, proper home in Grasmere, we find her suppressing some parts of herself just as fiercely as she insists on realizing others. This defiant but dangerous internal contest is at its most intense in her relationship with William. By aligning her life with his, and assuming from early womanhood that they would always be together in some kind of ménage or other, she discovered freedom and self-validation but also embraced self-denial.

Through most of the time that forms the centre of this book, the benefits of this paradox outweighed the difficulties. Wordsworth was a man of quite staggering egotism, even when judged by the standards of most poets, but the nursing (writing often made him

ill), the cooking (gallons of broth), the writing (not just transcrib-
ing the poems William composed on the hoof but handling most
of his post, including love letters), and the comforting (especially
during the time of his final separation from Annette Vallon) were
all things Dorothy willingly undertook. More than that, she felt –
and actually was – released by them. Released into forms of
behaviour that ranged from the boldly emancipated to the downright weird, but that were enjoyed freely and with a tremendous
sense of mutual benefit. Wilson gives all this the credit it deserves,
and quite properly balances the Wordsworths' 'sense sublime of
something far more deeply interfused' in their existence, with its
humdrum actuality. (It's good – isn't it? – to be reminded that on
the morning William wrote the opening line of the 'Immortality
Ode', he was interrupted by the arrival of a load of dung for the
garden.) But the longer she pores over the Journals, and the more
carefully she peers between their lines, the clearer it becomes that
Dorothy's devotion came at a price she hardly knew she was paying. Or maybe just didn't mind paying. Her almost endless
migraines are recorded as mere matters of fact; local gossip is
ignored; her exclusion from men other than her brother and his
close friends is made to sound normal.

Disaster feels inevitable – and it comes, of course, in the form of
William's wedding. Except that the marriage turned out to be
exceptionally happy, and Dorothy never did anything but support
it and call Mary 'dear'. Yet in the last part of Dorothy's long life (she
stayed under her brother's roof until her death at the age of eighty-
four), the strains finally emerged, and drove her to the edge of
madness. These were emphatically not the strains of guilt, though
some biographers have suggested as much. They are much more
probably, as Wilson says, the result of a severe depressive boredom.
Her role in William's life had been usurped – not entirely, and not
only by his wife but by a veritable harem of helpers. It means that
we close this book with a crushing sense of Dorothy's isolation –
while at the same time feeling we have been told a story that is
important and moving, and has at its heart a mysterious tenderness that has never before been so closely approached.

JOHN CLARE

1 A Life at Last

'Neglect is the only touchstone by which true genius is proved': like a lot of poets who feel hard-done-by in their lives, John Clare looked to posterity for his reward. He had more reason than most to do so. Whereas Keats had to deal with incomprehension and ridicule, Clare spent at least half his writing life actually unpublished – ignored by the readers who had once welcomed him, and latterly removed from the world into the confines of High Beech then Northampton General Lunatic Asylum. After his death in 1864 the neglect continued. Due partly to a long collective failure to appreciate him, and partly to the immense muddle of his manuscripts, it's taken nearly one hundred and fifty years for his work to gain the reputation it deserves.

'Muddle' in this case hasn't just meant the linked difficulties of deciphering his texts, and deciding how best to deal with the particulars of his spelling, punctuation and grammar. It has also had to do with a uniquely problematic issue of copyright. In 1965 the scholar Eric Robinson (who has no direct link to Clare's family or his original publishers) bought a mass of unpublished Clare manuscripts for the nominal sum of £1, thereby requiring other interested editorial parties to seek his permission to publish, and in some cases to pay a fee. This has generated what Jonathan Bate carefully calls 'the (not entirely accurate) perception that he would be hostile to any editorial approach other than his own method'. As Bate goes on to say, it is 'a strange situation', but that's putting it mildly. Robinson's actions are now being challenged in law, just as his 'own method' of editing the poems – which is one 'of rigorous fidelity to every particular of the manuscripts' – is being contested

John Clare: A Biography, by Jonathan Bate (Picador, 2003)

by other scholars, Bate among them. Poor Clare. Trampled in life; side-lined or fought over in death.

Still, thanks to Bate, at least we now have an appropriately ample and judicious biography. It rises from a passionate conviction of Clare's genius, and spreads into a calm appraisal of his experience. But there's cleverness in this calm: Bate knows the sadness of Clare's story has led previous writers to make false claims for him by sentimentalizing his achievement. His own tactic is to take nothing for granted, to stay as close as possible to Clare's intentions, to resist the temptation to read all the poems as being strictly autobiographical, and to admit ignorance where ignorance exists.

Clare's first twenty years are especially murky, and rather than struggle to assemble a chronological sequence, Bate takes a thematic approach, winding chapters on heredity, childhood, social environment and friendship around the few available facts of birth, family and upbringing. Far from making Clare seem vague, this has the good effect of allowing him to exist in a kind of dream. It's a dream which combines elements of bliss – the blazing delights in his home village of Helpston in Northamptonshire – with more nearly nightmarish components: the death of his twin sister, his family's poverty, the gruelling certainties and equally miserable uncertainties of manual labour, the threat and upheaval of Enclosure.

There has long been a body of opinion which claims that Enclosure was uniformly a disaster for those who worked the land. Bate challenges this argument, pointing out that in some cases it actually increased agricultural productivity and rural employment – before saying, rightly, that 'what matters to individual lives is personal experience, not economic statistics'. As far as Clare was concerned, Enclosure meant the end of the world he had known from birth. He could still breathe the air of paradise in Helpston, but he felt pushed out – an 'alien' at the centre of his own universe.

In this respect, we can see Clare's poetic impulse as something born of the wish to preserve, as well as to celebrate; even the most simply joyful early pieces such as 'To the Fox Fern' are soaked in the same regret that we find in later and more candidly mournful pieces like 'The Moors'. He was never 'a party man', never overtly revolutionary in his sympathies, 'but political opinions he certainly had', and these opinions are manifest in his reaction to everything around him. This in turn explains why the act of seeing mattered to him, and why he so relished details. For years there has been a tendency for readers to fall on these details simply as proof of his vigilance as a 'nature writer', but they are more than that: the extraordinary brilliance of his prose (light-rings 'widening and quavering on the water with the plunge of a Pike'), the myriad dazzling close-ups of his poems (the 'olive' feathers of a robin), are all a means of registering feeling. Like his local, vernacular language ('blea', 'crizzling', 'proggling', 'stulp'), they root him in his place even as they suggest his uprootedness.

Thomson's *The Seasons* set Clare on the road to poetry, and although he sheltered 'under the example of their popularity', and felt encouraged by the success of 'peasant poets' such as Robert Bloomfield, he was also aware that writing aggravated his condition as well as easing it. It confirmed his position as an oddball, an exception in his community. When his poems reached the London publisher John Taylor, the differences grew even more complicated – though Bate's job as a biographer simultaneously becomes somewhat easier. By joining the 'mainstream' Clare enters the realm of event-and-consequence, and the story of his life submits more readily to a chronological treatment. Most of the bare facts have been well known for some time now, but Bate takes us through them with proper vigilance, challenging misconceptions and adding details.

Bate is especially good on Clare's relationship with his publisher. In the past, Taylor has often been accused of mangling Clare's manuscripts, editing out their politics and curbing their originality. In this account it's clear that Taylor did indeed show some naivety in his original presentation of Clare, but broadly speaking he carried out Clare's wishes with a real respect for the original intention, and a genuine desire to resolve the rhythmical and textual problems they both knew needed sorting out. Bate follows

Taylor's lead in his own new selection of Clare's poems (*John Clare: Selected Poems*, Faber and Faber, 2003), where he makes a sensible distinction between 'normalization' and 'alteration'. The result is the broadest and most reliable sample of Clare's work now available, ranging from 'early poems' through to poems written in the Northampton asylum. We can see clearly, as Clare meant us to see, the scope as well as the substance of his work: the density of his sonnet-writing as well as its detailing ('Bumbarrel's Nest'); the structure as well as the strangeness of his satires ('Don Juan'); and the discipline as well as heartbreak of his natural elegies ('To the Snipe', 'The Lament of Swordy Well'). Taylor would have been grateful to Bate for carrying on his work, and we should be too.

Taylor wasn't valuable to Clare only as an editor. He also helped him to deal with the patrons who came forward when the first collection was published in 1820, he was generally generous about money matters, and encouraged him to be true to himself. 'I like your Independence, Clare,' Taylor says in one letter, 'and am sorry that any persons should be so ill judging as to try and screw you up the Squeak of Flattery. Take your own Course; write what you like.' At moments like this we can hear the same decency and kindness that Taylor showed to another of his authors: Keats.

Initially the public liked what Clare liked to write. But as the 1820s went by, the market for poetry dwindled, and 'peasant poets' became yesterday's fashion. Although every one of Clare's last three books (published in 1826, 1827 and 1835) is stronger than its predecessor, they brought him diminishing returns. For this reason and others, the last twenty-three years of his life make desperately sad reading. His wife seems never to have visited him in the Northampton asylum. His friend William F. Knight (who helped him finish some eight hundred poems between 1841 and 1849) left the vicinity. By 1852 he was virtually invisible to the outside world, and although generally calm around others, deeply troubled in himself. Bate reaches the end of the story on the same level note that he holds throughout, and the effect is all the greater for his restraint. For the first time, we can see the whole canvas of an extraordinary life, and marvel as we should at the quality and extent of its achievement. Clare may not have the epic sweep of Wordsworth, or the compact excellence of Keats, or the intellectual depth of Coleridge, but his best writing combines sharp seeing and deep feeling to an extent that means he deserves a place beside them in the pantheon of great Romantic poets.

2 Images from Nature

Quotations from John Clare's writings are taken wherever possible from *John Clare: Selected Poems*, edited by Jonathan Bate (Faber and Faber, 2003); texts not included in that book are taken from *Selected Poems and Prose of John Clare*, chosen and edited by Eric Robinson and Geoffrey Summerfield (OUP, 1967).

At first glance, John Clare and John Keats don't have much in common, beyond the fact that they shared the same publisher, John Taylor; one day in the late spring of 1820, in Taylor's offices, Keats revised his poem 'Lamia' on the back of an envelope recently sent by Clare. That was as close as they came to each other. They never met. They never corresponded. Their styles – Clare's earthy and unadorned, Keats's urban and allusive – suggest they came from and belonged to strictly separate worlds.

It's not as simple as that. Clare was the son of a labourer, born at Helpston in Northamptonshire into a family which struggled to make ends meet. He was briefly patronized but more often excluded by what we now call the Establishment. Keats, whose family had more money than Clare's, was nevertheless also brought up on the edge of things – his father ran a stables off the City Road in the east of London.

Clare spent his childhood in the fields. Keats was a Cockney, poised between the city, the suburbs and the country. He was one of those millions who, as the forces of the Industrial Revolution gathered strength at the end of the eighteenth century, found themselves caught up in a new and complicated process of class definition. The old, broad distinctions between employers and employees were elaborated as a huge middle class began to emerge. Clare came from the old world: he was agricultural working class. Keats was one of the new men, living somewhere between lower-middle class and middle-middle class.

In certain respects Keats was liberated by his social position. It allowed him to feel that he could re-describe himself – as a poet, in the event, and thereby become altogether déclassé. At the same time he felt that his world was unstable. He responded to this by learning the poetical manners of those he recognized as his superiors – Homer, Virgil, the great Elizabethans, and Milton – and adapting them to his own purposes. His gods and goddesses, his notion of literary grandeur, his transformation of immediate political circumstance into long-established mythic narratives: all these things are signs of conformity, yet also of social and cultural disturbance. They apprehend the Establishment, but they are apprehensive.

Clare's dislocations are much more obvious. He knew that his best chances in life were likely to stem from a sense of rootedness, but he was raised at a time when he was never able to feel securely at home. And his response? Rather than deciding to learn the accents of central authority, as Keats did, then bend them to suit his own ends, he challenged them. He remained stubbornly and exhilaratingly true to what he called his 'provincialism'. The choice brought him a lot of short-term trouble and even more long-term neglect. By remaining authentic, he became alternative.

This could easily have made Clare impatient with Keats, suspecting the younger poet had sold out to authority. But it didn't. His few criticisms have more to do with ways of looking than with ways of talking. He regrets the 'frequency' of 'classical accompaniment' in Keats's poems because it means Keats 'often described nature as she appeared to his fancies and not as he would have described her had he witnessed the things he describes'. (Keats, incidentally, responded in kind – to Taylor, not to Clare himself – saying that Clare's 'Images from Nature are too much introduced without being called for by a particular sentiment . . . Now and then he feels as if the Description overlaid and stifled that which ought to be the prevailing Idea.')

Clare's sympathy with Keats far outweighed his doubts about him. When Keats's *Poems* (1817) was published, Clare asked Taylor to 'give [him] my sincere Respects . . . and tell him I had a great desire to see him and that I like his first Vol. of poems much'. Thereafter, on separate occasions, Clare referred to him as 'Friend Keats' and as 'Poor Keats . . . a brother wanderer in the rough road of life'. He said 'I heartily love him', called him 'a child of nature, warm and wild', and, when news of his death reached England in April 1821, he sent Taylor a commemorative sonnet and told him: 'With the affection that one brother feels at the loss of another do I lament the end of poor Keats.'

All this has something to do with hostile criticism and – via this criticism – with class. Clare felt a protective affinity with Keats because he knew that he himself was vulnerable in the future to the sort of attacks the younger poet had endured in the past – the attacks in *Blackwoods Magazine* in May 1818, for instance, which had chastised Keats for his allegiance to Leigh Hunt and the 'Cockney' school of writing. When Clare's own first collection came out in 1820, even his supporters felt that he was 'too profuse' with his provincialisms. 'There is', Charles Lamb told him, 'a rustick Cockneyism as little pleasing as ours of London.' Clare's detractors, of course, would make the same objection – more violently, and for many years to come.

In those same years to come, Keats would be rehabilitated. By the middle of Victoria's reign, his place was fixed in the national pantheon. He had been spotted as someone whose intense admiration of Shakespeare had helped him develop certain Shakespearean kinds of greatness. Matthew Arnold said so. Tennyson said so. Palgrave said so, and included thirteen of his poems in the *Golden Treasury*. Yet this promotion involved suppressing the political element in his work. The brotherhood to which he was elected by the Victorians was a band of sweetly singing lyricists – poets who were hardly on speaking terms with the fraternity Clare meant to invoke when he called Keats 'brother'.

While Keats rose into the light of popular acclaim, Clare sank into obscurity. The political content of his work was almost entirely ignored, and throughout the nineteenth century he was served up – where he appeared on the menu at all – as purely and simply a lyricist. Even in this respect his reputation was limited. Not a single line of his work appeared in the *Golden Treasury*. Edmund Gosse crushingly referred to him as 'a camera, not a mind'.

Saying this, Gosse captured in a phrase most of the doubts about Clare that existed even as his career began. His publisher, Taylor, knew that Clare would suit the contemporary taste for 'peasant poetry' – Robert Bloomfield and before him Stephen Duck had already proved there was a market for it. Sure enough his first book, *Poems Descriptive of Rural Life and Scenery* (1820), went through four editions in its first year. But listen to how Taylor introduced the book. The poems, he said, 'are the genuine productions of a young Peasant, a day-labourer in husbandry, who has had no advantage of education beyond others of his class; and though Poets in this country have seldom been fortunate men, yet he is, perhaps, the least favoured by circumstances, and the most destitute of friends that ever existed.'

Taylor here makes out that Clare's circumstances were even more desperate than they were in fact: clearly he meant to boost sales by exciting sympathy. But he is defensive about his author, as well as promotive. His introduction admits that readers will find some aspects of Clare's work objectionable, and rather than give a proper justification for them, he merely apologizes. This somewhat misrepresents the role that Taylor played for Clare; now and later he gave a good deal of welcome editorial advice. But this is not to say they agreed about everything. Although Clare relied on Taylor for corrections, he also had to endure a good deal of active criticism. Taylor edited out parts of the poems that Clare sent him for this 1820 book, tidying up the idiom here, changing the punctuation there – not always with Clare's approval. He mangled passages of Clare's next book, *The Village Minstrel* (1821). He dithered over publication of the third, *The Shepherd's Calendar*, which he eventually brought out in 1827, mightily doctored. He gave the same treatment to the last collection to appear in Clare's lifetime, *The Rural Muse* (1835), which Clare had battled for years to bring out as *The Midsummer Cushion*.

From the outset, Taylor was supported in his editorial efforts by

Clare's patron, Lord Radstock. Although Radstock was prepared to give Clare a small annual allowance, he would not tolerate 'radical slang'. At his insistence, many more passages were excised from Clare's manuscripts. Passages, for instance, about Enclosure. Passages which reported on signs of unrest or upheaval, like the lines describing the Scottish drovers in *The Shepherd's Calendar*. Passages of passionate plain-speaking such as we find in the love poem 'My Mary'.

Clare resented this. 'Damn that canting way of being forced to please I say,' he wrote to Taylor. 'I can't abide it and one day or other I will show my Independence more strongly than ever.' One day or other. Clare knew that if he wanted his poems published at all, he would have to make compromises with Taylor, Radstock, and others. He also accepted that he would have to make certain deals with himself. We can see him doing this in his letters, for instance, when he turns his anger at interference into self-deprecation. It is a way of disguising what might otherwise seem a bumptious devotion to poetry, and it effectively conceals poetry's potential for polemic. He describes himself to one benefactor as 'a Clown', to others as 'a scribbler', and he says that his poems are 'scribblings' which lack a grand design. ('I am shortwinded', he told Taylor in 1820, 'and if ever I mount my old rawbone hack of a pegasus determind for a long journey we are sure to be both of us d–d–ly cut up ere we end it and often cussedly sick ere the half way is accomplished.')

Gosse's objections to Clare at the end of the nineteenth century are predicated on these original criticisms and self-woundings, and they have continued to resonate ever since. Of course there have been occasional champions. There was Edmund Blunden, one of Clare's first and most pioneering editors, as well as one of his most sensible commentators. There was John Middleton Murry, insisting that poems do not necessarily have to depend on a developing argument for their structure, but can rely instead on 'the visualising word'. And there was Edward Thomas, who as well as appreciating that Clare 'reminds us that words are alive, and not only alive but still half-wild and imperfectly domesticated', also understood his political purposes. Distinguishing between overtly polemical poetry ('active') and lyrical poetry ('passive'), Thomas discovered both kinds in Clare, and argued that each does the different but complementary job that is required of it. Clare's poems attend to the visible world, and at the same time they evoke the invisible one. 'Poetry', Thomas said, 'is and must always be apparently revolutionary if active, anarchic if passive. It is the utterance of the human spirit when it is in touch with a world to which the affairs of "the world" are parochial.'

In the last twenty-odd years – years which have seen Thomas's own reputation securely established – the lessons of these early sponsors have at last been more widely learnt. Why? In one way the answer is simple: we now have more reliable texts of Clare's work. The other explanation is more complex. These texts have been published as we have become increasingly aware of the diversity of our own culture. As a result, we are especially interested in matters vernacular – in dialect writers, in regional voices generally, in the politics and attitudes these voices convey, and in what Tom Paulin calls the 'shimmering' of 'words like moozing, soodling, crumping, drippling, soshing, brustling'.

This takes us straight to Helpston. Clare reckoned it was a mixed-up village – a 'rum place', he called it. Originally in Northamptonshire, today it is in Cambridgeshire, but two other counties encroach upon it so closely they also seem about to claim possession. It's between elements, too. To the north, west and south lies gently rising land, sprinkled with woods. To the east are the Fens: wind-swept, flat, towered over by enormous skies. In Clare's day, the difference between the two landscapes was even more marked than it is now. Although Cornelius Vermuyden had started to drain the Fens in 1630, many parts still had their original watery wildness: Whittlesea Mere, for instance – three thousand acres of water, shrinking to eighteen hundred in summer. It was known nationally as a place for bright regattas and water-picnics, but Clare was attracted for other reasons. He skulked and botanized there as boy and man, discovering 'beautiful or peculiar flowers that have not been honoured with christenings'. He knew and liked the idea that it had been sailed on by King Canute. When it was eventually drained in 1851, people discovered religious relics from far-off Romsey Abbey in the mud, and the skeletons of wild boar and a wolf.

The land in Clare's other direction was just as ancient-seeming, and just as engrossing. Lifting gradually towards Stamford, and sliced in two by the Great North Road, it was a place of winding tracks and dense woods with open patches of common grazing. Wandering through its shadows, Clare tells us that he felt magically in touch with the past. It was somewhere he might stumble out of solitude into a gypsy encampment, or scare himself with a will o' the wisp; mainly it was somewhere he could be alone. Every bend in the tracks, every strangely shaped tree, every landmark had a history which had remained intact for generations.

It was the same in the immediate vicinity of Helpston itself. Wriggling paths linked it to the neighbouring villages of Glinton, Woodcroft, Bainton and Barnack, each of which were home to no more than a few hundred people. (Two hundred and seventy-six people lived in Helpston in 1810, three hundred and seventy-two ten years later.) These places gave Clare a sense of community, but what he liked best about Helpston was how secluded it made him feel, how snugly safe. Spinneys and copses ran along the southern edge of the village, forming an almost continuous woodland which eventually gave way to the large gorse-covered tangles of Helpston Heath, Southorp Heath and Emmonsales Heath, before opening out into grazing as it swelled up to Peterborough.

These woods and commons were a kind of screen – comforting, concealing, and coded. From the 'roomy and comfortable' cottage in which he grew up, Clare could step immediately into a labyrinth of 'lonely nooks'. He tells us: 'I loved the pasture with its rushes and thistles and sheep tracks I adored the wild marshy fen with its solitary hernshaw sweeing along in its melancholy sky I wandered the heath in raptures among the rabbit burrows and golden blossomd furze I dropt down on the thymy molehill or mossy eminence . . . as full of rapture as now I marked the varied colors in flat spreading fields checkerd with closes of different tinted grain like the colors in a map.'

Clare slipped through the net of this world three times as a child, and each fall made him realize there was nowhere else he belonged. Once he nearly drowned 'when wading in the meadow-pits'; he said later: 'I felt the water choke me and the thunder in my ears and I thought it was all past.' Another time he toppled out of 'a large tree in which was a buzzard's nest'. The third was the most telling: 'I had a feeling to wander about the fields,' he tells us in his autobiography, then describes how he set off across 'the large heath called Emmonsales' because 'I had imagined that the worlds end was at the orizon and that a days journey was able to find it'. Eventually, he says, 'I got out of my knowledge where the very wild flowers seemed to forget me and I imagined they were the inhabitants of new countrys the very sun seemd to be a new one and slung in a different corner of the sky . . . I knew not which way to turn but chance put me on the right track and when I got back into my own fields I did not know them everything looked so different.'

While he was still a boy, Clare's expectations were familiar enough: he hoped to avoid hard work (he frequently admits to his own laziness); to hang on to the solitude he 'grew so fond of'; to make 'a better figure in the world'; and to avoid any shame his ill-directed or thwarted ambitions might bring him. His terrors were more particular: he was frightened of poverty (his childhood coincided with a sequence of notoriously poor harvests, and with mounting economic distress created by the cost of the war against France); he worried about invasion (the French again); most of all he dreaded enclosures.

We tend to think that Clare saw every one of the many dramatic changes which came with enclosures. In fact, they had started to take their toll before he was born; within walking distance of Helpston, common heaths had already been abolished, woods uprooted, hedges planted, roads straightened. The area immediately round the village wasn't seriously affected until 1809, when a Local Enclosure Act was passed. It was only then that he suffered the traumatic experience others had already endured. By the time he began writing, half a dozen years later, what W. G. Hoskins (in *The*

Making of the English Landscape) calls 'the small world of heath and wood' had been opened to the sky, and 'a feeling of nakedness and rawness, as well as dispossession, entered the landscape and those who lived in it'.

Rural people had suffered a complete transformation, and an extraordinarily quick one. A generation before, in 1760, only four hundred thousand acres of the English countryside had been enclosed – one per cent. But between 1761 and 1844 (the year before the General Enclosures Act), two thousand and five hundred Local Acts were passed, and 4 million acres of 'open fields' were affected. As far as other kinds of common land were concerned: heaths (or 'wastes') were mainly enclosed after 1800, when the cost of the French war brought more and more land under cultivation. Eventually a million and a quarter acres of these were appropriated. As this happened, the cost of living rose sharply because of the war, the greed of landowners, and the increasing population. In other words, life became more expensive for people like Clare just as they lost the means to fend for themselves.

As Clare scrabbled around to make ends meet, he was compelled to take part in the process of his own destruction. 'I usd to work at setting down fencing and planting quick-lines [young hawthorns],' he tells us. This, of course, only added insult to injury. At every turn he felt simultaneously confined and exposed. His secret places were vandalized. His private and collective memories were destroyed. His remaining pleasures were mingled with elegiac regrets. 'Nothing is lasting in the world,' he would later write in his journal (on 29 September 1824). 'Last year Langley bush was destroyd an old whitethorn that had stood for more than a centry full of fame the gipsies shepherds and Herdsmen all had their tales of its history and it will be long ere its memory is forgotten.'

The young Clare foraged for consolations. He shared his parents' relief at the small size of his family. He welcomed their indulgence of him – which, as his grandson later said, prevented his early years from becoming 'the round of drudgery that it has been made out to appear'. He seized what this same grandson called a 'fairly good education' as the best and most obvious means of improving his lot. By the time he had left the local church school at Glinton, aged twelve, he had developed an appetite for learning. But because it could not easily be fed, it irritated him even as it gave him heart.

Heart enough, anyway, to 'twitter with joy' the next year (1806) when he read James Thomson's poem *The Seasons* for the first time. Over the next several years, as he bumped his way through a series of part-time jobs as a clerk, a gardener, an incompetent member of the militia, and a lime-burner, he read Thomson and other poets whenever he could – especially Shakespeare, Milton and Wordsworth. Inevitably, reading bred writing – descriptive poems to start with, then poems which mingled his feelings about landscape with feelings about his first important love, Mary Joyce. She was the daughter of a relatively well-to-do couple in Glinton, and her parents disapproved of the lowly Clare. While this obviously disappointed him, it developed his existing attraction to secrecy. Local and large-scale threats had already made him value the concealing and concealed things in nature. Mary, unobtainable but not unresponsive, became identified with them ('O Mary,' he writes in an early poem dedicated to her, 'thou that once made all/What youthful dreams could pleasure call,/[You] once did love to walk with me/And own thy taste for scenery.')

Clare's second great love, Martha (Patty) Turner, whom he met in 1818, when he was twenty-four, and shortly afterwards married, had a similar effect. He tells us in the autobiography that he 'planned and wrote some of the best poems in my first volume among [Casterton's cow pasture, near where Patty lived] . . . My love-rambles then made me acquainted with many of the privacies of night which [Patty] seemed wishing to keep as secrets.' Like Mary, Patty eroticized the elements he most valued in landscape. She also expressed their vulnerability. Both women were Eve in Eden – with the difference that where the original Eve had a life before the Fall, they were already the victims, as Clare was himself, of those tyrannical demi-gods, the local landowners.

The poems in Clare's first (1820) volume were introduced to John Taylor in London by Taylor's cousin, who lived near Clare in

Market Deeping. The book contained a selection of the work that Clare had been producing since 1814, sometimes at the rate of six or seven poems a day. Its success changed his life completely, but also deepened existing wounds. Although he was perfectly well aware that his triumph had something to do with 'fashion', and that fashion was 'cobweb praise', he couldn't adequately protect himself against the ways in which fame aggravated his feelings of dislocation. His work cut him off from those he lived amongst, yet never won him a secure place in any alternative society. When he wrote to Taylor after visiting him for the first time in London, in the same year that his book was published, we can already hear a note of distress. 'I am at home again,' he says, 'and hear things which I formerly was accustomed to this puts all thoughts of other things out of my head and I think will be the only means of getting well.' He thought wrong. Two years later he wrote to Taylor again: 'I live here among the ignorant like a lost man in fact like one whom the rest seems careless of having anything to do with.'

While Clare's volume prospered, these feelings were a tolerable woe. As the cobweb praise blew away, and his work began to lose its audience, they became unbearable. Through the second half of the 1820s, and into the 1830s, he continued to write steadily, but received less and less support from Taylor. His dreams of glory faded. His family grew but he lost his sense of living among companions. His earnings shrivelled up. Occasionally his patrons offered him hand-outs, but these were never enough to make him feel safe, and in one instance turned out to be actually disastrous. In 1832 the well-meaning Earl Fitzwilliam offered him a cottage in Northborough, a few miles north of Helpston. Although the distance between his old and new homes was short, it was absolute. Clare was uprooted, lost, devastated. By the mid-1830s he began suffering periods of delusion and memory loss. In 1837 he decided that he was beyond the help of his wife or local doctors, and became a voluntary patient in Dr Mathew Allen's asylum in High Beech in Essex. (Allen had that year published his *Classifications of the Insane*, which immediately won him a reputation as an unusually sympathetic student of mental illness.)

By all accounts, including his own, Clare's disorientation was now so acute that he no longer had a reliable sense of identity. His old self was uninhabitable – it had been destroyed along with the countryside which had been his birthright. In its absence, Clare strove to adopt separate and different selves: he fancied that he was Lord Byron and wrote two long poems called 'Childe Harold' and 'Don Juan'; that he was Lord Nelson; that he was the boxer Jack Randall.

None of these other identities satisfied him. How could they? They had nothing to nourish them but a sense of loss – a loss which intensified steadily. When Clare fled from High Beech in 1841, and foot-slogged his way home back up the Great North Road, he arrived back in Northborough asking for Mary Joyce. She had died three years earlier, in 1838. For a few months, Patty and the children cared for him, but he was too much for them. Before the end of the year, he was taken into St Andrew's Asylum in Northampton, where he lived for another twenty-two years until his death in 1864, aged seventy-one.

During this time, Clare wrote a further eight hundred and fifty poems, songs and scraps. Whichever broad category they fall into, they all develop themes which had obsessed him from the start. They are filled with the idea that – left to itself – Nature 'chooses joy', and wants to communicate this to anyone able to appreciate it. Yet they also remind us how rarely nature is left to itself, how the choice can seldom if ever be made. When we think of Clare in old age, therefore, sitting in the churchyard near St Andrew's, or in his single room in the asylum, we realize that he might have forgotten who he was, but always remembered how he had lost his life.

Clare blamed enclosures for most contemporary ills, but they never turned him into the sort of radical who only faces one way. Nowhere, for instance, does he suggest that they might be replaced by a system which spread wealth more equally though society. What he wanted was a return to the old, time-honoured ways – ways which were feudal but benevolent. (William Barnes would take the same approach in Dorset thirty-odd years later.) In 'The

Parish', for instance, Clare celebrates 'That good old fame the farmer's earned of yore/That made as equals not as slaves the poor'. And again: 'Each guest was welcomed and the poor was fed/Where master son and serving man and clown/ Without distinction daily sat them down.'

In such a poem, as in many others – 'The Moors' would be a good example – Clare shows that enclosures and the 'blundering plough' turned the old relationship between squire and peasant into a drama of venality and exploitation. In the process, they destroyed an entire way of life, an entire consciousness. Almost a century later, we find Edward Thomas making the same point. But by the time Thomas took up Clare's cause, the traditions they both honoured were more thoroughly broken down. Thomas called himself 'a superfluous man', belonging nowhere. In Clare's poems we read about such figures. We often find him writing about gypsies, for instance – people who once lived in comparative security on the fringes of society, but are now pushed over its edge – and there are other kinds of Wordsworthian wanderers, too, such as the Scottish drovers in *The Shepherd's Calendar*. They are all scratching a living, and all sharing the experience of dispossession that Clare talks about in 'The Flitting':

> Time looks on pomp with careless moods
> Or killing apathys disdain
> – So where old marble citys stood
> Poor persecuted weeds remain
> She feels a love for little things
> That very few can feel beside
> And still the grass eternal springs
> Where castles stood and grandeur died.

While such eruptions have a magnificent resonance, the main burden of Clare's politics is carried more quietly. Insisting, as ever, that he 'became a scribbler for downright pleasure', Clare realized that his own dialect – which was 'as common around me as the grass under my feet' – had to negotiate with 'a sufficient knowledge of the written language of England before I could put down my ideas on paper even so far as to understand them'. What he means to suggest is that the language of his poetry is in fact two languages – one official, and one local. We can see this duality everywhere: in the battle he fought to publish his third collection as *The Midsummer Cushion*, not as the more decorous *The Rural Muse*; in the discrepancy between a lofty form of inherited poetic language and vernacular speech; in the juxtaposition of abstract nouns and things which he describes as their exact physical selves; in the relationship between echoes of his literary heroes, and his evocation of traditional songs and ballads; in the difference between his formal stanza shapes and the unpunctuated rhythmical patterns which create the impression of a speaking voice.

Clare's language may be part meeting-place, part battle-ground, but there's never any doubt where his sympathies lie. The great weight of his love and interest is given to what he calls 'each trifling thing'. The marvellously seen details in his poems are their own capacious reward, and their ordinariness is valued so highly that it becomes extraordinary. We have only to think again of 'My Mary', where he sees Mary 'Waddling like a duck/O'er head and ears in grease and muck'. Or of the crow 'flopping on heavy wings' in 'January' from *The Shepherd's Calendar*. Or of the cows in 'February' 'Tossing the molehills in their play/And staring round in frolic joy'. Or of 'Little Trotty Wagtail' who 'went in the rain,/And tittering, tottering sideways he ne're got straight again'. Or of the haymakers sheltering from a storm in 'The thunder mutters':

> all the gang a bigger haycock make
> To sit beneath – the woodland winds awake
> The drops so large wet all thro' in an hour
> A tiney flood runs down the leaning rake.

Reading such lines, we feel that everything in Clare's world is held out to us at eye-level, and shown as it most plainly and thrillingly is. But the closer he looks, the more sharply we realize that we're seeing more than just a brilliantly delineated world of actual things. The trees, birds, animals and people in his poems are like an enormous and acutely sensitive nervous system – one which is constantly wincing, quivering, pulsating and cowering as it records impressions.

Consider the size of the creatures which most interest him. They're small – the 'pismires [ants] round the hill', the 'tiney [insects] on the barley's beard', 'the lady bird [which] climbs the tall grass', the 'clock a cley', which 'in the cowslip peeps'. Of course these things are made charming by their size, but they are also made vulnerable. We hear about worms which 'leave their homes in fear'; about 'the snail from the shell peeping out/As fear full and cautious as thieves in the rout'; about the 'timid' and 'haunted' hares; about the fly 'Hiding in crowding beans and benty balks'; about the hedgehog which 'hides beneath the rotten hedge/And makes a great round nest of grass and sedge'; about 'The Fern Owl', which knows 'The weary woodman' will 'trample near its nest'; about the quail, for which Clare himself is the bright-eyed but unwitting danger 'When from my foot a bird did flee/The rain flew bouncing from her breast/I wondered what the bird could be/And almost trampled on her nest', and about the snipe in one of his best poems:

> Lover of swamps,
> The quagmire overgrown
> With hassock-tufts of sedge – where fear encamps
> Around thy home alone
>
> The trembling grass
> Quakes from the human foot
> Nor bears the weight of man to let him pass
> Where thou alone and mute
>
> Sittest at rest
> In safety neath the clump
> Of huge flag-forest that thy haunts invest
> Or some old sallow stump

Thriving on seams
That tiny islands swell,
Just hilling from the mud and rancid streams,
Suiting thy nature well –

In order to see these creatures minutely – and because he knows how timorous they are – Clare treads very gently in his poems: creeping, slinking, soft-footing, stealing in silence. Yet his caution is more than a good naturalist's sensible tactics. It's a sign that he shares the fearfulness of the creatures he describes. Although they might be able to evade enclosure as he never can, they are nevertheless in danger. The boundaries of their lives have changed. They are all likely to lose their secrets. Their plight is actual and pitiable, but it reflects his own.

It's hardly remarkable for a Romantic writer to be interested in nature both for its own sake, and for its metaphorical value. Yet Clare's reputation as a 'camera' went unchallenged for so long, it's worth emphasizing how well he balances self-scrutiny with his interest in the world around him. Although enclosures might threaten them, roads might rattle them, and ploughs might ruin them, Clare never quite stops believing that the creatures can be a comfort to him. He keeps sight of the visionary gleam which shines at the centre of the Romantic ideal. How do we explain this? Take these lines from the poem 'Childhood'. 'The past is a magic word', Clare tells us, 'Too beautiful to last,/It looks back like a lovely face –/Who can forget the past?/There's music in its childhood/That's known in every tongue,/Like the music of the wildwood/All chorus to the song.' On the face of it, the poem is resigned to the disappointment of adult life. Nevertheless, Clare admits that he might be able to hang on to 'beauty', if he could only escape 'thought' and all its allies: reason, argument, articulation, and the world of power to which they belong. This is why he aligns himself with the creatures and the birds: they are not subject to the dictates of reason; they are not hindered by the limits of language.

Much as Clare relishes language, he spends a great deal of time longing for a state it cannot come near – the state of delight which fills him in 'A Scene', for instance, when he says 'Language fails the pleasure to express'. He comes to the same point from the opposite direction in 'Remembrances', where 'words' are 'poor receipts for what time hath stole away'. In one sense, this gap between language and experience represents a specifically Romantic failure. In another sense, it represents a triumphant success: it records a 'joy' which is wordless because it is literally unspeakable.

This kind of rhapsodizing might easily become sentimental. Yet in so far as Clare's apprehension of 'joy' entails a pleasurable form of self-forgetting, it is automatically linked to his other, grimmer sorts of identity-loss. At the beginning of his writing life, he tells us that his need for dissolution is inseparable from his fear of dislocation, in much the same way that his love of solitude is connected with his need for escape. Through the middle and last part of his life, and especially once he had moved from Helpston to Northborough, these connections continue to give his work its dramatic shape – in the two long Byron poems, for instance, or his extraordinary sonnet 'The Mouse's Nest', which describes how a terrified 'old mouse bolted in the wheat/With all her young ones hanging at her teats', or his masterpiece 'I Am':

> I am – yet what I am, none cares or knows;
> My friends forsake me like a memory lost:
> I am the self-consumer of my woes –
> They rise and vanish in oblivion's host
> Like shadows in love-frenzied stifled throes –
> And yet I am and live – like vapours tossed
>
> Into the nothingness of scorn and noise,
> Into the living sea of waking dreams
> Where there is neither sense of life or joys
> But the vast shipwreck of my life's esteems;
> Even the dearest that I love the best
> Are strange – nay, rather, stranger than the rest.
>
> I long for scenes where man hath never trod

A place where woman never smiled or wept,
There to abide with my Creator, God,
And sleep as I in childhood sweetly slept,
Untroubling and untroubled where I lie,
The grass below – above, the vaulted sky.

If the poems Clare wrote in the last half of his life were merely accounts of a mind collapsing, we would value them differently. We would feel they were sympathetic, as we feel some of the poems that Ivor Gurney wrote in his asylum are sympathetic. But we might hesitate to say they spoke to us meaningfully or movingly about experience we recognized. As it is, we can be more full-blooded. We can say that the forces tearing his life apart also united his obsessions. The ties that bound him to his childhood, to Mary, to Patty – these were all tested, and were all strengthened.

They were strengthened because Clare never wavered in his devotion to the act of looking: his thought depended on it. He is an intensely individual but vitally emblematic figure – one whose double achievement takes us back to where we began, to Keats. 'A Man's life of any worth', Keats wrote to his brother George in the spring of 1819, 'is a continual allegory . . . Shakespeare led a life of allegory; his works are the comments on it.' So did Clare live a life of allegory; his works are the comments on it.

Leigh Hunt
In the Political World

Poor Leigh Hunt. So famous in his youth, so well connected, so effective – and then, when the quick current of the Regency channelled into the broader flow of Victorianism, so soon swept aside. The precocious poet, the fearless editor and the friend of Keats, Shelley and Byron, finally appeared as the original of Harold Skimpole in *Bleak House*: a model of fecklessness. It's a classic literary rise and fall, and has a lot to say about the unreliability of initial reputations, as well as the fate of characters who live too variously to leave a single distinct impression. Hunt wrote a couple of popular anthology pieces ('Abou Ben Adhem' and 'Jenny Kissed Me'), but substantial parts of his achievement (other good poems like 'The Fish, the Man and the Spirit', as well as his lobbying, befriending and journalism) don't register clearly on history's radar. What made him significant in his early days became a part of the explanation for his later obscurity.

Nicholas Roe doesn't deal with Hunt's fall in *Fiery Heart*: he ends his account in 1822, just after the death of Shelley, when his subject's life has been shaken to its foundation but has thirty-seven years left to run. The disadvantages are obvious. We don't get a sense of completion, long-term consequences are veiled, the fascinations of historical change are diminished. But there are big gains, too. We feel Hunt's power at its most intense, we concentrate on his greatest achievements, and – most important of all – we experience him as he appeared to the most significant people in his life. Roe is an exceptionally shrewd critic of Romanticism, uncannily alert to the political dimensions of innocent-seeming texts. In this new book he plays to his strengths; everything he says is well turned and reliably clever.

Given our continuing absorption in Romanticism, it's remark-

Fiery Heart: The First Life of Leigh Hunt, by Nicholas Roe (Pimlico, 2005) and *The Wit in the Dungeon: A Life of Leigh Hunt* by Anthony Holden (Little, Brown, 2006)

able that no proper attempt to write Hunt's life has been made since Edmund Blunden began his biography in the 1920s. Remarkable, too, that now Roe's *Life* is here, another should coincide with it. Anthony Holden's *The Wit in the Dungeon* can't match the forensic subtleties of *Fiery Heart*: it's much less informative about the big picture, and sometimes rather breathlessly cheerful in the Huntian manner. But it is enthusiastic and sensible, and it does follow its subject all the way to the grave, having especially useful things to say about Hunt's relationship with Dickens. While Roe's book is the more impressive piece of work, Holden's will suit general readers.

What can we learn from the two books appearing at the same time? Some might say that all the larger lives have been taken, and Hunt's was left at the bottom of the barrel. But that misjudges things. It's actually to do with our contemporary interest in the Romantic context. We're more alert than ever before to the connections between individual writers, more concerned with understanding how they reflect the life of their times, and more willing to explore links between the first generation (Wordsworth et al.) and the second (Keats et al.). Hunt worked at the point where these things coincided – as a champion of liberty in an oppressive age, as an editor, as an advocate, as an essayist and poet, and as the sociable stoker of a warm hearth. Reading about his more famous contemporaries, it's customary to find him flickering in the background. Yet as far as the contemporaries themselves were concerned, he dominated the foreground, though not always for reasons that history has found it easy to recognize or reward.

The story starts in America, where Hunt's father, Isaac, combined a radical spirit with patriotic loyalty to such an exceptional degree, and often in such tempestuous circumstances, that any biographer in search of a subject would do well to give him a look. Isaac eventually made life so uncomfortable for himself that he had to bring his brood to the old country, where he was ordained in 1777. Leigh Hunt was born seven years later, by which time the family finances had collapsed: Hunt's infant memories of debtors' gaol, and his parents' decision to become Unitarians, Universalists and Republicans, crucially shaped his later thoughts about liberty and justice, as well as his primitive need for snugness and good cheer. School – Christ's Hospital for eight years – reinforced these early lessons. He said later that it was run according to 'a system of alternate slavery and tyranny, fitted to make alternate slaves and tyrants in the political world'. But it was also the place which drove him to explore consolingly seditious books – especially those by the radical dissenters Tooke and Spence, which a generation later would have a similarly liberating effect on Keats – and to evolve ideas about poetry which mingled safety with defiance. In his first collection, *Juvenilia*, published in 1801 when he was only sixteen years old, he challenged orthodoxy by flaunting his youth, but embraced the Establishment in his list of subscribers.

He played fast and loose in other ways too, fixing his affections on Mary Ann – eventually Marianne – Knight, then including her sister Bess in a *ménage à trois*. (Hunt thought the arrangement reflected his liberal politics in a domestic setting.) But at the same time he also began to show the kind of steadiness that Isaac had always found difficult. He took a job in the War Office, and started writing theatre reviews when his brother John, who had trained as a printer, established the *Weekly News*. It was while working on the *News* that Hunt discovered the alert yet amiable style that was his greatest contribution to journalism, and which he would apply to a much wider range of subjects after he and John launched the *Examiner* in 1807. As Hunt gave his views about everything from the slave trade to military reform, as he published Hazlitt, as he launched Keats and Shelley, as he provided some of the best contemporary criticisms of Wordsworth, he dominated and united one of the key documents of the Romantic period.

The achievement came at a high price: personal exhaustion and – after repeated 'libels' of the Prince Regent – gaol. As history so often proves, this attempt at suppression lifted Hunt to a new level. He continued to publish successfully from his cell, he became a magnet for all left-leaning writers, he found something comforting in confinement and, when he eventually regained his liberty, he was called a hero. A less dynamic personality, and a differently needy one, might have taken this as a cue for quiet. But Hunt went on working furiously. His home in the Vale of Health, Hampstead, became a forcing-house for other people's talent. He wrote his own new poems to illustrate beliefs he had espoused in his journalism (including 'The Story of Rimini'). He nagged and mocked and attacked the government while helping at least one of his protégés, Keats, to find a way of writing poetry that was at once engaged with politics and Shakespeareanly wary of having 'a palpable design' on the reader.

His world started to end when Keats died, but Hunt didn't know this. He had always had more time for Shelley than 'Junkets' (as Keats had sometimes signed himself in letters to Hunt), and after Shelley's escape to Europe he dreamed of following him – ideally with a view to including Byron in their circle, and setting up yet another magazine, which would continue the old battles in a new place. The dream turned almost immediately into a nightmare: arguments, poverty, muddle, illness, and eventually a funeral pyre at Lerici. No matter how many times this part of Shelley's story comes round, it triggers a dismal pathos. But because Roe sees it from an unusual angle – through the eyes of a man who is generally only a bit-player – it has a special force here. Although Hunt continued to promote and protect Romantic ideals in later life, he never entirely recovered from the Italian debacle; he was disappointed and sidelined.

Roe's account of the love between Shelley and Hunt, and of the way in which they stimulated an astonishing array of interests in each other (everything from electricity to paganism), is a really significant addition to our appreciation of the period. It would frankly have been impossible to extend this sense of achievement had Roe followed Hunt's life to the bitter end. As Holden shows, the material simply isn't there to support a case. A handful of decent poems, some important friendships, several pages of useful journalism – but nothing which catches the spirit of the age, and the whole performance disrupted by pathetic bids for money, position, attention. On the last page of Roe's book, Hunt is stricken by grief, yet oddly noble. By the close of Holden's, death feels like a merciful release.

JOSEPH SEVERN
Painter, Friend, Consul

Everyone who loves John Keats feels affection for Joseph Severn. When Keats left England for Italy in the autumn of 1820, already desperately ill with tuberculosis, Severn was the only friend willing and able to go with him. His companionship, his nursing, and his devotion have always been inseparable from the story of Keats's own suffering. More than just inseparable: to a great extent, Severn's witness actually *is* the story. His intimate gaze, and his unshakeable conviction that Keats was a genius (in spite of dismal reviews, poor sales, and the rest of it), make the letters he sent back to England during the winter of 1820–21 invaluable to scholars and irresistible to general readers.

But what exactly have we been reading? The first significant collection of Severn's papers was published by William Sharp in 1892, and even though subsequent biographers have always doubted the accuracy of his transcriptions, and wondered about omissions, his *Life and Letters* has remained the standard text. Grant F. Scott has finally done the decent thing and put it out of its misery. He has found hundreds of 'new' letters, rescued a long and largely unknown memoir from obscurity, re-edited everything, and surrounded it with a briskly written critical commentary. It's an important job, and difficult to see how anyone could have done it better. For the first time, we have a reliable foundation for our appreciation of one of the great early nineteenth-century also-rans.

Maybe 'also-ran' is too harsh. Scott goes to great lengths to show that Severn's time at Keats's bedside was just part of a long and busy life (1793–1879). He was a painter, for one thing. When he first met Keats in 1816 he was already trying to make his name – he'd been admitted to the Royal Academy Schools the previous year –

Joseph Severn: Letters and Memoirs, edited by Grant F. Scott (Ashgate, 2005) and later he exhibited frequently at the RA. Scott calls him 'exceptionally versatile', and reproduces a good number of things in the hope of proving his point. They seldom do so: although they are always painstaking and sometimes ambitious, they seldom convey much flair or originality. The figure-painting is generally awkward, and the historical/allegorical scenes are at once stiff and melodramatic.

If praising the paintings doesn't quite work as a way of re-dignifying Severn, what about his life in politics? Here again, Scott gives honour where honour is due, outlining the tasks Severn undertook after being appointed British Consul in Rome in 1861. Even allowing for the turbulence of the times, it has to be said that Severn's diplomatic skills were still less well developed than his painterly ones. He was accused of incompetence by the government at home, narrowly escaped being sacked, and eventually retired amidst sighs of relief in 1872, at the grand old age of seventy-nine.

Does this mean Scott is wrong to make the case for versatility? No: his book straightens the record of Severn's life and gives us a more complete sense of his whole character. But it does leave Severn's reputation more or less where it has been for many years: the brief Keats-contact is without doubt the most compelling part of the story. Still – and this is important – we can now judge its mood and effect more accurately than ever before. The strongest effect is just what we would expect: desolating sadness. As Keats watches his English friends sink over the horizon, as he frets about his absence from Fanny Brawne, as he refuses the comforts of religious faith, and as he submits to the ravages of the disease (which his medical knowledge allowed him to understand all too well), Severn creates scenes of appalling pathos: 'I had seen him awake on the morning of this attack . . . When in an instant a Cough seized him, and he vomited near two cup-fuls of blood – In a moment I got Dr Clarke, who saw the manner of it, and immediately took away about 8 ounces of blood from the Arm – it was black and thick in the extreme.'

Such descriptions are unforgettable, and have decisively shaped the whole course of Keats's posthumous fame. But in Scott's spruced-up versions, we see more than just tragedy. It transpires (and this is the book's single greatest biographical revelation) that Severn had an illegitimate child shortly before volunteering to accompany Keats to Rome. As well as helping to explain his motives for going, this also lets us understand some of his psychological imperatives as a nurse. In particular, it makes us think differently about his reasons for making clear the extent of his own exhaustion. 'My spirits dropt – at the sight of his suffering,' he keeps saying, emphasizing how seldom he leaves Keats's side, how no other nurse is acceptable, how compassion and 'dread' fight an endless battle in him. Over the years, a number of Keatsians have interpreted these moans as self-pitying, and it's easy to see why. Even some of Severn's grateful contemporaries thought he was overdoing things, and Keats's friend Isabella Jones was more critical still. 'I never saw so much egotism and selfishness displayed under the mask of feeling and friendship,' she told Keats's publisher John Taylor. But there's something else here too. Severn's whine is the sound of someone asking for forgiveness, as well as sympathy.

This is why Severn remains likeable, in spite of all the faults and weaknesses his letters put on display. He is a muddler (Keats's friend William Haslam, urging Severn to write regularly from Italy, says exasperatedly: 'Do this Severn, tho' at some sacrifice of your inherent dislike of order – and of obligation to do a thing – do it, if but because I ask it –'). He fusses about his health in a way that can't help but seem small-minded. In later life he has a horrible tendency to sound simultaneously snobbish and fawning when writing about his posh connections, and almost explodes when mentioning to his brother 'what the King does for me'. Most troubling of all, he is thrown into confusion when Keats's letters to Fanny Brawne finally come to light in the late 1870s. Before reading them, he gallantly supposes 'they must be even superior to his poetry & will be a boon to the world quite unlooked for –'. Once he has seen their anguish he can hardly bear the fact that Keats didn't confide in him: 'I think he must have been sensible this passion was destroying or he would have made it known – to me. He referred at times to his being cut of[f] from his world of poetry as his great misfortune but never to Fanny Brawne . . .'

There's a sense of injured pride here, as well as genuine puzzlement, and those who take the Isabella Jones view of Severn will be quick to say it proves how much less a man than Keats he was. He was. On the other hand there's plenty of recognizable humanness in his response to the Brawne letters, just as there's also a lot of generosity in his self-regard. Severn used his link with Keats to give himself a leg up in the world. He too eagerly stressed his significance as a friend (and even got himself buried next to Keats, as though he was something like a wife). But he also worked hard to keep Keats's reputation alive, and then to extend it. For those reasons, and because he lovingly helped Keats to die when no one else could or would, he deserves a memorial as painstaking as this book.

Christina Rossetti
Stories and Secrets

Christina Rossetti liked to create the impression that she had a secret, perhaps because she was a naturally self-revealing writer. It was her way of keeping something back, of guarding herself while giving so much away. One of her best and best-known poems, 'Goblin Market', is a case in point: the sinuous lines overflow with suggestions about appetite and its dangers, but they keep us guessing – in the same way that her love-lyrics also throw a veil over the narrative that impels them. Did she love and lose someone, and if so, how? Biographers have given various opinions, but uncertainty lingers. It is essential to the method and the atmosphere of her work; she is a haunted writer as well as a haunting one.

The same is true of her long short story 'Commonplace', which she wrote some time between 1852 and 1870, and was first published with other pieces of short fiction by F. S. Ellis, who also published her brother Dante Gabriel. Although it lacks the sensuality of her best poems as well as the plangent beauty of her characteristic music, it resembles the rest of her work in being at once forthright and withheld. This isn't to say it's fascinated by mystery as such – rather that its actions are dealt with very quickly and their consequences treated at much greater length. Rossetti is more interested in mood than event: when a boat sinks, we don't see it happen; when a woman has a daughter, we hear next to nothing about the pregnancy; when a man dies, it's over in a sentence. Furthermore, she doesn't identify herself with a particular character, but refracts herself through several, and so confirms a sense of puzzlement in the reader. We finish the story feeling that its clear utterances are less significant than their implications.

Which is as well, considering how often and how badly Rossetti's engine stutters as she tries to drive her characters forward in

'Commonplace': 'On the morning when our story commences', she says, or 'Forty years before the commencement of this story', or 'The last chapter was parenthetical, this takes up the broken thread of the story'. These are not the remarks of a proto-modernist, drawing our attention to the idea of fiction as a construct; they are simply awkwardnesses, which show a lyric poet grappling with the unfamiliar demands of a prose narrative. And there are other problems too: occasionally the shape and pace of the story are damaged by an unjustified surge of description; at other times it sounds perfunctory where it means to be allusive.

Yet these imperfections are insignificant compared to the seriousness of Rossetti's achievement. The three central characters – the sisters Catherine, Lucy and Jane Charlmont – are a means of exploring the plight of mid-nineteenth-century middle-class women as they swirl down the marriage-stream towards a lonely old age. Catherine has promised her dying mother 'to stay here [at their childhood home in Brompton-on-Sea] ready for your father' – who has previously vanished in a boating accident – thereby condemning herself to a fate of 'self-postponement'. Lucy has been disappointed in love and still feels so wounded she can't face visiting London with her sisters, because it will mean having to meet her former admirer – Mr Hartley – who is now married to another woman. And the youngest, Jane, is determined to have money at all costs, even if it means attaching herself to the crassly vain Mr Durham of Orpingham Place.

Jane's single-minded pursuit of her goal is condemned by her sisters, who think it venal and sad, but there are hints that Rossetti thinks desperate situations require desperate remedies: Jane's marriage is arid, though not actually appalling. The other two girls look likely to go unrewarded for their finer feelings: Lucy only escapes becoming a life-long spinster at the last minute, saved by the sincere but passionless love of Mr Tresham, and Catherine finally accepts that her happiness will not come on this earth. 'My dear,' she tells Lucy in the closing lines of the story, 'my future seems further off than yours; but I certainly have a future, and I can wait.' Rossetti is not giving her casting vote to the pious life here; she knows it has its rewards, but she also understands the sacrifices involved.

In her other short prose fiction, Rossetti explored similar and related themes – in 'The Lost Titian' we find her imagining the loss, perhaps irrevocable, of Titian's greatest masterpiece; in 'Vanna's Twins' she examines the stoic devotion of a woman toward the twins of her landlord and lady; in 'Pros and Cons' a rector and his parishioners debate the abolition of pews from their church; and in 'The Waves of This Troublesome World', Rossetti describes the journey of a woman from her childhood, through a disapproved marriage to a Methodist, back to the church and place of her birth, and contentment.

The balance of sympathies in 'Commonplace' is reinforced everywhere: Lucy grows to like the woman now married to the man she loved, and even Jane's husband, the ghastly Mr Durham, realizes that he is 'inferior' to the Charlmont sisters. In other words, Rossetti squeezes a doctrine of forgiveness and mutual understanding through the veins of her story, and is generally at pains not to leave her characters feeling antagonistic to one another. Lest this should make 'Commonplace' seem sentimental, she is also at pains to show that the problems associated with love and age are ubiquitous. The difficulties faced by the three sisters are mirrored in all the minor players. The sisters' one-time governess Miss Drum, for instance, who is 'mainly describable by negatives', yet capable of seeing that women must 'do one thing or do the other', on the sole condition that they 'do not become ridiculous'. Whatever their ages, social positions, characters and beliefs, Rossetti's women are all touched by the desperation that Lucy feels in Chapter 7:

It is easy to ridicule a woman nearly thirty years old for fancying herself beloved without a word said, and suffering deeply under disappointment; yet Lucy Charlmont was no contemptible person . . . Alone in her own room she might suffer visibly and keenly, but with any eye upon her she would not give way. Sometimes it felt as if the next moment the strain on her nerves might wax unendurable: but such a next moment never came, and she endured still. Only, who is there strong enough, day after day, to strain strength to the utmost, and yet give no sign?

In this passage we hear the same note that strikes again and again in Rossetti's poems: melancholy and wretchedness, mingled with stoicism. And as the title of her short-story collection makes plain, she knew it was a commonplace problem for women in her time. It is her sense of this pain and its pervasiveness that gives 'Commonplace' such raw power. What makes that power twist into our memories is the suggestion that even a money-fixated marriage like Jane's, or a cautious courtship like Lucy's (in which the only 'romantic moment' comes when her fiancé jumps onto the carriage-step of a train as it steams her away from him), is preferable to the singleness of Catherine. Coming from a writer as eagle-eyed about heavenly rewards as Rossetti, this is a remarkable and touching compromise.

WILLIAM BARNES
An Introduction

William Barnes (1801–1886) is a major lyric poet and much neglected. It's easy to see why. Most of his poems are written in a Dorset dialect, which looks bewildering on the page and puts people off. Several of his earliest and best-known admirers realized this, and did what they could to give reassurances. Francis Kilvert called him 'a great idyllic poet'. Tennyson cited him as an influence on 'The Northern Farmer'. Hopkins called him 'a perfect artist and of most spontaneous inspiration'. Thomas Hardy was his friend and elegist, and introduced a selection of his work. In the years immediately following Barnes's death there were signs that these recommendations might do the trick. The 1879 collected edition of his dialect poetry was reprinted four times before the end of the century, and the *Saturday Review* said in its unsigned obituary: 'There is no doubt that [Barnes] is the best pastoral poet we possess, the most sincere, the most genuine, the most Theocritan; and that the dialect is but a very thin veil hiding from us some of the most delicate and finished verse written in our time.'

Since then, famous voices have continued to speak up for him. Vaughan Williams set 'Linden Lea'. Geoffrey Grigson compiled and introduced an edition of his work. W. H. Auden said, 'I cannot enjoy one poem by Shelley and am delighted by every line of William Barnes.' Philip Larkin referred to him as 'one of the most scrupulous metrists, [and] vowel and consonant balancers in our tongue'.

None of these golden opinions has had much popularizing effect – and neither has Bernard Jones's two-volume edition of the poems, published in 1962, nor a handful of subsequent selections. Year by year, Barnes has been pushed to the side of the English tradition, waiting for a change to occur in our attitude to vernacular

William Barnes: Selected Poems (Faber and Faber, 2007)

writing so that we might see and hear his genius for the thing it is.

Dialect is not the only obstacle. Barnes further increased the likelihood of his own neglect by resisting categories – as Hardy acknowledged when he called him 'probably the most interesting link between the present and past forms of rural life that England possesses'. Barnes spent most of his writing life as a Victorian, yet his attitudes to Nature linked him to the Romantics: to Wordsworth, obviously, but in idiom and emphasis also to Burns, Clare and Crabbe. (The poems in his first dialect collection were divided into seasons, like Clare's *Shepherd's Calendar* of 1827.) At the same time, traces of Augustanism survived in Barnes's standard English writing. Everything about him was at odds with his own time, even his appearance: he could be seen strolling round Dorchester in the late 1870s wearing buckle shoes and knee breeches, wielding a staff. His aim was a kind of heroic individualism, a style of living and writing which set him at an angle to his contemporaries.

Much of the inspiration for this came from Barnes's childhood. He was born at Rush-Hay, by Bagber Common, two miles west of Sturminster Newton in the Vale of Blackmore, Dorset. His grandfather had inherited but been forced to sell a small farm of his own; his father John described himself in a Population Return compiled during the year of William's birth as a 'labourer in husbandry', and raised his family in an atmosphere that mingled restraint with anxiety.

In 1806, when Barnes was five, he was sent to live with his father's sister Ann and her husband Charles Rabbetts (or Roberts), who farmed nearby at Pentridge in the Vale of Blackmore, on land which ran down to the River Stour. This big clay valley, extending south and east of Sherborne, in an arc west of Shaftesbury and up beyond the Somerset border, had changed very little by the time Hardy came to describe it almost a century later in *Tess of the D'Urbervilles* (1891):

The traveller from the coast, who, after plodding northward for a score of miles over calcareous downs and corn-lands, suddenly

175

reaches the verge of one of these escarpments, is surprised and delighted to behold, extended like a map beneath him, a country differing absolutely from that which he has passed through. Behind him the hills are open, the sun blazes down upon fields so large as to give an unenclosed character to the landscape, the lanes are white, the hedges low and plashed, the atmosphere colourless. Here, in the valley, the world seems to be constructed upon a smaller and more delicate scale; the fields are mere paddocks, so reduced that from this height their hedgerows appear a network of dark green threads overspreading the paler green of the grass. The atmosphere beneath is languorous, and is so tinged with azure that what artists call the middle distance partakes also of that hue, while the horizon beyond is of the deepest ultramarine.

Barnes later remembered his life with the Rabbetts and their family (they had eight children of their own) in many poems, notably 'Uncle an' Aunt' and 'Rustic Childhood'. Yet while the world they depict is compactly detailed, it has an air of remoteness about it. Barnes had scarcely finished his schooling (at a Church of England-endowed school in Sturminster Newton) when the Vale of Blackmore fell victim to the agricultural depression which ravaged Dorset in the years following the Napoleonic wars. Charles Rabbetts went bankrupt, and the farm was sold. 'The young men were in reckless mood,' Barnes wrote later, 'the girls bewildered. Then were driven away the cows ... then went the wagon in which the merry haymakers had so many times ridden to the feast of harvest-home; in short everything that was dear from familiarity was taken away.' He associated the disaster with the plight of his father and grandfather, and began to idealize the remoter past of the place even more wholeheartedly.

At the same time, Barnes rebelled against his misfortune. He had excelled at school and, soon after his thirteenth birthday, he started working as a clerk for a solicitor in Sturminster Newton. In 1818 he moved to Dorchester, where he got a similar job with Thomas Coombs and Son. In the evenings after work, he studied the classics with a local priest, drew, played music, and learned how to engrave on wood and paper. 'It was always in my mind', he said later, 'that I would try to rise to a higher standing than that to which my father had fallen.'

For a while Barnes toyed with the idea of making his living as an engraver. He did some work for a bookseller in Weymouth and sent specimen drawings to a fine-art dealer in London. He was told there was no vacancy. He tried again, submitting work to Edward Scriven, a London bookseller, and got the same answer. Reluctantly he accepted that his hopes of 'following a career in art' would have to be redefined. (A watercolour self-portrait he painted when a young man shows an easy but unexceptional talent, as do the two hundred or so engravings he cut over the years to illustrate technical, linguistic and architectural pamphlets.)

Just as Barnes was trying to get work in London he discovered a reason for wanting to stay in Dorchester. In the summer of 1819, when he was eighteen, he noticed a family clambering down from the stage coach outside the King's Arms Hotel in High Street East. Many years later Barnes's daughter would say that her father immediately 'found his heart . . . awakened [as] a slight elegant child of about sixteen sprang easily down with a bright smile. She had blue eyes, and wavy brown hair [and] the unbidden thought came into his mind, "that shall be my wife".' This 'child' was Julia Miles, and she was fourteen, not sixteen years old. Her father James, a Supervisor of Excises who had previously lived in Saffron Waldon in Essex, was understandably keen to shield her, and parried Barnes's first advances. For his pains, he was transformed by Barnes into a domestic tyrant. In 1820 Barnes published a small collection of clumsy *Poetical Pieces* – in standard English – which are remarkable chiefly for their hostile accounts of fathers who value money more than affection:

> Her father he lik'd the pecun'ary ore,
> Insomuch that in one of his passions he swore
> That Julia should ne'er again enter his door
> If to him she her hand should impart.

Two years later the same complaints reappear in 'Orra: A Lapland Tale' (a narrative poem influenced by Ambrose Philips's 'A Lapland Lovesong', which Barnes had read in the *Spectator*). While singing 'the sorrows of a faithful pair' Barnes reprimands those who prefer 'A life of luxury and splendour', spurns the idea that 'young love could not brook/The woes that from poverty spring', and dismisses the adage that 'gold's the best passport thro' life'.

In 1823 Barnes accepted that if he was going to marry Julia he would have to conform to her father's expectations and find a respectable job. This led him to take on the headmastership of the Market House School in Mere, ten miles north of Shaftesbury, and before leaving Dorchester, he applied once more to James Miles. He was again rejected. '[My father] told me plainly,' Julia reported, 'that he had no objection to you in the least ... But then he told me I must remember that when you first walked with me I was but a mere child and it was his duty as an affectionate father to make objections.'

Mere was bleak compared to Dorchester. In the year Barnes arrived, its population was only two thousand five hundred, it had no public systems of lighting or water or sewerage, and disease was rife among the people and livestock. None of this prevented Barnes from improving his lot – becoming, in Larkin's phrase: 'a kind of successful Jude Fawley' – but it was a lonely process. During his first five years at Mere, he and Julia saw each other only occasionally (at first in Dorchester, then in Nailsea, Somerset, after the Miles family moved there in 1825), and the letters they exchanged were kindly but guarded. As their editor says: 'A natural pedagogue, [Barnes] gave [Julia] lessons in perspective and reproves her for writing crooked-backed Ds. He never mentions her errors, but frequently correctly uses the misspelled word or incorrect name in the next letter.'

Market House School was a modest, one-roomed stone building in Mere's central square; every evening its desks were cleared away and it was used as the town's theatre. During the twelve years of Barnes's headmastership, the number of pupils never rose above two dozen, and the diet of their learning remained constant:

'Reading, English Grammar, at three guineas per annum; and if required Drawing, Music and Latin at three guineas per annum.' (In other words, Barnes's annual income from teaching never rose above £144.) What this meant in practice was an education based on the formulas laid out in Locke's *Essay on Education* (1752). The *Essay* was touched with the idealism Barnes had already shown in his other walks of life, yet it also emphasized the virtues of pragmatism and self-help. Practising what he preached, Barnes spent his evenings continuing the studies he had begun at Dorchester. He investigated ancient British history. He rapidly developed an interest in languages, learning French from a Frenchman who had settled in Mere, and also studying Persian and Welsh. His education, his daughter Lucy said later, 'could have been nothing but elementary [but] this was of little importance, for the learning which made his name was no grammar school knowledge . . . No school teaching gave him his faculty of penetrating to the root of every study which came his way, it was the natural instinct of a keen and penetrative mind.'

By the spring of 1827 Barnes's school was securely based, and he was able to think of living more comfortably. He rented the large and beautiful Chantry House in the centre of Mere, overlooking the church, and immediately wrote again to James Miles asking for permission to marry Julia. Judging by the terms of his letter, recent experience in Mere had turned a defiant young man into a soberly self-confident adult. 'I have always', he said to Miles, 'been taught to rely on my own exertions and this has brought all my powers into action and given me a greater variety of resources than those who have always followed one pursuit.' This time Miles needed no cajoling: Barnes and Julia were married in Nailsea on 9 July 1827, eight years after they had first met.

With his wife to help him, and a roomy house at his disposal, Barnes was able to take in boarders as well as day-pupils. The school flourished, increasing its range of courses as Barnes's own studies embraced new areas of knowledge, yet remained faithful to his original ideals. Trevor Hearl, one of his biographers, tells us: 'The keystone of education at Chantry House' combined Locke's principles with 'moral training based on the Christian gospels' – and Barnes was also 'deeply influenced by the [great figures of the] Enlightenment . . . whose ideal [in education] was to speak fluent French, write Italian poetry, admire Greek culture; to pen emotion in verse, have music and art at the fingertips, and reveal a knowledgeable enthusiasm for classical learning.' Barnes was renowned, too, for the kindness he showed his charges. 'During his thirty-nine years as a schoolmaster he was never known to strike a pupil or speak harshly to one.'

In the same year that he married, Barnes began contributing to the local weekly paper, the *Dorset County Chronicle,* a stoutly conservative broadsheet. He submitted prose essays to start with, but was soon sending poems in both dialect and standard English – as he continued to do throughout his life. (He also wrote for the *Gentleman's Magazine, Fraser's Magazine, The Reader,* and *Macmillan's Magazine.*) His first three articles were entitled 'Linguiana' and initialled 'WB'. After that he branched out, and over the years his topics ranged from the means by which language should be classified to the attractions of going to auctions.

Barnes's success as a journalist, combining with the good reputation of his school and his exceptional happiness at home with his wife and children, gave his life the stability it had lacked since leaving Pentridge. Yet as his family grew he needed to earn more money, and this meant taking in more pupils. He found Mere 'out of the way', and in 1835, when he heard of 'an opening for a boarding school at Dorchester', he took it. He stayed for the next twenty-seven years. 'I put my hopes of afterlife in work at [Dorchester],' he said, modifying still further the attitude he had once taken to 'gold'.

The relief the thirty-four-year-old Barnes felt when he left Mere is suppressed in his farewell poem, 'To A Garden – On Leaving It': 'My eyes no more may see this peaceful scene./But still, sweet spot, wherever I may be,/My love-led soul will wander back to thee.' In fact his years in Mere had set his life on its adult course without allowing him to develop his full potential. In Dorchester – a comparatively busy and well-off market town – he was much better able to develop his many interests.

Barnes's first school was in Durngate Street, which after two successful years he said was too small. In 1837 he moved to Norman House in South Street. In both places he kept faith with the principles he had tried and tested in Mere: 'preparing middle-class children for the professions, the army or navy or . . . the universities'. He also continued to produce a steady stream of poems – in what he called 'national' English, and in Dorset dialect as well. A first collection of dialect work appeared in 1844 with a fifty-page dissertation on the principles of his ideas about language, and a fifteen-hundred-word glossary; another, in 'national' English, in 1846; a second dialect collection in 1862; and another in standard English in 1868. In addition, he persevered with his essays for the *Dorset County Chronicle* and elsewhere. He read extensively in the large library belonging to John Richmond, the former headmaster of Dorchester's grammar school. He was also 'so lucky as to find . . . a friend who was a good Oriental scholar, Colonel Besant, theretofor of the Bengal Infantry and author of the *Persian and Urdu Letter-writer*, with whom for some years [he] read a little Hindustani or Persian once almost every week'. He compiled large-scale grammatical works, including *The Elements of English Grammar* (1842) and *A Philological Grammar* (1853) which demonstrates in its three hundred and twenty pages that Barnes had a competent understanding of no fewer than sixty-five languages. He also published *A Grammar of the Dorset Dialect* (1863); and *A Glossary of the Dorset Dialect* (1886).

Despite the breadth of his learning, Barnes lived between strict boundaries. He visited London only a handful of times – once to meet the poet Caroline Norton, an admirer of his own work; once to visit the Great Exhibition. His single trip abroad was to France in 1845. Yet it was a packed existence. As well as teaching and writing, he studied throughout the 1830s and most of the 1840s for a Bachelor's Degree of Divinity at Cambridge – a course which required him to spend three full terms in college. In 1845 he helped to found the Dorset County Museum. In 1847 he was ordained at Salisbury and became pastor at Whitcombe near Dorchester.

These demands were matched by dramas in his personal life. In

May 1837 his only son Julius died, aged three months. Three years later a friend he had known since childhood, Edward Fuller, also died – and was elegized in the poem 'The Music o' the Dead'. When his wife Julia died on 21 June 1852, nine days after her forty-seventh birthday, from an 'ulcer' of the breast, his world was even more profoundly shaken. 'Oh! Day of overwhelming woe!' he wrote in his diary. 'That which I greatly dreaded has come upon me. God has withdrawn from me his choicest world gift. Who can measure the greatness, the vastness of my loss? I am undone. Lord have mercy upon me!'

Barnes took charge of his 'six children, the youngest young' and at the same time tried to maintain standards in his classroom. Even with Julia beside him, his daily work had become increasingly difficult during the late 1840s. Now that he was alone, he made unreasonable demands on his oldest children and on himself ('I took in my sadness to constant work,' he said) – especially after the death in 1853 of his mother-in-law, who had lived with him and Julia for the last twenty years, and had also helped in the school. No matter how hard he worked to augment his income by publishing, lecturing and giving public readings of his work, his livelihood steadily ebbed away from him. At the beginning of the summer term 1859 his daughter Laura 'went into the school to find her father sitting alone at his desk with not a single pupil. He remarked gravely: "You see, I am at my post."'

Barnes persevered for another three years, reminded by his own failure of the disappointments that his grandfather, father, uncle and aunt had once endured. The struggle took its toll. The formerly 'alert and vigorous teacher' became increasingly eccentric, growing a long grey beard and, when teaching, wearing a 'long light-blue, rough-faced, flannel-textured dressing gown'. As his biographer Alan Chedzoy says, it was a way of advertising that he had 'ceased to live emotionally in the world he actually inhabited'.

Barnes's school eventually closed in 1862, teaching him a difficult lesson about 'the mockery' of life: on the very day he shut up shop, *The Times* announced that one of his former pupils had come first in the Indian Civil Service examination; it brought him a flood of applications. Soon afterwards, however, his prospects brightened again: the government gave him a Literary Pension of £70 a year, and he was offered the living of Winterbourne Came, two miles south of Dorchester. He was sixty-one years old, but still full of energy – walking long distances every day as he carried out his pastoral duties, helping to develop the County Museum in Dorchester, and in 1875 founding the Dorset Field Club.

As Barnes settled into his new home – a thatched, shaggy-browed rectory – Coventry Patmore eulogized his second dialect collection in *Macmillan's Magazine*, brushing aside questions of linguistic difficulty. 'Mr Barnes', Patmore wrote, 'is not only one of the few living poets of England, but . . . in one respect he stands out in a remarkable way from other living English poets . . . Seldom before has the precept "Look in thy heart and write" been followed with such integrity and simplicity; and seldom before have rural nature and humanity in its simpler aspects been expressed in verse with fidelity so charming. We breathe the morning air while we are reading.' This article not only confirmed Barnes as a local celebrity, it turned him, briefly, into a national figure. His books sold steadily if not spectacularly. He became an object of curiosity and a port of call for passing worthies, including Tennyson. Like Hardy, he was credited with the power to articulate the spirit of 'Wessex'.

Barnes lived the last part of his life quietly. To some, his reserve seemed to show a 'morbid' form of modesty; to others he appeared 'deficient in determination and spirit'. His admirers realized that he looked picturesque but intended to be practical. Hardy, for instance, admitted that Barnes was 'quaintly attired', but also knew that 'he warble[ed] his nature wood-notes with a watchful eye on the predetermined score'.

Patmore sensed the same element of calculation when he made his last visit to Winterbourne Came in September 1886: 'I found him', he said,

> in bed in his study with his face turned to the window, where the light came streaming in through flowering plants, his brown

books on all sides of him, save one, the wall behind him being hung with old green tapestries. He had a scarlet bedgown on, a kind of soft biretta of dark red wool on his head, from which his long white hair escaped onto the pillow. His grey beard has grown very long upon his breast. His complexion . . . has become bleached by keeping indoors, and is now waxily white where it is not waxily pink. The blue eyes were half shut, restless under languid lids; the whole body was very restless, rousing and falling in bed by means of a very gorgeous bedrope, with an action like rowing a boat. I wish I could paint for you the strange effect of this old, old man, lying in cardinal scarlet in his white bed, the only bright point in the gloom of all these books. You must think I make too much of these outer signs, but it seemed to me that this unconsciously theatrical *mise-en-scène* in the solitude of this out-of-the-way rectory was very curious and characteristic.

Two months later, on Thursday, 7 October, Barnes died; four days after that he was buried in the churchyard of Winterbourne Came. In his elegy, 'The Last Signal', Hardy tells us that as he set out from Max Gate for the funeral half a mile away across the fields, the sun flashed off the coffin-lid, which was made of polished elm: 'Thus a farewell to me he signalled on his grave-way,' Hardy wrote, 'as with a wave of his hand.' Tennyson felt a similarly personal loss. He wrote to Barnes's daughter: 'Your father seems to me one of the men most to be honoured and revered in our day.'

*

Rescuing Barnes from obscurity means showing his weaknesses as well as his strengths; he is a poet who needs some apologies, as well as apologists. His religious conviction, for instance, can sound sentimental and smug. He moralizes too easily on the basis of Nature's example. He can seem unduly trustful of authority ('Let other vo'k meake money vaster/I don't dread a peevish measter'). He is inclined to endorse a culture in which outcasts are pitied but not protected, and opportunities for self-help – which he preached earnestly in the classroom – are neglected. But if we allow these things to persuade us that he was someone who unthinkingly preferred the past to the present, and brought no artifice to his art, we would fall foul of the danger that Hardy warned about, and succumb to 'the popular impression of him as the naif and rude bard'. Barnes's religion may be too secure for some tastes, and his liking for the status quo too uncritical for others, but his imagination is contradictory and perturbing, and his views about versification and language all combine innocence with cunning. Hardy was right again when he said Barnes 'really belonged to the literary school of such poets as Tennyson, Gray and Collins, rather than to that of the old unpremeditating singers'.

Barnes's 'cunning' is easy to establish: many of his homely-seeming structures are in fact exotic imports. A Persian verse form is used in 'Woke Hill', Hebrew in 'White an' Blue' and 'Melhill Feast' – and elsewhere he borrows from Norse, Irish and Welsh. The same goes for his dialect itself. When E. M. Forster, for instance, said that 'the veil of the Dorset dialect . . . is slight: anyone can lift it after half an hour's reading', he meant to recommend Barnes, but in fact made him seem a much less conscious artist than was the case. Regional dialect, as a written form, had largely disappeared from books published in Britain within a century of Chaucer's death: to pretend that Barnes is not an anomaly is to play down the extent to which his work is deliberately provocative.

When Barnes published his first dialect collection in 1844, his claim to be using a 'real' language was evidently far-fetched. In the years following, it became increasingly obvious that he was not so much maintaining a distinct local tradition as using his skills as a philologist, historian and archaeologist to create a language that appeared to be common to all Dorset but was in reality his own. He spruced up the spellings in his dialect work as successive editions appeared. He demanded that 'foreign' words be excluded from ordinary speech and that Anglo-Saxon alternatives be provided. He ornamented his Dorset research with references to the Welsh language. In nearly every respect, Barnes's efforts led him further and further into oddity – and today most philologists agree that both his linguistic principles and his vocabulary were substantially of his own invention. The evidence is everywhere. Among his many other theories we find the idea of 'hard-', 'dead-' and 'half-pennings', which refer to varieties of vocal stops and chords. (The word 'penning' is not even in his own Glossary, let alone the *OED*.) Elsewhere he speaks of 'wordheads' (initials), 'lessening meanings' (diminutives), and 'clippings' (consonants). And in his *Outline of English Speech Craft* (1878) we find him offering a host of substitutes for familiar existing words: 'skysill' (for 'horizon'), 'mind-glee' (for 'delight'), 'song-mocking' (for 'parody') 'thing-name' (for 'noun'), and 'many-wedder' (for 'bigamist').

Barnes's philological arguments are flawed by comic strangeness: in his wish to keep language accurately local, he made it arcane. Tellingly, the London-based Philological Society never asked him to become a member. As Chedzoy says: 'The great work of the Society was the preparation of its dictionary, which was eventually published as the *Oxford English Dictionary* in 1888, two years after Barnes's death. In their prospectus, the editors of the dictionary declared the principle that there should be no exclusions on the grounds of "obsoleteness, foreignness or localism", yet they almost completely ignored hundreds of revived items or neologisms suggested by Barnes in his various publications.'

In the face of such evidence, it's obvious that if we want to appreciate the power and purpose of Barnes's dialect poems, we have to accept their element of inventedness. Barnes claimed that he was producing something pure, simple, and old as the hills. ('I cannot help' writing in dialect, he once said; 'it is my mother tongue, and is to my mind the only true speech of the life that I draw.') In fact his work is immensely intricate, sometimes a little crazy, and new. It is more like Burns than Clare, and more like Hugh MacDiarmid than either – a manner of speaking which is at once quaint (and therefore socially tolerable, however strange), and subversive (and therefore marginal).

Barnes's first dialect poems, written in 1834, were a series of eclogues modelled to varying degrees on Virgil's originals. They have been described and generally accepted as 'a half-humorous set of observations [of country working] people', which Barnes himself bracketed with all his other poems as merely 'pictures . . . I see in my mind'. In fact they are much more ambitious than that. Before writing the eclogues, he had dealt with conventional themes in standard English. Now he created a language which allowed him to deal directly with urgent contemporary problems.

The issue which forced Barnes to this creative crisis was Enclosure – the subject of his first eclogue 'Rusticus Dolens, or Inclosures of Common', which was later retitled 'Eclogue: The Common A-Took In'. The year he wrote this poem (1834), Dorset had been agitated by the Swing Riots, a series of disturbances during which farmworkers protested about low wages, the price of bread, Irish labour, and the loss of traditional common land. (The rioters rode through Hampshire, Wiltshire and Dorset, urging labourers to burn ricks and smash machines.) Barnes sympathized with the rioters but, being a cautious man and preferring to avoid confrontation with authority, his response was not to show outright support. Instead, he offered a dramatic presentation of their cause – in poems like 'Father Come Hwome' and 'The 'Lotments', as well as 'Eclogue: The Common A-Took In' itself. In this earliest example, two labourers, John and Thomas, discuss the effect of enclosures. John explains that he has to sell his geese because 'they do mean to take the moor in', and adds that he expects to have to sell the cow for the same reasons. Barnes suggests that once the two men lose their traditional rights, they will also lose their independence and their sense of belonging:

> 'Tis handy to live near a common;
> But I've a zeed, an' I've a zaid,
> That if a poor man got a bit o' bread,
> They'll try to teake it vrom en.

'Eclogue: The Common A-Took In' ends with Thomas saying that 'I wer twold back – t'other day,/That they be got into a way/O letten bits o' ground out to the poor.' This hint of compromise no doubt derives in part from Barnes's reluctance to offend either the editor of the conservative *Dorset County Chronicle*, on which he depended for supplements to his income, or the parents of his pupils, who were his mainstay. Most of it, though, stems from his enduring respect for the status quo – a respect which underlay all his political and educational beliefs. (He was silent, for instance, about the conviction of the Tolpuddle Martyrs in 1834, having supported their claim for a living wage but opposed their means of achieving it.) He disapproved of organized labour (his poem 'The Times' depicts a typical Chartist as a cunning crow who deprives the labourer, a pig, of his roots). He extolled the virtues of the independent smallholder – 'my uncle Charles Rabbetts when he was free of debt and danger' – working in a feudal system. In *Views of Labour and Gold* (1859), his idiosyncratic textbook on economics, he states 'the squire and his lady are a great social good when they live among the poor, and keep before their eye the graceful pattern of Christian life, and raise the tone of feeling by kindness and sober expectation'.

In other words, Barnes's ideal society is a mixture of paternalistic conservatism and Christian socialism, combining elements from the writings of Ruskin, Morris, Kingsley and Samuel Smiles. But whereas his thinking often seems naive when he is writing prose or standard English, it becomes much subtler and more allusive when he turns to dialect. His poem 'Air an' Light' is a good case in point. Its third verse, in the 'national English' version, runs as follows:

> The Morning sun may cast abroad
> His light on dew about our feet,
> And down below his noontide road
> The streams may glare below his heat;
> The evening light may sparkle bright
> Across the quiv'ring gossamer;
> But I, though fair he still may glow,
> Must miss a face he cannot show.

Compare this to the more energetic and evocative dialect version:

> The mornen zun do cast abroad
> His light on drops o' dewy wet,
> An' down below his noontide road
> The streams do gleare below his het;
> His evenen light do sparkle bright
> Across the quiv'ren gossamer;
> But I, though fair he still mid glow,
> Do miss a zight he cannot show.

The great majority of Barnes's dialect poems have a similar power: they may lack what Larkin called Hardy's 'bitter and ironical despair', but they prove that dialect widened his eyes and turned him into a poet who 'noticed things'. His Dorset is not a flimsy Arcadian paradise but a real place full of real people doing real work, and feeling real anxiety about change. In this respect, his work looks back to the Romantics, and forward to Edward Thomas, whose own poems often use definite characters and hard characteristics to create a landscape which is at once intimate and removed (in 'Lob', 'The Gypsy' and 'The Manor Farm', for instance). 'A Haulen o' the Corn' is a good example, with its attention to the sheer hard work of harvesting. So is 'Shroden Fair', with its celebration of seasonal rituals, and 'Leady-Day, an' Ridden House', with its attention to domestic practicalities. These poems combine people and places and customs to create the picture of a community which has been superseded, but is still secure in the imaginative present. 'The Wold Wagon' is yet another example. Its technical terms and details make the poem part evocation and part elegy:

> Upon his head an' tail wer pinks,
> A-painted all in tangled links;
> His two long zides wer blue, – his bed
> Bent slightly upwards at the head;
> His reaves rose upward in a bow
> Above the slow hind-wheels below.

The imaginative pressure of these poems depends on more than a general feeling of dispossession: it is accelerated and deepened by three personal losses. One was the death of his son Julius, whom Barnes commemorated in 'To a Child Lost', 'Our Little Boy' and 'The Turnstile'. Another was the death of one of his brothers from sunstroke, which he remembered in 'The Child an' the Mowers', when writing about another boy in the neighbourhood who suffered the same fate. The lines derive a great deal of their power from remaining practical and pragmatic; they remind us that in the actual lives of labourers, shade is welcome and necessary:

> Then they laid en there – right on the ground
> On a grass-heap, a-zweltren wi' het,
> Wi' his heair all a-wetted around
> His young feace, wi' the big drops o' zweat;
> In his little left palm he'd a-zet,
> Wi' his right hand, his vore-vinger's tip,
> As ver zome'hat he woulden vorget
> Aye! Zome thought that he woulden let slip.

The death of Barnes's wife Julia had an even more pervasive effect. He produced several elegies for her, in dialect and standard English, and they stand at the centre of his work in much the same way that 'Poems of 1912–13' do in Hardy's – but with no guilt stirred into their melancholy. In earlier poems, written during their courtship, Barnes often told the story of his feelings by means of images to do with water. Water is cold and sometimes frozen in 'Orra', his narrative of frustration; in 'To Julia' it is unlocked as 'the bright waves of the Frome'; in 'The Aquatic Excursion' it is 'glittering . . . up the stream' – and so on. This imagery returns in the best of his later poems about his wife, 'The Bwoat', where water carries the couple apart rather than uniting them:

> Then, lik' a cloud below the skies,
> A-drifted off, wi' less'nen size

An' lost, she floated vrom my eyes,
Where down below the stream did wind;
An' left the quiet weaves woonce mwore
To zink to rest, a sky-blue'd vloor,
Wi' all so still's the clote they bore,
Aye, all but my own ruffled mind.

Barnes bends towards details under the weight of his bereavements: they are his consolation in a world stricken by bad luck, limited opportunities, and mortality. But he never loses his sense of larger consolations. When his reasons for despair are strongest, and his feelings of alienation most acute, he is still able to appeal to something outside himself for comfort – God, or Nature, or cyclical time. 'Time alone shall lead me on/At last to where my love is gone,' he writes in another poem for 'My Dearest Wife'. This leaves his work, like his life, rich in contradictions. His poems speak of a particular historical moment, yet his methods make him a voice apart. It was a combination Barnes often claimed not to notice in himself; in fact he knew it from first to last. When he had finished dictating his final poem, 'The Geate A-Vallen To', he turned to his daughter and said:

'Observe that word gate . . . that is how King Alfred would have pronounced it, and how it was called in the Saxon Chronicle, which told us of King Edward, who was slain at Corfe's gate.' He paused again, and continued: 'Ah! If the Court had not been moved to London, then the speech of King Alfred, of which our Dorset is the remnant, would have been the Court language of today'.

THOMAS HARDY
The Dynasts

The Dynasts has always had defenders but few actual fans. Thomas Hardy discovered this in 1904, when the first of its three parts was published (the others appeared in 1906 and 1908). Friends and insiders admired its ambition – Max Beerbohm said it was 'a noble achievement'; most reviewers and general readers agreed that it was 'uncouth', 'halting', and 'stiffly brocaded'. The hostility depressed Hardy. It also goaded him into the same sort of defiance with which he had previously responded to criticism of his novels. The more questions people asked about his play's style, and the more aspersions they cast on its philosophy, the more obstinately he protested its merits.

He had particular reasons for feeling protective. The idea of writing *The Dynasts* had originally occurred to him in 1875, nearly thirty years before its first part saw the light of day, and once the play's life in print had finally begun, he went on tinkering with it more or less until the end of his life. It was, in other words, a favourite child – one made all the more dear by unpopularity. It wasn't so much the form that made it special, nor even its vulnerable grand design. It was the subject. Sweeping from 1805 to the eventual defeat of Napoleon at Waterloo, *The Dynasts* dramatizes the painful birth of the world on which his life and imagination depended.

For all its cosmopolitan interests, its scenes in Parliaments and ballrooms, its set-piece battles, its political discussions and intriguing cameos, the play's most lively interest is the interplay between humble lives and great events, between individual desires and the unchangeable plans of an Immanent Will. And while much of the out-fall from these contests pours through impressive cities and across the mainland of Europe, its effects and some of its

The Complete Poetical Works of Thomas Hardy volumes iv and v, edited by
Samuel Hynes (Clarendon Press, 1995)

origins were clearly observable right under Hardy's nose in Wessex. The local geography of *The Dynasts* – the Dorset villages from which soldiers went to war, and the Dorset cliffs where people watched for Napoleon's invasion – is the drama's most powerful motivating force. Hardy meant to capture the clang and clash of events, but also to excavate 'the primal rocks of history' which lay underneath.

He set about his task with exceptional energy. He compiled and studied a huge collection of Napoleonic literature; he interviewed interested parties; he trekked across battlefields; he pondered relics and remains – such as the 'outhouse door' he mentions in the preface to *The Trumpet-Major,* 'riddled with bullet holes, which had been extemporized by a solitary man as a target for firelock practice when the landing was hourly expected'. At the same time, he juggled ideas about which form would best suit a mixture of mythic, epic and personal incident. Should it be a stage play, or a series of ballads? In the end, he settled on something described in the cumbersome subtitle as 'An Epic-Drama'. What he meant was a mind-play, a piece for the inner theatre, which he bristlingly insisted was 'the only way' he could 'present such a wide subject within reasonable compass'.

In theory, all this research and all these plans are admirable – tightly concentrated on strengths that Hardy knew he should play to, and also strikingly original. But he evidently found it difficult to reconcile the competing demands of his various ingredients. Having decided against the immersed narrative of a straightforward play, and having also refused the tone-steadying pattern of orthodox lyric, he found himself writing instead in a style which could never quite relax into a familiar thing, nor transform itself into a wholly persuasive new one.

The problem is obvious in the opening pages, where we meet the Spirits ('The Spirit of the Years', 'The Spirit of the Pieties', et al.) who make regular appearances through the rest of the piece. Their function is to explore the tension between individual will and the pre-determined pattern of fate, but whether their voices are satirical or speculative, they are invariably raised by Hardy to a pitch of

abstract utterance which is often unintentionally comic, or baffling. Here is 'The Spirit of the Years':

> These are the Prime Volitions – fibrils, veins,
> Will-tissues, nerves, and pulses of the Cause,
> That heave throughout the Earth's compositure.
> Their sum is like the lobule of a Brain
> Evolving always that it wots not of.

Here and everywhere else in the Spirits' speeches, we understand the points they want to make without quite seeing how their
imagery works, and certainly without feeling its intended force.
The same sort of thing also happens when ordinary mortals speak.
There is no corresponding effort to make them as humanly human
as the Spirits are spiritually spiritual, but there is a similar effect of
stultification. Hardy wants to show us that the lives of his characters are not their own – that their stories were written even before
they began making history – and as he presses this point home, he
makes them too merely the 'flesh-hinged mannikins' their over-
seers reckon them to be. They are stuck like insects in amber. Their
vernacular dash and their instinct for a higher poetry are fatally
inhibited.

This means no character develops at all interestingly. Most of
the big names come on stage only to deliver their burden of the
narrative and depart – Pitt in Parliament, Wellington in the Peninsula. It's possible that a few such appearances wouldn't do much
harm – provided there were at least some people, or even one person, whom we felt to be evolving through suffering. Napoleon
himself, of course, is the best bet – many of those British writers
who were his contemporaries, and stood to lose most by his cam-
paigns, show a fascinated ambivalence about him. Hazlitt, for
instance, while condemning his ravages and rampages, could not
help admiring his mythic boldness.

Hardy is more settled – clearly engrossed by the scale of
Napoleon's operations, even more obviously deploring him. Early
on, we read about his 'vulpine smile', and thereafter we're deluged

with tales or displays of his treachery, rapacity, heartlessness. Even the pathos which springs from discovering that he is not a free agent but a cipher for the Immanent Will is muffled. Late in the third part, for instance, with defeat staring him in the face, Napoleon's speech is restrained by Hardy's linguistic awkwardness, and his pro-British bias:

> The fates had served me best
> If in the thick and thunder of to-day,
> Like Nelson, Harold, Elector, Cyrus, Saul,
> I had been shifted from this jail of flesh,
> To wander as a greatened ghost elsewhere.

Given so much stiffness at the centre of *The Dynasts'* stage, it's tempting to overpraise action nearer its wings – action at a local level and especially in Dorset, where the 'primal rocks of history' are most nearly exposed. In truth, the language of the Wessex folk shouldering their arms and peering from their cliffs is also blighted. Like everyone else, they are marooned in history, illustrating it rather than exemplifying it, their mouths full of library-speak and their spirits broken by the weight of Hardy's research into their lives. Here, typically, is a 'rustic' preparing to burn an effigy of Napoleon before Waterloo: 'Says I, please God I'll lose a quarter to zee he burned! And I left Stourcastle one o'clock to a minute. And if I'd known that I should be too late to zee the beginning on't, I'd have lost a half to be a bit sooner.'

The Dynasts only flickers into life when Hardy changes tack: in the few poems and songs, for instance, which perhaps remember his original idea of casting the whole play into ballads, and convey the sense of being inside an experience rather than providing a documentary comment upon it. At one point – and they're the most evocative lines in the whole play – even the Spirit of the Years suppresses its instinct for abstraction and starts using its eyes:

> The mole's tunnelled chambers are crushed by wheels,
> The lark's eggs scattered, their owners fled;

And the Hedgehog's household the sapper unseals.

The snail draws in at the terrible tread,
But in vain; he is crushed by the felloe-rim;
The worm asks what can be overhead,

And wriggles deep from a scene so grim,
And guesses him safe; for he does not know
What a foul red rain will be soaking him!

This has the watchfulness, the sense of a wide world in miniature, that gives Hardy's other writing – in novels and poetry – so
much of its character. The same qualities also exist in many of the
prose scene-settings which punctuate the play's action: Europe
'disclosed as a prone and emaciated figure, the Alps shaped like a
backbone, and the branching mountain-chains like ribs'; or 'the
purple rotundities of the heath [which] show like bronze, and the
pits like the eye-sockets of a skull'. These have often been praised
for their cinematic clarity, and the source of their power – like the
source of the poem's excitement – has a great deal to do with a certain kind of detachment. By panning above his scenery, by pinning
himself inside a lyric, Hardy forgets the duty he feels that he owes
both to his narrative and to the philosophy he hoped it would
exemplify. His gigantic project works best when it is least determined to be itself. His imagination is most engaged when it has
least to answer for.

However carefully we weigh these successes, they can't prevent
The Dynasts from seeming at worst a failure, at best a curio. Yet like
all the failures of great writers – Keats's plays, for instance, or Tennyson's – it has its importance and its fascination. What we lose in
terms of achievement we gain by seeing abiding inspirations laid
bare. *The Dynasts* defines the whole scope and focus of Hardy's
historical imagination; it exposes the theories and attitudes which
are made flesh and blood in the poems and novels. In this sense,
therefore, it does seem a kind of primal rock: a foundation stone.

Robert Frost

1 Accounts of the Life

Jay Parini's *Life* of Robert Frost is always competent – but is it necessary? Parini himself puts the question in his Afterword, where he considers 'Frost and his Biographers'. He sees them advancing on their subject in three distinct waves. The first presented their man as 'a classical humanist', full of Yankee good sense and slow-talking fireside wisdom. It was an image that conformed more or less exactly to the one Frost presented in the flesh, and was bound to provoke a doubtful counterblast in due time. The only surprise was the source of this second wave. Lawrance Thompson, whom Frost invited to become his official chronicler, trampled down everything he was expected to preserve, and created instead the portrait of a 'monster' (the word appears several times in the text of his three-volume assassination) – 'selfish, egomaniacal, dour, cruel, and angry'.

Parini says Thompson's attack was an aspect of his 'naivity', adding that (in order to make a coherent shape from the scattered facts of Frost's career) a 'mythos' was developed which 'distorted, rather than clarified, the material in hand'. This sounds more like a repetition of the charges against Thompson than an explanation of the case – but at least it makes us consider the likelihood of prejudice and presupposition.

The third wave was a reaction to the reaction. William H. Pritchard, whose excellent *Robert Frost: A literary life reconsidered* (1984) read 'the poetry back into the life rather than the other way round', created a context in which other level-headed accounts could flourish. In the years since it first appeared, there have been several high-spots of criticism (such as Seamus Heaney's essay in 'Homage

Robert Frost: A Life, by Jay Parini (Henry Holt, New York, 2001)

to Robert Frost'); there have been intelligent attempts to bridge the gap between Frost and the modernists – notably Mark Richardson's well-argued *The Ordeal of Robert Frost* (1997); and there have been jobbing summaries, such as Jeffrey Meyers's over-heated and under-researched biography. By and large, though, the Frost now lodged in the minds of his readers is a poet in whom stark alternatives have been reconciled. His orneryness is as widely accepted as his grace; his ingenuity is as warmly praised as his charm.

So to put the question again: is Parini's book necessary? Well, yes, according to the three-wave theory. In a case like Frost's, where the flight into posthumous existence has been bumpy, there is always a need for steadiness, which this *Life* sensibly provides. Parini's prose is generally reined in, and his character judgements cautious. They allow a clear light to fall over the whole of Frost's story, and create logical connections between its various parts and performances.

The price is a lack of surprise, not just in terms of insight about the relationships between different people, but about the relation between Frost and 'mystery'. We learn early on that, according to one friend, 'Robert believed he could hear voices, real voices. His poems came to him like voices from nowhere.' While Parini squeezes some religious significance out of this, he does not develop any important connection with Frost's theories of poetic voice and 'the sound of sense' – though these things take up a significant part of his book.

This is a pity, since in many of Frost's beautiful remarks about writing he allows for an element of not-knowing, and of givenness, which has an interesting association with the spiritual development he described as 'Presbyterian, Unitarian, Swedenborgian, Nothing'. It is the same whether he is dealing with single images (such as the idea that a poem, like a piece of ice, should 'ride on its own melting'), or in more elaborate thoughts such as his notion that

the living part of a poem is the intonation entangled somehow in the syntax, idiom, and meaning of a sentence. It is only there for those who have heard it previously in conversation. It is not for us in any Greek or Latin poem because our ears have not been filled with the tones of Greek and Roman talk. It is the most volatile and at the same time important part of poetry. It goes and the language becomes a dead language, the poetry dead poetry ... Words exist in the mouth, not in books.

In all his remarks about 'the sound of sense', Frost expects the familiar to produce something marvellous; what is inherent will be inspirational. This is clear enough. But there are difficulties, too. When Frost says that we are able to identify the 'living part' of a poem only by associating it with something 'previously' heard 'in conversation', he under-represents the role that he believes music can play in poetry. That is to say: his poems repeatedly establish a brilliant interplay between conversational rhythms and the trace-memory of more formally perfect lines. One side-effect of this is to suggest that the perfectly clear communication of a definite 'meaning' might not be his primary intention. Rather, in fact, that he wants to produce a sound that is designed to carry the weight of inarticulate thought – a sound of longing and dread and confusion. Frost may have said that poems 'begin with a lump in the throat', with 'lovesickness' and with 'homesickness', but he was less willing to admit they often end by referring to the same state. Did the practical Yankee in him jib at the idea? Maybe. All the same, it is there in many of his best (and best-known) poems – as though the words on the page represent an interval between two mysteries:

> The woods are lovely, dark and deep,
> But I have promises to keep,
> And miles to go before I sleep,
> And miles to go before I sleep.

Parini is good on what is clearly visible and audible in Frost's work, and gives sensitive readings of his formal effects. But even when not believing everything Frost said about his aims (he quotes another friend saying that Frost 'wanted to be found out –

by the right people in the right way'), he is reluctant to explore the contradictions in his verse-theories. The sense in which the easy affability of the poems is built over a ghastly silence, and the skill with which that silence is worked into their cadence, are not adequately realized.

The same sort of thing applies to the book's other main concern: the narrative of the life itself. The story is told with a kindly sympathy no matter what the circumstances – even the last part of his career, which was almost all surface (readings, politickings and honourings), is handled with a surprising degree of excitement. On the other hand, the tensions in Frost's marriage, and his relationship with his family, which caused Thompson so much irritation, are not given adequate attention. Frost's recurring illnesses, his wife's, the personal tragedies which afflicted several of their children: Parini dutifully logs all these things without seriously asking whether it was such a good idea for Frost to be 'a self-professed believer in monogamy', or whether, when his friend Louis Untermeyer went through a crisis in his personal life, it was more than 'scolding' of Frost to write:

> What I dread most now is that you will go [i.e. that Untermeyer would end his second marriage] on the assumption that, though it was folly and landed you in tragedy, it was on the way somewhere and somehow prepared you for greater and fuller life. Shut up. To hell with such comforts. It was all time and energy lost, as I have said before.

At such moments, Parini's refusal to pass judgement seems evasive, not tactful. For one thing, it prevents him from wondering about the secret engines that drive poems other than the obvious narratives of distress like 'Home Burial'. For another, it keeps him from asking questions about the nature of Frost's friendship with other men – and especially about his crucial brotherhood with Edward Thomas. Frost and Thomas met when Frost was living in England between 1912 and 1915, and certain aspects of their alliance are now well known: how Frost released Thomas as a poet, how

Thomas did Frost some big favours in reviewing his poems, how they tramped and talked through the last summer before the war. Given what Thompson (not Parini) says about the state of Frost's marriage during this time, and given the condition of Thomas's relationship with his own wife Helen (which she at once publicized and misrepresented in her memoirs), it seems clear that the intellectual and imaginative sympathy between the two men was fed by other kinds of mutual recognition: by a rich brew of marriage-inspired frustration and self-dislike.

By underplaying this aspect of Frost's time with Thomas, Parini does nothing so disastrous as create a travesty. Rather, he once again shows himself bound by certain vows of moderation – all of them essentially decent, but all made rigid by his reluctance to echo Thompson's harsh judgements. As a result, the English episode has the same strengths, and the same weaknesses, as the book as a whole. When we get towards the end, and find Lionel Trilling, at Frost's eighty-fifth birthday party, causing consternation by referring to him as 'a terrifying poet', we see what he means, without feeling it on our pulses. Parini shows us how Frost wrote poems to make 'a momentary stay against confusion', but does not let us understand the confusion itself – not the desolate impulse which led him in 'The Wind and the Rain', that poem with the Hardyesque title, to ask the Hardyesque question:

> Oh, should a child be left unwarned
> That any song in which he mourned
> Would be as if he prophesied?

2 The Secret Places

'We were a strange pair in our at-variances. We kept it up between us in a kind of magnanimity of high-minded tolerance of each other's taste.' Robert Frost's summary of his friendship with Sidney Cox strikes a characteristically wry note. But here as elsewhere in his poems and letters, the tone masks and protects strong feelings. Throughout his life, Frost seems to have needed not merely

Robert Frost and Sidney Cox: Forty Years of Friendship, by William R. Evans
(University Press of New England, Hanover, 1981)

praise, but hero-worship, and in Cox he found an almost ideal acolyte: during the forty years of their correspondence, it is Cox who sounds the more active friend. Yet Frost's comparative diffidence is in fact demanding. He required to be approached – and to pontificate – just as badly as Cox needed to live his life within sight of an irreproachable example. The story of their relationship, as it is revealed in their letters, makes for tense reading.

In 1911, when they originally met, Frost and Cox were both working as teachers. Frost was thirty-seven, had published very little poetry, and was profoundly dispirited by the restlessnesses and disappointments of his past. Cox was fifteen years younger – energetic, idealistic, and innocent. He had been brought up a Baptist, and although this had helped to develop a rather orthodox, upright streak in his personality (initially he was disgusted by Frost's scruffiness and iconoclasm), he was romantically impressed by literature. When Frost showed him some manuscript poems, Cox's admiration was awoken, and the seal was set on their friendship. '[Frost] is spontaneous', he was to tell his parents. 'He never gives praise when it is sought. He likes nothing because it is esteemed. He does not gush over anything or anybody. Show him a picture of a dear relative, and he will not try to say something nice about it . . . He does not hesitate to expose defects and reveal follies in notions and in people. But he is, invariably, kind. And his dry humor saves all the delicate situations as well as glorifies the pleasant ones.'

Shortly after their first meeting, Frost left for England, intent on making his name as a poet. Within two years he had published two collections (*A Boy's Will* in 1913 and *North of Boston* in 1914) and had established himself prominently in literary London. At regular intervals he relayed news of his triumphs to Cox, passing on gossip about writers and trying out various poetic theories. But Cox's value at this time was not simply his capacity to be impressed. He was also a means by which Frost could prepare the way for a successful return home. Cox faithfully disseminated copies of Frost's good reviews, taught his poems, and kept an eye on the American market. A good deal of Frost's wheeling and dealing now looks pretty distasteful, particularly since it involved him in taking a strikingly selfish attitude to the war: 'It ends my little literary game', he complained, '– that's all. No more books from anybody for the present. And the fact seems to be that I needed just one more book to clinch my business.'

Frost need not have worried. By the time he eventually returned to America, in 1915, his own and Cox's efforts had guaranteed him a warm reception. He found himself at once set on the course that over the next fifty-odd years led him to become his country's best-loved poet, its unofficial laureate. It is clear from Lawrance Thompson's biography that this affectionate acclaim was often achieved – in America as it had been in England – by ruthless operating, and at considerable cost to his family and friends. Like Hardy, he projected an image of himself as a natural, homely, wise old boy (he told Cox in 1929, 'I fight to be allowed to sit cross-legged on the old flint pile and flake a lump into an artefact'), and he worked hard to cover the tracks of his ambitious manipulations. As one might expect, therefore, it is not hard to find plenty of unpleasant bossiness in Frost's letters to Cox. But equally, there is ample compassion and care. Frost continually and kindly checked Cox's uncritical sentimentality, helped him to obtain jobs as a teacher and gave good advice about teaching methods. Frost was never so sure of himself and his position that he could afford to threaten Cox's friendship.

In spite of his evident commitment to Cox – who must have been, often, an infuriatingly smothering friend – there is a striking and persistent restraint in Frost's letters. For one thing, he makes surprisingly few judgements about other poets and poems. When he does, they are usually competitively derogatory. On one occasion he calls Carl Sandburg 'probably the most artificial and studied ruffian the world has had'; on another he asks, 'Why doesn't someone discover that T. S. Eliot is no more than an extremely competent voice of human giving-up, first in sneers and then in prayers?'; and on a third he ridicules I. A. Richards's talks on Basic English as 'Basic Balls'.

References to the methods and intentions of his own poems are similarly few and far between. This is partly due, no doubt, to Frost's understandable fear of afflicting his writing with self-consciousness. The correspondence abounds with remarks like 'You *must not* disillusion your admirers with the tale of your sources and processes', and 'I don't want to search the poet's mind too seriously'. The one exception Frost makes to this rule is his willingness to discuss his now celebrated verse theory, 'the sound of sense', which was shaped during his time in England. With considerable help from his friend Edward Thomas, who had independently developed similar beliefs, Frost refined his conviction that 'The living part of a poem is the intonation entangled somehow in the syntax, idiom and meaning of a sentence.' Cox played a vital part in the evolution of this theory: his rapt and enthusiastic response made him an ideal sounding-board.

From a strictly literary point of view, Frost's letters about 'the sound of sense' were the most important he sent to Cox. But while their insight and originality are remarkable, it is hardly surprising that Cox should have received them. He was, after all, one of Frost's closest friends. This makes the other outstanding element of reserve in Frost's correspondence all the more striking. Although quick to discuss verse theory, Frost steadfastly refused to explore the relationship between his own experience and the situations created in his poems. In fact he told Cox virtually nothing about his family and personal life, not even during his traumatic late middle age. Frost's sister died in 1929, his daughter in 1934, his wife in 1938, and in 1940 his son shot himself – and he scarcely mentions any of these events to Cox.

Frost's silence on these subjects is related to his habitually wry tone of voice: it is a more extreme form of his shyness and containment. And among other things, it helps to explain his hostility to Helen Thomas after she had published *As It Was* and *World Without End*. These candid evocations of life with her husband Edward broke all the rules Frost had laid down for himself:

In one [chapter] she has him invite to the house a girl [Eleanor Farjeon] he has met and come home full of admiration of. She gives herself away by calling the girl 'this paragon of women'. But she finds the minute she sees her (how homely she is) that she can conquer her with magnanimity. All women are sisters that the same man loves, she tries to make herself think. Once in the woods listening to a nightingale in the dark E says to the two of them We are knowing, but the nightingale knows all. Then he kisses his wife and to keep the score even his wife makes him kiss the other woman. She pretends to think that it is large and lovely but I happen to know it was a dose she was giving him and rubbing in. These things are hard to do sincerely. And unridiculously.

Frost's dislike of self-revelation also illuminates his fondness for narrative poems. To create a dramatic structure, and to incorporate fictional details or characters, was his way of drawing on intense personal feelings without embarrassment. It allowed him the chance to give a general application to the intimate hurts and anxieties which thrust themselves upon a writer. Hence, partly, the power of 'Home Burial', and Frost's own liking for the poem. It both objectifies his grief for the premature death of his first son, and explores the subsequent difficulties in his relationship with his wife:

> The little graveyard where my people are!
> So small the window frames the whole of it.
> Not so much larger than a bed-room, is it?
> There are three stones of slate and one of marble,
> Broad-shouldered little slabs there in the sunlight
> On the sidehill. We haven't to mind *those*.
> But I understand: it is not the stones,
> But the child's mound . . .
> 'Don't, don't, don't, don't', she cried.

Cox understood Frost's strategies for discretion, and appears to have accepted the implication that even the closest friends could not expect to be told everything. Yet as a young man it seems he could never quite resist the temptation to push his luck, and in later life he paid a price for it. Cox was keen to celebrate his relationship with Frost by publishing a critical study, but Frost stubbornly resisted him. 'I have written to keep the overcurious out of the secret places of my mind both in my verse and in my letters to such as you', Frost once snapped. Eventually, though, Cox had his way, and his eulogistic – and tactful – appreciation *A Swinger of Birches* was published posthumously. Frost was even prevailed upon to write an introduction, in spite of his refusal to read the book itself. But he must have known that Cox would loyally and revealingly concentrate on discussing 'the sound of sense'. If he had imagined less well of the book, he would have referred to their friendship in less self-deprecating terms. The introduction's modesty is a form of grateful pride: his affection for Cox, Frost says, 'was a curious blend of differences that if properly handled might prove an almost literary curiosity'.

IVOR GURNEY
Beaten Down Continually

Ivor Gurney was certified insane in 1922; for the previous ten years he had suffered periodic bouts of acute depression (he refers to it as 'neurasthenia', in the vague terminology of the day). This was given an obvious focus by his experiences in the First World War, but was further exacerbated by his sense of displacement in the ensuing peace. The last fifteen years of his life were spent in Stone House mental hospital in Kent. The poems he wrote there continue the celebrations of the English countryside and its history, and the ruminations about the war, that had dominated the two collections with which he had first made his name as a poet: *Severn and Somme* (1917) and *War's Embers* (1919). But while the themes are consistent, the treatment is fascinatingly different. Predominantly Georgian qualities are consistently pressed out of shape by a mind which – for personal as well as literary reasons – can no longer trust them.

For years Gurney's poetic qualities have not simply been undervalued or misunderstood – they have been almost completely neglected. If he has been known at all widely, it has usually been as a song-writer, and as the author of a few poems such as 'To His Love' and 'Song' ('Only the wanderer . . . '). Although his first two books were well received, a third – to have been called *Rewards of Wonder* – was turned down in 1919, and no successful efforts were made to publish other collections during his lifetime. In 1954, seventy-eight mostly uncollected poems were edited and introduced by Edmund Blunden but they created little interest. In 1973, about half this selection was reissued with the addition of a further ninety-seven previously uncollected poems chosen by Leonard Clark. Gurney's hour still had not come, and the book has long been difficult to obtain.

Collected Poems of Ivor Gurney, edited by P. J. Kavanagh
(Oxford University Press, 1982)

It has not only been literary taste which has prevented Gurney from getting the attention and praise he deserves. During his years in Stone House, his friend and mentor Marion Scott lovingly typed out and preserved his work, but over the years her concern for its safety hardened into something like jealous hoarding. Gerald Finzi had some success in extracting songs from her private archive, and he was also the moving force behind the Blunden edition. But Blunden's selection, like Clark's, was textually corrupt. This is hardly surprising, in view of the fact that he had no easy access to the original manuscripts. Only in the last few years have the majority of Gurney's papers found their way to the library of his home town, Gloucester, and their collection has coincided with signs of awakening general interest in his work and life. He has been promoted by anthologists and critics such as Geoffrey Grigson, Jon Silkin and Paul Fussell, and in 1978 Michael Hurd published a full-length biography. Now at last we have an authoritative *Collected Poems*.

P. J. Kavanagh's editorial task has been a difficult one, and he has done it with insight and affection. His edition selects more than three hundred poems (one hundred and seventeen of them previously uncollected) from the nine hundred-odd that Gurney wrote. If this seems rigorous, it is only because Gurney wrote a number of poems on closely similar subjects, and habitually produced wholly new poems rather than revising those that he thought had gone off the rails. Kavanagh has also tried to establish a chronological order, but since relatively few of the manuscripts are dated, he has had to rely on the loose structure dictated by the main events in Gurney's life. The period 1919–22 is the best represented; after 1926 – when Gurney's illness often prevented him from working coherently – the most sparse. There is an introduction which avoids saying much in the way of literary criticism, but is sympathetic in its effort to interest 'the general reader'. For 'the Gurney student' there are annotations which are intended as a guide 'through the Archive' in Gloucester. There remains, of course, a nagging wish for a *Collected Poems* which is a *Complete Poems* – but Kavanagh has successfully avoided the dangers of making Gurney seem (as

Blunden surprisingly did) a thoroughly mad modern, or of representing him too absolutely as a Georgian. He has, in effect, restored to us a poet whose achievement can be compared to that of the contemporary who has also had to wait for more than half a century for recognition: Edward Thomas.

Having said that, it is important to insist on the differences between the two poets. Gurney was more strongly influenced by Thomas than by any other writer; he borrows phrases, cadences and situations from him, as well as emulating his subtle playing of sentence against line. His work nevertheless expresses a quite distinct poetic personality. This is partly a matter of landscape: where Thomas is involved with the south of England and its (usually) specifically British past, Gurney turns again and again to Gloucestershire, and sees the landscape as a palimpsest in which traces of the Romans mingle with indigenous relics. (The more disturbed Gurney's mind became, the more frequently he referred to the Romans – because of the order associated with them, and because as an invading force they allowed him to refract his recollections of the war.) In 'Cotswold Ways', for example, some of the 'strangest things' he 'comes across' walking are:

> Stream-sources happened upon in unlikely places,
> And Roman-looking hills of small degree
> And the surprise of dignity of poplars
> At a road end, or the white Cotswold scars,
> Or sheets spread white against the hazel tree.
> Strange the large difference of up-Cotswold ways;
> Birdlip climbs bold and treeless to a bend,
> Portway to dim wood-lengths without end,
> And Crickley goes to cliffs are the crown of days.

This poem, typically, takes a greater risk with its syntax than one usually finds in Thomas. Where Thomas is ruminative and scrupulous, Gurney is impetuous, occasionally naive, and enthusiastic. The pace of Thomas's thoughts, as suggested by his poems' rhythms, is slower than Gurney's – who often looks and speaks

and – worst of all – there was no hope of recovering the comrade-
liness he had found in the trenches. 'As for rest or true ease, when
is it or what is it?' he asks in one poem. 'With criss-cross purposes
and spoilt threads of life,/Perverse pathways, the savour of life is
gone.' In another, 'Strange Hells', he beautifully imagines the waste
of spirit in humdrum living which his former companions now
suffer.

Where are they now, on state-doles, or showing shop-patterns
Or walking town to town sore in borrowed tatterns
Or begged. Some civic routine one never learns.
The heart burns – but has to keep out of face how heart burns.

For all its unpleasantnesses, the army checked Gurney's instability by imposing some order on his life. Without it, his old characteristics returned and were stimulated by the memories of what he
had lost. In spite of making various efforts to pick up the threads
of his former life – he returned to the Royal College of Music
(where he had been given a scholarship in 1911), wrote, and visited
friends – he could settle to nothing. And although tramping round
England could still rekindle his feelings for its landscape, even
these had a new, disturbing dimension. The act of walking, and the
hardships he imposed on himself when undertaking a long journey, were almost a parody of his 'moving and shifting about' in
France, and therefore filled him with thoughts of the war. When he
was confined, it was because he could envisage only one way out of
his unhappiness:

Death is not here, save mercy grant it. When
Was cruelty such known last among like-and-like men?
An Interview? It is cried for – and not known –
Not found. Death absent what thing is truly man's own?
Beaten down continually, continually beaten clean down.

Until the end of Gurney's writing life, the war and Gloucestershire remain interlocked and dominant in his imagination. So

much so, that almost all his late poems avoid mentioning the facts of his confined existence. But evidence of his plight is evident everywhere. His original Georgian poetic addresses ('O blow here, you dusk-airs . . .') are transformed into tormented appeals to God, Death and even the police for deliverance. The early, strict and lucid lyric forms are twisted and packed to contain the bulging, irrepressible shape of Gurney's distress, and are frequently interrupted by comments which both welcome the idea of formal order, and recognize that he cannot obey its requirements entirely:

> I musician have wrestled with the stuff in making,
> And wrought a square thing out of my stubborn mind –
> And gathered a huge surge of spirit as the great barriers bind
> The whole Atlantic at them by Devon or west Ireland.

Even the stable sanctities of the English landscape can no longer provide the comfort they once did. Instead, they become a kind of hallucination: closely and lovingly recalled, brilliantly lit by memory, but never to be enjoyed in the present except as a thought. He writes about his country, as he does about the war, as if he were a ghost. He is almost as much out of life, the poems imply, as if he had been killed in France – but instead of being actually dead, or 'happy alive', he is condemned to a 'liberty' in which he can only envy death and yearn for the past:

> Madness my enemy, cunning extreme my friend,
> Prayer my safeguard. (Ashes my reward at end.)
> Secrecy fervid my honour, soldier-courage my aid.
> (Promise and evil threatening my soul ever-afraid.)
> Now, with the work long done, to the witchcraft I bend
> And crouch – that knows nothing good.
> Hell uncaring. Hell undismayed.

Criticism is disabled by poetry of such urgency and pain. Yet one cannot help feeling that for all their poignancy, and in spite of the sympathy they evoke, these late poems might well have become repetitive had Kavanagh not printed only thirty-five poems from '1926 and after': Gurney sometimes wrote too entirely to 'keep madness and black torture away/A little' for the good of his poems. If this is the price readers pay for his achievement, the achievement itself is never in doubt. Although his madness meant that he was effectively locked out of England for much of his life, Gurney was one of the very few poets of his time to adapt the jaded literary traditions he grew up with, and allow them to accommodate the anxieties and preoccupations of the post-war years. The result is a large body of work which is extremely powerful in its own right, and also a significant landmark in literary history. Gurney – like Thomas – secured and sustained a poetic line that was specifically English but nevertheless flexible and inclusive, at precisely the moment when the radical, cosmopolitan techniques of Pound and Eliot seemed to overwhelm it. For a long time we have been told that the modernists were a race completely apart, and the only people to face up to the modern period. Now we are beginning to know better.

WILFRED OWEN
The Last Two Years

One might expect the poets of the First World War to have been done to death by biographers: the 'pity' in their work depends greatly on the circumstances of their lives. Yet for a variety of reasons, some of their number have been sparsely served. Ivor Gurney has Michael Hurd's amiable but ambling *Ordeal*. Edward Thomas has R. George Thomas's inadequate *Portrait*. And Wilfred Owen? Owen has only been properly tackled once before – by Jon Stallworthy in 1979.

When Stallworthy's *Life* came out, it was much praised and prized, and most readers accepted its view that Owen had been 'shaped for his subjects' by the entire course of his life – not just by his experiences in the trenches. Philip Larkin was one of the few to raise a doubting voice. He rejected Stallworthy's implication that Owen's journey to poetic maturity had been 'a smooth and harmonious development', saying 'much as one sympathizes with his impatience at the instant maturity legend it remains a convenient shorthand for the evidence as we have it'. Guessing what the reasons for Owen's sudden convulsion into greatness might be, Larkin couched most of his points in social rather than literary terms. He registered the impact on Owen of 'belonging to a common enterprise' in the Manchester Regiment. He admitted the importance of the famous 'encounter with Sassoon' in Craiglockhart Hospital in Edinburgh. He argued that '[Owen's] association with homosexuals [in the last year or so of his life] introduced him to an emotional climate that at the time he found liberating and relevant'.

Since Stallworthy says next to nothing about homosexuals in his biography, this final point seemed especially striking. He asks no questions about Sassoon's proclivities, nor about the role they

Wilfred Owen: The Last Year, by Dominic Hibberd (Constable, 1992)

played in his friendship with Owen at Craiglockhart and later. Neither does he properly characterize the London world opened up to Owen by Sassoon once the two men had left hospital – and before they returned to France. By far the most important player in this world was Robbie Ross. Stallworthy's book includes some references to Ross (and a picture) – but they are few, far between and misleading in their meekness. Ross is introduced merely as 'Oscar Wilde's friend and editor': we are not told that he was the first boy Wilde slept with, and neither do we learn about his courageous protection of Wilde's posthumous reputation. When Sassoon introduced him to Owen, Ross's past was in the process of being investigated and criticized by Lord Alfred Douglas, polite society was preparing to be scandalized, and shades of the prison house were about to close around him. He was a dangerous as well as an exciting person for Owen to associate with.

Inevitably, this friendship led Owen into the company of other, only slightly less risqué figures. Charles Scott Moncrieff, for instance (later to dedicate his version of *The Song of Roland* to Owen, whom he called 'my master in assonance'), and Philip Bainbrigge (Bainbrigge was 'a tall, weedy man with glasses' according to Stallworthy, who scrunches up his writing life in a footnote. In fact, Bainbrigge was the author of – among other things – an obscene dialogue between two schoolboys, and a scurrilous verse play: *Achilles in Scyros*). Mentioning these people is not just a way of showing that Owen's life was differently daring from how Stallworthy makes it sound. It confirms that when Owen wrote the poems on which his reputation depends, he was for the first time part of a milieu in which he felt simultaneously liberated and at home.

Dominic Hibberd is either too modest or too impatient to rehearse this background to the story he tells in the first of his two biographies of Wilfred Owen. (*Wilfred Owen: The last year 1917-1918* was followed in 2002 *by Wilfred Owen: A New Biography*. The later book usefully fleshes out much that is only sketched in the first.) In view of the continuing good reputation of Stallworthy's study, his own may at first appear ancillary or limited. As things turn out, it is a fascinating and important piece of writing. Hibberd begins his story at the moment when Owen, having fought in France for the first four months of 1917, is about to go to Craiglockhart. A brave warrior-poet, reprieved from slaughter? Hardly. Owen has recently been accused of cowardice by his commanding officer, and is now jittery, plagued by nightmares, angry with his existing circle (especially his non-combatant cousin Leslie Gunston), and at the same time unable to discover either people to replace it or an adequate language in which to speak his mind.

At Craiglockhart ('a decayed Hydro, far too full of officers, some of whom I know') Owen was put in the care of Dr Arthur Brook. Hibberd's description of the treatment offered by Brook – 'work-cure' or, in his pre-war coinage, 'ergotherapy' – immediately establishes the scope and intelligence of his book. He explains the various kinds of therapy Owen received, discusses the feelings of guilt, as well as fear, which contributed to his mental state, and illuminates the content and effect of other aspects of the work-cure. Two of these, 'synoptic seeing' (seeing the world as a whole), and expeditions with the hospital Field Club (studying stones and plants in the Pentlands), were particularly valuable to Owen. They sharpened his descriptive powers, while reminding him that he was 'out of battle'.

These feelings of security changed and deepened when he met Sassoon, his fellow patient in the Hydro. In certain respects, the older poet had already made the imaginative journey that Owen was anxious to begin. He had spent his pre-war days in a blissful rural daze, then opened his eyes in France – opened them to suffering, and to the suspicion that the British Government had changed its aims from 'defence and liberation' to 'aggression and conquest'. By removing him to Craiglockhart, Sassoon's friends were trying to save his skin as well as heal his shell-shock – but once incarcerated, he began insisting that most of his 'drifting' and 'haunted' companions were in fact shirkers. When he first encountered Owen, therefore, Sassoon was not just a celebrated and admired poet, but a troublesome and outspoken protester: someone who was as keen to end the war as he was to criticize those not shouldering their responsibilities. Within a matter of days, Owen was striking the same note – initially in 'The Dead-Beat'. The poem marked the beginning of his *annus mirabilis*: Owen would soon stop balancing himself against Sassoon's poetic example, and speak in his own tough yet lush voice.

The literary relationship between Owen and Sassoon has been well publicized and deeply explored; Stallworthy gives a sensible account of it in his biography. Yet it also, as Larkin pointed out, had a complex and neglected social dimension. On the one hand, Sassoon's wealth, posh connections and aristocratic manner appealed to the snob in Owen: on the other, Sassoon's homosexuality admitted Owen to a style of living and thinking that he found naturally sympathetic. It was now – when he left the Hydro and spent time in London, and then continued his training with the Manchesters in Scarborough and Ripon – that Owen fell under the influence of Ross, Scott Moncrieff, Bainbrigge et al. They complemented and corroborated everything that Sassoon had done. They gave Owen, for the first time in his life, an environment in which he could feel both different and himself. No wonder his links with his old world – Leslie Gunston – weakened still further. No wonder his gifts blossomed.

Hibberd investigates these things with an almost exaggerated sensitivity; he never refers to Owen as 'a homosexual', for instance, and he is hampered by the lack of any precise evidence about Owen's tastes, deeds and desires. (We get a glimpse of what these might have been in 'Shadwell Stair', when Owen cruises the waterfront in the East End, half admitting, half disguising his purposes: 'I walk till the stars of London wane/And dawn creeps up the Shadwell Stair./But when the crowing sirens blare/I with another ghost am lain.') Nevertheless, as we enter Ross's gold-painted London apartment, hear again the story and consequences of his association with Wilde, and tune in to the camp chat of Ross's pals, Hibberd provides us with the fullest and most balanced account we have of Owen's true adult personality. 'Lone Wolf', the nostalgic poseur and fuggily religious introvert, becomes self-confident and adversarial.

At the same time his poems are revolutionized. The soldiers

who make up his subject are no longer just 'the fallen', but admired physical types. Their wounds are specific outrages; their sufferings the more terrible because they now offend a sensibility that is not only sympathetic but eroticized. Everywhere we look, we find him communicating a delighted sense of his male companions which stimulates and dignifies his sense of their imminent or actual loss; in the horrible inertia of 'The Dead-Beat', for instance; in the 'Awful falseness' of the 'set-smiling corpses' in 'Mental Cases'; in the tenderness of 'Futility'; in the threatened pastoral of 'Spring Offensive', where the resting troops 'ponder the warm field/And the far valley behind, where the buttercups/Had blessed with gold their slow boots coming up,/Where even the little brambles would not yield,/But clutched and clung to them like sorrowing hands'; in the beautifully weighted and weighed-down cadences of 'Fragment':

> I saw his round mouth's crimson deepen as it fell
> Like a Sun, in his last deep hour;
> Watched the magnificent recession of farewell,
> Clouding, half gleam, half glower,
> And a last splendour burn the heavens of his cheek.
> And in his eyes
> The cold stars lighting, very old and bleak,
> In different skies.

Once Owen has returned to Boulogne, and begins travelling south-east towards his own death, it doesn't seem likely that Hibberd will be able to spring many more surprises. Stallworthy's book deals ably with Owen's last few months, even though it contains moments of startling descriptive inadequacy: 'like storm clouds blocking their way, the dark hills held by the enemy shook out their thunder and lightning'. Yet Hibberd's book manages to make even this familiar territory seem new. It points out that the last part of the war was utterly unlike the first four years: fast-moving, fluid, decisive. Hibberd shows the once-uncertain Owen functioning as a notably brave and well-liked officer (comforting his men, winning the MC). He follows the Manchesters in full cry until they are facing Germany's last substantial line of defence, the Hindenburg Line, dramatizing his story with detailed first-hand accounts.

All this makes for exciting reading, though one might wish Hibberd to slow down and examine more carefully the letters and poems that Owen continued to write. Most of these letters – now as hitherto – were sent to his adored mother, and although they keep the quality of their affection there are signs that his recently discovered life with Ross and company had changed things. Instead of coming on to her as though he would willingly suffocate in her love, he performs for her – showing off his new literary daring. This bravado, as in the poems, often leads him to juxtapose the expectations of the old, safe, godly world with the realities of the new barbarous one. We find him, for example, peppering the letters with descriptions of battle which use the sort of religious imagery we might normally expect to find in a peaceable context (fighting 'like an angel', dodging bullets which come 'like the gentle rain from heaven'). If Hibberd had spoken about this, he might have been able to relate it to a larger discussion of Owen's irony – how he adapted the effective but comparatively simple devices of Sassoon, and created instead subtle strategies of contrast and comparison. Much of the force of Owen's work, after all, comes from his apprehension that the full weight of present horrors can be felt only if they are connected to past pleasures. (As in the quotation from 'Spring Offensive' above.) His poems gauge the depths of contemporary depravity by evoking it in language which sometimes recognizes old values, sometimes discredits them, but never ignores them altogether.

Hibberd ends the story in his original volume by falling into the habit that he has elsewhere corrected in others: flushing away a revelation into a footnote. We have understood from all previous accounts of Owen's death, Stallworthy's among them, that he was shot and killed on the banks of the Sambre Canal, as he encouraged his men to attack the enemy on the other side. Hibberd tells us in his main text that 'several people' fighting beside Owen at the time remembered that he had 'boarded a raft and been hit while out on the water'. In the small print, we are reminded that Dr Brook, at Craiglockhart, had a painting of Hercules and Antaeus above his desk. When Owen identified his true, strong homosexual self, he discovered his genius. When he lost contact with the earth, he was vulnerable.

JOHN BETJEMAN
Serious Feelings

In the course of his long life (1906–1984), John Betjeman became the most popular British poet of the late twentieth century. Several of his lines entered the national bloodstream (mainly from 'lighter' poems such as 'Slough', 'A Subaltern's Love-song', 'How to Get On in Society'), and – as a writer and as an architectural historian – he became a television celebrity before the term was invented. Yet even at the height of his fame he divided literary opinion. Modernists accused him of being a throwback; admirers felt that he offered a delightful break from obscurity. Inevitably, this created problems for him, and for his audience. It meant that readers who defended his use of traditional forms, his moments of music-hall comedy, his accessibility and his apparent lack of writerly guile were branded as reactionaries, while people who attacked him risked seeming doctrinaire, academy-bound, and interested in newness to the exclusion of everything else. No one talked about this better than Philip Larkin. In the longest of several essays he wrote on Betjeman – the Introduction to a *Collected Poems* for a largely uninterested American audience – Larkin admitted: 'The quickest way to start a punch-up between two British literary critics is to ask them what they think of the poems of Sir John Betjeman. For while their author has attained nearly every honour open to a writer of verse in this country, his work and its reputation still evoke a remarkable variety of response here.'

Twenty-two years after Betjeman's death, and in the centenary of his birth, this 'variety' is still evident. On the one hand there is still a flourishing Betjeman Society, and a sizeable audience for his work. On the other hand, there is still a lack of academic interest in his work (university English departments have generally voted

The Collected Poems of John Betjeman (Murray, 2006)

with the modernists), and no properly edited edition of his poems or prose.

Betjeman's reputation has been unstable from the outset: in his first collection, *Mount Zion* (1931) – which was elaborately designed by his friend Edward James – he went to considerable lengths to complicate the question of how seriously his readers should take him. Were the fancy type-faces and the decorations a leg-pull, or a serious act of homage to earlier ages? And what about the poems? Some were obviously skittish ('The Varsity Students' Rag'), some were obviously sombre ('Death in Leamington'), but many walked a fine line between those two tones, or actually partook of both, in a way which confused categories. The subjects and titles of several poems compounded the problem, and its pleasures: 'An Eighteenth-Century Calvinistic Hymn', 'For Nineteenth Century Burials', 'The Sandemanian Meeting-house in Highbury Quadrant'. Nine years after *The Waste Land* was published, poetry-readers were used to seeing the old laws flouted – but Eliot, Pound and Co. did their flouting in the open, using broken forms which reflected the fragmented interior worlds of their poems. Betjeman's rebellion was to put his new wine in old bottles, to make the staid Victorians dance, and to see the insignificance as well as the pathos in fast-vanishing things (all those place names and ecclesiastical sub-groups) while producing unofficial elegies for them.

There's a word for this. Camp. Meaning: to make light of what is in fact taken very seriously. And what *Mount Zion* did was to introduce into British poetry a voice that makes better use of the camp range, of its subtle opportunities, unexpected depths, and defended tendernesses, than any other modern poet. It is the single most significant quality of the early work in Betjeman's *Collected Poems*. But because the register of his camp is so readily mistaken for mere silliness, it might also count as a drawback. So it's worth emphasizing that although Betjeman wrote a lot of funny poems, and said a lot of funny things, his camp (and the instinct for self-protection upon which it feeds) has its origin in very un-funny experience. It's this experience that forms the bedrock of all his work, and guarantees its fundamental seriousness.

In his verse autobiography *Summoned by Bells* (1960), Betjeman
admits to the embarrassments and difficulties of growing up in
wartime England with a name that sounded German:

'Your name is German, John' –
But I had always thought that it was Dutch . . .
That tee-jay-ee, that fatal tee-jay-ee
Which I have watched the hesitating pens
Of government clerks and cloakroom porters funk.
I asked my mother. 'No,' she said, 'it's Dutch;
Thank god you're English on your mother's side.'
O happy, happy Browns and Robinsons!

It wasn't just the 'tee-jay-ee' that was 'fatal'; there was the question of whether his name ended in '–n' or '–nn'. And although Betjeman would have poo-poohed the idea of submitting the
name-problem to a thorough Freudian analysis, there's enough
readily available evidence in the poems to prove that his upbringing was fraught with questions about belonging, identity and tradition. It helps to explain why, through his prep school, then
Marlborough, and even more decisively at Oxford, he went out of
his way to cultivate the cultivated, as well as the rich and titled. It
also sheds light on why he preferred the old forms in his writing.
He wanted to be himself, to maintain a watchful distance, but he
also needed to develop contacts with the national past, and particularly with the Victorian period – which represented stability and
prosperity – because his personal past was less than he wished it to
be.

Not only less in the sense of awkwardly foreign, either. Less
because less grand. Around and beneath the formative name-
drama lies an even more vitalizing difficulty: Betjeman's relationship with his father as both man and trades-man. Betjeman senior
spent all his life in the family firm (founded 1820) making furniture and suchlike – most of it for the luxury market ('Maharajah's
dressing cases', 'the Tantalus/On which the family fortune had
been made', 'The Alexandra Palace patent lock', 'the Betjemann

trolley', etc.). Although many of these objects were extremely beautiful, and produced to a very high standard, the young Betjeman spurned them, along with the idea that he should enter the family Works. He would have been the fourth generation to do so, but this was not the kind of tradition he wanted. It was trade, and therefore beneath him.

Betjeman senior was understandably upset by his son's decision, and by the feelings that informed it. (He might have felt a little baffled, too: weren't these Tantaluses and so on a domestic counterpart to much of the architecture that Betjeman spent his life defending?) Their relationship suffered accordingly – though Betjeman generally had the good grace to keep quiet about this, in print at least, during his father's lifetime. After his father died, he turned to writing about him at regular intervals in poems that are at once honest and touching. So touching, in fact, and so haunting, that Betjeman senior lives through the *Collected Poems*, let alone *Summoned by Bells*, as a quietly admonitory spirit – deaf, suffering, pathetic, and terminal:

> 'Oh, little body, do not die.
> You hold the soul that talks to me
> Although our conversation be
> As wordless as the windy sky.'

> So looked my father at the last
> Right in my soul, before he died,
> Though words we spoke went heedless past
> As London traffic-roar outside.

Poems such as this ('A Child Ill') appear to be a far cry from the campery of *Mount Zion* – and indeed many of Betjeman's best poems have the same shrinking clarity of utterance and directness of gaze. Yet they spring from similar ground. The campery is a form of protection for Betjeman's deepest feelings: it converts them into forms and a diction that is entertaining and unthreatening. The poems about his father show deep feelings with the pro-

tective veil ripped away. They are studies of remorse and self-accu-
sation, howls about death in general and the prospect of his own
death in particular, and frettings about time. They prove his
remarkable range as a poet, but they also show that its two opposite poles are connected.

Given this, it's not surprising to find Betjeman searching repeatedly for a mood or a place he can consider safe. The word 'safe', or
'safety' appears like a nervous tic in his poems – 'safe in bed', 'safety with old friends', 'safe in G. F. Bodley's green and browns,/Safe in
the surge of undogmatic hymns': there are at least ten uses of the
word in the one hundred-odd pages of *Summoned by Bells*, and
they link with every one of his interests and allegiances. His passion for the seaside (especially Cornwall), which distils secure
childhood memories of feeling coddled. His enthusiasm for parish
churches, and their time-honoured reassurances. His addiction to
Victoriana, with its elaborate manifestations of solidity. Even his
snobbishness forms a part of the pattern: it wasn't greed or the
wish for an easy life that drew him to posh people, it was his sense
of their ancient rootedness. And there's a camp manifestation, too:
Betjeman's notorious teddy bear Archibald, much mentioned in
his poems, much filmed in his films, and evidently much loved, is
an image of childhood security that he worked hard to blend with
his own public persona.

It is only a short step from Betjeman's search for safety to his
devotion to things – to objects that defy the passage of time, and
accumulate significance as they do so. The few people to have written well about his work have often commented on this, enjoying
the skill with which he uses hard facts and proper names to evoke
time past. They are right to do so: he has a wonderfully sharp eye
and a brilliant memory, and a sure sense of the pathos that lurks in
half-forgotten or easily missed details. In this respect (and paradoxically) his work recalls James Joyce – a modernist who revelled
in the everyday, but whose experimental forms seem entirely at
odds with Betjeman's own styles.

It is not simply that, for Betjeman, things and the names of
things are a source of (often nostalgic) pleasure. Rather, they

become for him a means of conveying strong feelings that he may well choose not to deliver directly – either because the subject is especially inaccessible or awkward, or because his poetics require him to deal with 'sensations' rather than 'thoughts'. One of his best poems, 'Devonshire Street W.1' is a good example. The street and consulting room, which we see at the beginning of the poem, act both as a background for the reticence that forms an important part of the poem's subject, and also as a way of dramatizing the unspoken fears of the two central characters – an elderly husband and wife. Readers are then allowed into the mind of the man, and hear him wondering, 'Why was I made/For the long and the painful deathbed coming to me?' It's a moment of shocking candour – from which Betjeman characteristically turns away in the final quatrain to daily things. But this turning away is not evasion. It is the means by which the wife simultaneously accepts her husband's reserve, finds brief comfort in the familiar, and registers a literally unspeakable sadness:

> She puts her fingers in his as, loving and silly,
> At long-past Kensington dances she used to do
> 'It's cheaper to take the tube to Piccadilly
> And then we can catch a nineteen or a twenty-two.'

Time and again in the *Collected Poems,* and throughout *Summoned by Bells,* objects of one kind or another are trusted to carry the emotional burden of the poetry. This has the great advantage of making it feel intimate, and of allowing lines to deliver their blow with a force that would have been impossible if their conclusions had been more obviously spelt-out. A good example is 'That wide bedroom with its two branched lighting' in 'Oxford: Sudden Illness at the Bus-stop'; others are the hock, the seltzer, the astrakhan coat, the Moroccan portmanteau, and the 'palms on the staircase' in 'The Arrest of Oscar Wilde at the Cadogan Hotel'. Such details are adornments, of course, and often very enjoyably actual and shrewdly positioned. Yet they are much more significantly the means of conveying whatever fear, dread, desire, sorrow, delight is the poem's main subject.

There's another side to this. Things anchor Betjeman – they allow him to show his heart without speaking his mind – and to that extent they offer some comfort and pleasure. But they can have the opposite effect. Death-things terrify him (the crumbling teeth, failing limbs, deaf ears, and rotting corpses we find in some of his finest poems – 'On a Portrait of a Deaf Man', for instance, or 'I. M. Walter Ramsden'). And living bodies can shame him – either because they are trapped in a situation that he regrets (being 'that strange, rather common little boy'), or because they are repellent. The 'large behinds and jingling chains,/And riddled teeth and riddling brains' of an early poem like 'The City' manifests a discomfort that swells with time and eventually includes himself ('For I am bald and old and green').

This awkwardness gains a special edge in Betjeman's love poetry. Typically – and certainly in keeping with his interest in camp – he makes a joke of his feelings by showing off about how much he likes big girls. He seems to be saying: look, these women are obviously slightly grotesque, so how could anyone believe I like them really? Think of 'Pam, I adore you, Pam, you great big mountainous sports girl', or the 'Ringleader, tom-boy and chum to the weak' that is 'Myfanwy' ('Were you a hockey girl, tennis or gym?'), or the 'golden hiking girl' of 'Senex', or Miss Joan Hunter Dunn with her 'speed of a swallow' and 'grace of a boy', or the 'sturdy' and 'flannel-slack'd' legs in 'The Licorice Fields at Pontefract', or the beefy racket-squeezing Amazon of 'The Olympic Girl'. In every case Betjeman seems to be letting himself off the charge of being taken seriously as an admirer. Yet as the evidence accumulates, we realize the joke is on us. These big girls truly are desirable – and for reasons that fit very interestingly with his other thoughts about safety. They are made unthreatening by recurring as a type, they are reassuringly familiar to the extent of being part-male (Betjeman always insisted that none of us is wholly straight or gay, but a variable percentage of both), and they take charge.

One of the highest accolades Larkin gave Betjeman was to call him 'an accepter, not a rejecter, of his time and the people he shares

it with'. This quite properly emphasizes what is democratic in Betjeman, in spite of his reputation for being a snob preoccupied by
the horrors of 'ghastly good taste'. But Larkin might have added
that Betjeman accepted his own self, too – his flaws and fears and
primitive needs, as well as his sociable gifts. This helps to explain
why the nostalgia in his poems, and their instinct to run for cover,
does not often turn into sentimentality. Betjeman is generally a
tough-minded poet, as well as a tender-eyed one. That is reason
enough for thinking that his star will rise in the years to come. But
it will only reach its proper height if his readers can attune themselves to what is complex and highly unusual in his poems: their
cultivation of comedy for serious ends, and their reliance on familiar things to express unusually intense feeling. 'I do not think that
what is said or written matters, but what is felt. Often my most
"serious" feelings are expressed in a joke. I very rarely talk about
what I really feel.' Betjeman wrote that to his father in 1929. He
could equally well have said it every other day of his life.

ROBERT LOWELL
Like a Tennis Match

The Letters of Robert Lowell rekindles an old argument. When Ian
Hamilton published his *Life* of Lowell in 1982, five years after the
poet's death, various friends and family members thought the
book placed too much emphasis on Lowell's manic breakdowns
and undervalued what ran straight and true in his career. Other
people – including his second wife Elizabeth Hardwick and most
readers who had no first-hand knowledge of Lowell – felt Hamilton had got the balance about right. He's sceptical where he needs
to be, but cannily alert to the trajectory of Lowell's work, as it rose
from the muddle and madness that frequently swirled through his
days.

All the same, the doubters have now seized the chance to rectify
what they see as old wrongs. Several British reviewers of the *Letters*
have celebrated its depiction of a steadier Lowell, and in the *New
York Review of Books* Jonathan Raban has speculated that one reason for the recent slump in Lowell's reputation has been that
Hamilton misrepresented his life as 'madness punctuated by sani-
ty'. Hamilton's widow, Ahdaf Soueif, has ticked him off in the letters column, but there's not much reason to think the controversy
will end there. Which is Lowell to be, as he continues his long ride
into posterity: wild man or vulnerable spirit? Raw poet or cooked?
Life-messer or life-enhancer?

In her clever introduction to the *Letters*, Saskia Hamilton (no
relation) treads carefully. 'Because of the cyclical nature of Lowell's
illness,' she says, 'people's social experience of him was not consistent. He was neither always mad nor always sane; he was also either
mad or sane.' The strength of this position is evident. It allows her
to repudiate the over-simple idea that the manic Lowell was the
'real' Lowell – a poor, forked and maskless creature. At the same

The Letters of Robert Lowell, edited by Saskia Hamilton (Faber and Faber, 2005) time, it means she can oversee the sense in which the sane Lowell was the authentic one – and in turn encourage us to understand that at least one of the creative efforts of his life was to mediate between two versions of himself. It's an idea that illuminates everything – from the characteristic electric crackle of his lines (stretching for extremes, but also for order), to the effusive compliments he showers on fellow poets (registering his own authority, but also showing genuine kindness), to the complications of his love life (hurtfully reckless, but also filled with tenderness).

In the end – and this is a compendious edition, though not a complete one – it has to be said: the abundant, generous, well-judging Lowell dominates the book. True, there are terrible descents into madness, which demand a high price from his friends in general and his wives in particular. The relatively rapid collapse of his first marriage is painful enough, but the hysterical surge of his affair with Giovanna Madonia in the spring of 1954, and the roller-coaster ride and eventual crash of his marriage to Hardwick, are truly anguishing. So is the slew of fragmentary letters to his last wife, Caroline Blackwood, with which the book ends. But set against this, spread more generally and resounding just as loudly, is the evidence of real steadiness and truthfulness: with his lifetime friends Peter Taylor and Blair Clark, for instance, with George Santayana, and with virtually every English-language poet of note in his own generation, as well as the ones above (Pound, Frost) and below (Snodgrass, Larkin, Heaney).

For all the wealth of common human feeling on display, it's these letters to and about other poets that make the book exceptional. That, and the energy, attention and intensity of the composition. From the word go, we find Lowell pitching his tent high up Parnassus, and proving his devotion. 'You will probably think that I am very impudent and presumptuous,' he writes to Ezra Pound when only nineteen years old, 'but I want to come to Italy and work under you and forge my way into reality.' Once his career is launched, this zeal deepens as he draws round him (or at least develops contact with) the strong poets of his own age. Randall Jarrell, Allen Tate, Theodore Roethke, William Carlos Williams,

Elizabeth Bishop, William Empson: these and others are all coun-
selled and consulted. Sometimes the spirit of the exchange is com-
radely. Sometimes it's competitive. (Once again, the two – at least
two – Lowells are wrestling for control of the steering wheel.) But
where a smaller heart might have allowed the whole business to
slide into mere neurosis about the pecking order, Lowell embraces
the richness of his surrounding talents. Writing to a reviewer who
has described 'a Lowell Circle' in 1969, he says, 'I don't think I ever
heard the words till yesterday in your piece. A graver matter is the
competition, the boxing match. Without it, I think we miss some
of the pleasure of writing: part of it is rather like a tennis match.
Who would play without scoring? But how can you score in poetry? In what contest that means anything can we enter our poems
and books? The scales do not exist to weigh art. Yet some things are
better or greater. I must call the contest emulation.'

Of all Lowell's poet-correspondents, no one is more important
to him than Elizabeth Bishop. In a sense it's easy to see why; Lowell was quick to acknowledge her genius, and he simply and frankly
admired her: 'You have more to offer, I think, than anyone writing
poems in English,' he tells her in the early 1960s – and never devi-
ates from this view. There are other reasons for his attraction. Even
though Bishop had her own share of partner-problems and drink-
difficulties, the focus of her life and the apparently relaxed tone of
her poems spoke to Lowell of something he felt was beyond him
yet profoundly desirable. Something that helped him to keep track
of his own ambitions as he worked clear of a comparatively clotted
early style, into a cleaner yet still nervous mature manner. Something that taught him a lesson about how to use autobiography
(which was always his strong suit) with proper dignity and
metaphorical power. Lowell knew that he had it in himself to vulgarize the transmission of his own experience – and did vulgarize
it, spectacularly, when he included some of Hardwick's letters in
one of his late sequences, and gave great hurt. Bishop's decorum,
her 'manners', helped to make this a rare lapse.

Lowell's encouragement of Bishop is heartening, and even if his
compliments to other poets can seem like a way of not thinking

hard enough, or simply of keeping in their good books, it does create an overall impression of decency and kindness – and of a commitment to poetry as such. After the death of his English publisher Eliot, he said, 'There was no one else who could both write and tell us how to write, no one who spoke with such authority and so little played the role of a great man.' He told Empson: 'I have loved and reverenced you as my friend and teacher, as the most important teacher in England, the greatest Englishman.' He calls Pound 'a hero, full of courage, and humour and compassion'. And so on. Attractive as they are, these effusions would be less compelling did Lowell not also keep up a barrage of more detailed judgements – his dislike of Hughes's *Crow,* for example, or his feeling that Ginsberg and his 'people' were 'pathetic and doomed', or that Plath 'seemed rather gothic and arid' in comparison with Bishop. The point is not so much whether we happen to agree, but how it manifests Lowell's engagement. Here he is writing to Bishop about Larkin, for instance, in spring 1973:

Philip Larkin spent last weekend with us. He looked older than T. S. Eliot – six foot one, low-spoken, bald, deaf, deathbrooding, a sculptured statue of his poems. He made me feel almost undergraduate in health, and somehow old as the hills – he is four years younger. I asked him about a poem, 'Wild Oats', where he speaks of a girl he met a few times in his twenties – 'a bosomy English rose', and had kept two photos of her in his billfold – and there the two photos were, her breasts invisible under a heavy coat, small, the same, and no more than passport pictures. He is the best poet writing here I think, perhaps by far.

Saskia Hamilton may not be able to restore order overnight in the unruly house of Lowell's admirers, but her edition will go a long way towards steadying the balance of his reputation. Her selection, as far as one can judge, is excellent: it certainly gives a rounded picture of a marvellously jagged mind. Her notes are shrewd and reliable, even if they are on the brief side and sometimes leave us wanting to know more about the personalities involved as well as the bigger picture (there's always a risk of Lowell's family fixation overshadowing his achievement as a political poet). Best of all, her approach throughout is enthusiastic, as well as scholarly, and lets us see that even if Lowell wrote his letters in a way that's almost opposite to the way he wrote his poems (freely, and with hardly any revision), they nevertheless meet in a single concentration. They are, as he said of Hopkins, 'thoroughly made'.

W. S. Graham

1 It is Myself

'Only mediocrities develop,' said Wilde – implying that great writers are born, not made; they spring fully-formed into the world, always speaking in their own authentic voices and obsessed by their particular themes. Like many of Wilde's best aphorisms, this is both profoundly true and suggestively false. While some authors deepen by concentrating (Hardy, for instance), others (like Yeats) depend on change.

And what about W. S. Graham, who did a fair bit of both? Compared to the densely packed poetic language of his early work published in the 1940s and 1950s, which takes its colour from Joyce and Dylan Thomas, the conversations of his later work seem a model of achieved simplicity. Yet in spite of these 'developments', his subjects remain remarkably focused. Preoccupied by the tricks and limits of language, fascinated by the differences between sensory impressions and intellectual constructions, excited by the links and divisions in time, he spent his poetic life evolving so that he could say clearly at the end what he knew at the beginning.

When Faber published Graham's uncollected poems in 1993 (he died in 1986), his widow prefaced the book by saying that her husband felt 'every poem was relevant; that it was integrated into the whole body of his writing'. This means that any *Selected Poems* is likely to seem controversial. It is almost bound to promote the story of change at the expense of delineating recurrent themes, or vice versa. The editor of the present volume (Christopher Reid, his editor at Faber, though his identity is not revealed) has risen to the challenge bravely. Only three poems are included from Graham's first three books. The bulk are taken from *The Nightfishing* (1955),

W. S. Graham: Selected Poems (Faber and Faber, 1996)

Malcolm Mooney's Land (which appeared in 1970 after a fifteen-year silence), and *Implements in their Places* (1977). Dwelling on this later and plainer work reduces our understanding of the process by which Graham altered his style. As a compensation, though, re-orderings have been undertaken, and additions made from work that he decided not to collect in his lifetime – which stimulates our sense of his growing argumentative force. In the case of a writer as shamefully neglected as Graham, any kind of introduction should be warmly embraced. Because this *Selected Poems* is so cleverly compiled, it is especially welcome.

In the first poem we're given, 'Listen. Put on Morning', Graham says, 'A man's imagining/Suddenly may inherit/The handclapping centuries/Of his one minute on earth.' It's like hearing a theme announced briefly at the beginning of a symphony – a theme that is embellished and purified throughout the book. Initially, its suggestions that the imagination can cross boundaries of space and time are related to Graham's uneasy feelings about his native Greenock. While he sees it as a source of wonder, it is also shadowed by 'tenements', 'the poorhouse', and impossible odds. 'Everyone's name against them bled/In already the helpless world's bed', he says in 'The Children of Greenock'.

The Nightfishing dramatizes what he calls elsewhere this 'contrary shout'. Its long narrative of a moon-lit, storm-raddled expedition to catch herring is a commemoration of place (a kind of sea-salted Wordsworth) and a miniature epic of departure. As these two things clash in the poem, they provoke another and related theme – one that Graham had already raised in his earlier poems. Torn between loving his 'difficult home' and wanting to leave it, he realizes that in order to do justice to his mixed feelings he must come up with a language that is itself contradictory. It must not only register conflicting impulses, it must include the sense of its own opposite: silence. 'Who is the poor sea-scholar,' he asks at the height of the storm:

> It is myself,
> So he who died is announced. This mingling element

Gives up myself.
Words travel from what they once
Passed silence with. Here, in this intricate death,
He goes as fixed on silence as he'll ever be.

Graham's next major poem, 'Malcolm Mooney's Land', once
again casts the poet-self as an explorer, this time in bleak polar
wastes which are primarily a mental rather than an actual landscape. In the 'white-out in this tent of a place', the difficulties of
language are even more intense: 'My words get through the smoking air/Changing their tune on silence.' Graham's point, like Beckett's, is that as language struggles to convey simultaneous
experiences, it threatens to come to a standstill. Furthermore, if it
is to exist at all, it must admit to feelings which are hard to express
for other, social reasons. Because of sexual guilt, for instance,
which flickers and shudders in several poems from this period
('The Dark Dialogues'). Because of unresolved tensions in his relationship with his parents. Because of his fear of and fascination
with death – which even seeps into a comparatively light-hearted
poem such as 'Master Cat and Master Me':

> The way I see it is that Master
> Me is falling out with Servant
> Me and understairs is live
> With small complaints and clattering.
>
> The dust is being too quickly
> Feathered off my dear objects.
> On the other hand I find myself
> Impeded where I want to go.

As Graham moved into the last part of his life, he felt the power
of silence grow. His late work is perhaps best seen as a kind of noble
resistance. The more conscious he was of 'The inadequacy/Of the
living, animal language', the more calculatedly metaphorical he
became (often he uses images and places – particularly places in

Cornwall, where he eventually lived – with a sense of their totemic value). The more deeply he felt the sadness of passing time, the more willingly he celebrated the revitalizing power of love. The more he doubted the sufficiency of words, the keener he became to make them assume the reflective attributes of abstract art. His elegies for the artists Peter Lanyon ('The Thermal Stair') and Roger Hilton ('Lines on Roger Hilton's Watch') are two poems among many that prove the point:

> I called today, Peter, and you were away.
> I looked out over Botallack and over Ding
> Dong and Levant and over the jasper sea.
>
> Find me a thermal to speak and soar to you from
> Over Lanyon Quoit and the circling stones standing
> High on the moor over Gurnard's Head where some
>
> Time three foxglove summers ago, you came.
> The days are shortening over Little Parc Owles.
> The poet or painter steers his life to maim
>
> Himself somehow for the job. His job is Love
> Imagined into words or paint to make
> An object that will stand and will not move.

Graham never becomes complacent about the value of his strategies for coping with the threats and seductions of encroaching silence. On the contrary, he bolsters them by emphasizing his delight in surviving and writing. This is what makes his work so enjoyable: his pleasure in speaking keeps pace with his fears about its shortcomings. It also helps to explain why he has for so long been regarded as a 'poet's poet'. In fact, he is no more a poet's poet than Beckett was a playwright's playwright. His themes might have a particular application to people who write, but their wider implications touch everyone. During the middle and late part of the twentieth century, when the attention of poetry-readers was captured by the quotidian adventures of the Movement, he never found a large audience. Now that he has entered his posthumous existence, perhaps his different, difficult voice will get the credit it deserves.

2 The Blue Crevasse

In his Foreword to W. S. Graham's *New Collected Poems*, Douglas Dunn recalls Ian Hamilton's judgement that unjustly neglected poets can't be certain posterity will provide the reputations they deserve. 'It isn't true that "if it's good, it will survive", said Hamilton. 'Someone, somewhere has to keep saying that it's good – or if not good, exactly, then at least worthy of a small piece of the historical jigsaw, the map.'

When Graham died in 1986 he was certainly one of the most undervalued poets of the middle and late twentieth century – admired by other writers (Pinter said his work was 'an inspiration'), intriguing to the academy because of his modernist-Beckettian fascination with silence, but hardly a strong presence for general readers. Clearly, his publishers needed to take Hamilton's advice, and 'keep saying the work was good'. They have done. Since his death there has been an *Uncollected Poems* (1990), a volume of items from notebooks (1993), and a *Selected* (1996). Now there is this *New Collected*, which contains the seven volumes published during his lifetime and everything significant that has since come to light. Will it bring the wide audience that his admirers believe is his due?

The sorry answer is: probably not. Although this book is a necessary thing, because it shows the whole range of his achievement, and the exceptional dedication of his writing life, it exemplifies the problem that besets a good many collected editions. In particular, it shows Graham returning to his central themes so obsessively that what looks adventurous in small samples comes to seem predictable in bulk. All the same, when another *Selected* appears in the fullness of time, using the texts gathered here, this volume will have served an invaluable purpose. The best of Graham is very

W. S. Graham: New Collected Poems, edited by Douglas Dunn (Faber and Faber, 2004)

good indeed: ambitious in its forms and metrical variety, profound in its engagement with recurring human conditions, and highly original in tone.

Or rather, eventually highly original in tone. Graham's first four books, published between 1942 and 1949, are generally and rightly described as owing a great deal to Dylan Thomas. They are dense, voluptuous, bardic, determined to 'disturb the language', and do for parts of the Scottish landscape (Graham was born in Greenock) what Thomas did for Wales. 'The Narrator', the first poem in the *New Collected*, sets the standard: 'I worship a skylift of Nairnain blaeberry globed/Priestlike sealed in a tensile sac in a nerve/In the vein-geared bubble of vision.'

Graham himself stoutly defended these early poems, and Dunn does the same. But many readers will nevertheless recoil from them, not merely because they are unfashionable (a notion that goads Dunn into some short-tempered swiping at literary trend-spotters), but for subtler reasons as well. They aim to evoke specific places, to create a proper context for ideas about work and personal affairs, and to investigate the difficulties of communication. More than anything, they want to escape the 'genteel' tradition of British writing, and embrace an ecstatic, neo-Surrealist world – the world of Thomas himself, and of contemporary painters such as Paul Nash and John Piper. But like some of Thomas's poems they can seem the victims of their own energy: necessary hard details are often blurred or buried; poetic language becomes a private code.

If Graham himself hadn't felt some measure of disappointment with these early poems, he would hardly have worked so hard to change his style. The change gathered pace in 1955, with his long poem *The Nightfishing*, which describes a storm-tossed sea-trip to catch herring. The look, feel and sound of the sea's 'mingling element' are rendered with a new kind of simplicity, but the deeper (or at least other) success of the poem is to record a dramatic form of inward remaking. For the first time we see the clear shape of Graham's abiding obsession. In a world where the single self is constantly destabilized, the importance of work, and of communicating with others, becomes paramount. The poem looks hard at its own procedures ('Each word is but a longing/Set out to break from a difficult home'), and pays close attention to fortifying, practical actions: 'And the net fed out in arm-lengths over the side./So we shoot out the slowly diving nets/Like sowing grain.'

It took Graham fifteen years to complete his next collection, *Malcolm Mooney's Land*. Given the number of personal distress flares sent up in *The Nightfishing* (and in the 'Seven Letters' of the same volume), this is hardly surprising. For all its devotion to real things in real places, *The Nightfishing* was a book in which the tussle of words with meaning was always exacerbated by the equally fierce battle between language and silence. The even more intense struggles of the later work are dramatized by a shift from sea-scapes to ice-scapes (the title poem is set in a version of Franz Josef Island in the Arctic Ocean), and expressed in more outspoken accounts of 'trying to use the obstacle/Of language well'. Graham remains a defiantly Romantic poet, but the universe he surveys, both external and internal, is stripped down, bleak and punishing. The self appears increasingly isolated and increasingly unreal: 'maybe/The place and myself are both the one/Side of the allegory and the other/Side is apart and still escaped/Outside.' Art is a 'barrier of ice'. Silence prowls and swells everywhere, threatening both to overwhelm speech and to turn the landscape into nothing more than a blank canvas. Graham might sometimes have comforted himself by thinking of these poems as a form of 'abstract' writing, analogous to abstract painting, but this doesn't diminish their severity. The image that dominates the book is desperately plaintive: 'Yesterday/I heard the telephone ringing deep/Down in a blue crevasse./I did not answer it and could/Hardly bear to pass.'

Graham continued to explore these desolate themes for the remainder of his life. But for all its eventual and hard-won austerity, his poetry keeps the warmth of human contact. This is partly due to his exceptionally skilful manipulation of verse forms, which allows even the most conversational pieces to preserve a sense of anticipation and surprise. We come round his line-endings never quite knowing what to expect, and find that new life and tender-

hear Plath in her own words, to see her marriage in close up, and to watch the evolution of her dazzling last poems. At the same time, it removes an Estate-blockage which has unhelpfully fed the rumour-mill for the past many years.

Although an edited version of the *Journals* has been available in the US since 1982, this is their first appearance in the UK. The book contains every entry Plath wrote after 1950, apart from those contained in 'the two bound journals [she] wrote during the last three years of her life' – one of which was destroyed by Hughes, the other of which has 'disappeared'. After years of muddle and suspicion, everything that survives seems out in the open. But of course nothing with Plath is ever simple. Listening to her speak 'in her own words' does not mean getting unvarnished truths or unbiased accounts. It means feeling a furnace-blast of the imagination, which turns the most ordinary events into crises. It means hearing the soft voice of diary-intimacy drowned by a roaring torrent of subjectivity. It means never expecting any conclusion to consist in a single-minded judgement, but in a welter of paradoxes. The effect, over more than seven hundred pages, is profoundly 'weird' (a word Plath used of herself); by turns exasperating and engrossing, stifling and searing.

For all its mood-changes, *Journals* is clear about its obsessions. The first one hundred and eighty-odd pages, which follow Plath from 1950 in Massachusetts to 1955 in Cambridge, England, see her circling round boyfriends and poetic ambitions in a mood of fiery self-scrutiny. Frankly, the language during this section of the book is a great deal more interesting than its subjects and analyses: mawkishness, self-pity and an adolescent relentlessness are always impending if not actually present, and the lack of detailed attention given to other people (or other writers) is extraordinary.

So extraordinary, it is hard not to look on these early pages as a description of symptoms – as proof of Plath's instability, and of her wish to dominate, and of her equally strong longing to serve. Here she is in the summer of 1950, claiming she wants to find 'balance' in her relationships, but sounding distinctly un-balanced:

Sure, I'm a little scared of being dominated. (Who isn't? Just the submissive, docile, milky type of individual. And that is Not he, Not me.) But that doesn't mean I, ipso facto, want to *dominate*. No, it is not a black-and-white choice or alternative like: 'Either-I'm-victorious-on-top-or-you-are.' It is only *balance* I ask for. Not the *continual* subordination of one person's desires and interests to the continual advancement of another's! That would be too grossly unfair.

Over the months, Plath forges a style from this ranting: she discovers a way of making her 'weirdness' a part of her imaginative world, and of giving her college-crushes their adult focus. When she met Hughes she found her ideal. His value for her lay not simply in seeming to be a kind of genius sex-god ('dark, dishevelled, and with that queer electric invisible radiance'), but in his ability to connect her brilliant apprehension of surfaces with the dark currents that flowed beneath everything. He introduced her to first causes and also gave expert advice about final effects.

Hughes was not the only one to do this. Plath's therapist Ruth Beuscher also played a vital role, and the two therapy-journals Plath kept between August 1957 and November 1959, which have hitherto been off-limits but were unsealed by Hughes shortly before his death, are fascinating. They show the mingled admiration and resentment Plath felt for her father, and the guilt-riddled hatred she had for her mother, in the most naked terms imaginable: 'Me, I never knew the love of a father, the love of a steady blood-related man after the age of eight. My mother killed the only man who'd love me steady through life: came in one morning with tears of nobility in her eyes and told me he was gone for good. I hate her for that.' The things Beuscher encouraged Plath to know about her feelings for her parents, and the things Hughes dramatized in the same emotional area (by taking on the father's role and complicating it still further), were inevitably destructive as well as liberating. This paradox is a commonplace for most Romantic artists; in Plath's case, it became the definition of her whole imaginative response to life. Every step she took towards finding her true voice as a poet was also a step towards self-destruction.

Following Plath's move to Devon with Hughes in August 1961, her rages become wilder, and her moments of grateful tenderness more complete. (Hughes, in spite of all difficulties, remains 'the ideal, the one possible person'.) Her anxieties about money grow more acute. The flame of her language burns with a better-controlled heat. But while this is happening, and driving her more deeply inwards into herself, her attention is also drawn powerfully outside as well. Her marriage is ventilated by the feeling that she must keep her independence. Her two children – one born in 1960, the other in 1962 – hook her into different realities. Her village-existence, for all its longueurs, generates a strong sense of community, and provokes some wonderful writing about local characters, about her plans to keep bees, about the slow death of an elderly neighbour.

All readers are fascinated by the origins of work, and this final turning towards the world is one of the most remarkable things about the present edition of Plath's journals. (Admittedly, the impression might be different if we had the two missing volumes.) We close the book feeling we have been shown an important general truth while gaining any number of insights into a particular case. It is the final triumph of the symbolic style to affirm its deep connection with recognizable daily life.

Anne Stevenson
Putting the Bones to Bed

Introduction

In the biographical note to her collection *Granny Scarecrow*, published in 2000 when she was sixty-seven, we are told that Anne Stevenson was 'born in England of American parents, grew up in the States, but has lived in Britain for most of her adult life'. This is fair enough, but as a résumé it can only hint at the questions that dominate her work: how does a personality define itself within a family; how does child-love translate into loving as an adult; what role do places play in the creation of a sensibility; and – in particular – what is the relationship between thinking about questions of belonging, and observing the hard facts of location and habitat. At a time when political and social upheavals around the world have provoked a good many poets to consider the enigmas of arrival, Stevenson has produced a large body of work that is at once representative of common contemporary concerns, and highly individual. She is a voice for our age, and compellingly her own questing and questioning self.

Stevenson's originality is of a complex and multi-layered kind. As a student at the University of Michigan she began to write poetry while studying the challenges to puritanism in American writers such as Robert Frost and Elizabeth Bishop, of whom she later wrote a pioneering study. In the late 1980s she developed many related ideas in her biography of Sylvia Plath. (When it first appeared, this book was considered controversial in its even-handed treatment of Plath's marriage to Ted Hughes; other subsequent studies of the relationship have done a good deal to justify the approach.) Instead of trying to conceal the influence of these writers in her work, Stevenson openly addresses them in a number of poems, deliberately echoes them, and consciously allies herself to many of their practices. The effect is not in the least to compromise her authenticity; rather, it establishes the foundations of her work in a distinct tradition. She is herself a puritan writer who at once honours and contests her inheritance; writing in the heat generated by this personal conflict, she has forged a style that both registers and stands apart from the confessional modes and political dogmas of much late twentieth-century women's poetry.

Stevenson's longest and best-sustained poetic examination of the puritan past is *Correspondences* (1974), the volume that first established her reputation in England following her departure from America, and that provides a broad background to her work in general. Its piecemeal family history, in which a good deal of the material for the puritan Boyds is modelled on her mother's family, while her father's is represented by the more worldly Arbeiters, is comprised of letters, lyrics and prose-poems. It is at once a collection of wistfully entertained backward glances and a proof that Stevenson accepts the inevitability of change and challenge. In this respect, *Correspondences* anticipates her other and later long poem *A Lament for the Makers*, published in 2007, in which she converses with the poets who have meant most to her across the years. *Correspondences* presents a drama of identity in a domestic context, *A Lament* does the same thing in literary terms. For both poems, the issue is not how to escape the past, but how to accommodate the past in the present; how to preserve its values and authenticities without becoming trapped in nostalgia or sapped by historical example.

The same questions are present from the outset in Stevenson's shorter pieces. We find them in one of the earliest lyrics in her first *Collected Poems* (1996), 'To My Daughter in a Red Coat', where she says 'Child, your mittens tug your sleeves./They lick your drumming feet, the leaves./You come so fast, so fast./You violate the past,/My daughter, as your coat dances.' They emerge again in many of her narrative poems – 'The Dear Ladies of Cincinnati', for instance, in which we meet 'the aunts' who 'remembered the words of hit tunes they'd been courted to,/avoided the contagion of thought/so successfully that the game kept time to the music'. And they circle too in the majority of her later poems about family matters. 'Of course I love them,' she says of her children in 'The Mother'. 'That is my daughter and this is my son./And this is my life I give them to please them./It has never been used. Keep it safe, pass it on.'

For all their general resonance, many of these shorter family poems arise from the same particular circumstances that Stevenson remembers in *Correspondences*. She was brought up in the university environments of Harvard, Yale and Ann Arbor by parents she has called 'intelligent and sympathetic'. From her father, the philosopher C. L. Stevenson, she absorbed a love of classical music and an intolerance of unexamined, conformist opinion – as we discover in 'Elegy', where music (and by implication all the arts, including poetry) is described as a means of re-interpreting the past, and where philosophy is by implication commended as a way of challenging accepted truths. It was her mother, however, who instilled in her a love of history together with the sturdy compassion that lies at the root of her poetry. We can see this in 'Arioso Dolente', for instance, where Stevenson refers to her mother as someone 'who read and thought and poured herself into me;/She was the jug and I was the two-eared cup./How she would scorn today's "show-biz" inanity,/Democracy twisted, its high ideals sold up!'

Although Stevenson clearly owes debts to the traditions represented by her parents, these have done as much to provoke her sense of detachment as they have to stimulate a sense of belonging. For one thing, her father's work as a university teacher apparently bred in her a love–hate relationship with academies which often produces side-swipes at their reputation for desiccation and fustiness. In 'Ann Arbor' we hear about 'the usual/academic antipathies'; in 'Coming Back to Cambridge' we find dons and their wives who are 'arrogant/Within the compass of wistfulness'; and in 'By the Boat House, Oxford' we meet more academic wives 'in their own quenched country' who are half pitied and half scorned for believing their husbands are 'plainly superior'. For another, Stevenson's father, in particular, set her a vital example about the value of intellectual restlessness – restlessness that formed a part of her compulsion to move from America to England, and then to spend much of her adult life moving around and laying claim to different parts of her adopted country: Cambridge, Oxford, the Welsh borders, Wales itself, the North-East.

The question Stevenson wants to answer in many of her early poems is not 'when will I arrive at the one stable place I might call home', but 'how can I benefit from and understand what it means to keep moving'. In the work of her early maturity, it seems that sexual and married love might help her reach a conclusion. Yet for all their force and candour, her love poems habitually describe human tenderness in terms of landscape – suggesting that for her 'home' will finally involve places more reliably than people. In the brief and potent lyric 'New York', she wonders if 'love, love, love/is the only green in the jungle'; in 'Reversals', she asks '. . . is love in its last metamorphosis arable,/less than what was sometimes imaginary,/more than what was usually accessible –/full furrows harvested, a completed sky?'

This shift of trust away from individuals to their surroundings is often accompanied by forthright doubting of her self and others. 'There only is one love –/which is never enough' we hear in 'Theme with Variations', and in 'The Marriage' she says with wry deprecation: 'Even as it is,/there are compensations/for having to meet/nose to neck/chest to scapula/groin to rump/when they sleep./They look, at least,/as if they were going/in the same direction.' (Strikingly, the personal difficulties registered here are often connected to the complications of raising children – complications that are linked to the family matters raised more generally elsewhere. 'A woman's life is her own/until it is taken away/by a first particular cry', she says in 'Poem for a Daughter'.)

Throughout Stevenson's fully mature work, this question of how to continue living in transit, and yet have an adequate sense of belonging, becomes her dominant theme. The title of her first *Selected Poems, Travelling Behind Glass* (1974), suggestively indicates that a part of her restlessness derives from the sense that she is falsely protected from reality. (As she says in 'The Price', 'My dear, the ropes that bind us/are safe to hold;/the walls that crush us/keep us from the cold.') It is therefore not surprising that she should be strongly drawn to landscapes that are themselves fluid, or marginal – to borders and border counties, to water and shore-lines ('The sea is as near as we come to another world,' she writes in 'North Sea off Carnoustie'), and to objects that are either a kind of boundary in themselves (glass, for instance) or a reminder of mobility. Her large number of good poems about birds, for example, tend to celebrate migratory species (such as swifts); and her similarly strong poems about flora and fauna often dwell on ideas of escape or transgression. 'Ragwort' is characteristic:

> They won't let railways alone, these ragged flowers.
> They're some remorseless joy of dereliction
> Darkest banks exhale like vivid breath
> As bricks divide to let them root between.
> How every falling place concocts their smile,
> Taking what's left and making a song of it.

There is another and even larger reason for Stevenson to insist on the need to keep moving, keep enquiring. This has less to do with her sense of being adrift in the physical world than of being philosophically in two minds. In much the same way that she feels she is living between generations, between certain kinds of land-scape, between certain named places and certain loved individuals, so she also feels divided between different kinds of response to experience. Early in her writing life, there are signs that Stevenson feels tempted to heal this division by abolishing herself. In the poem 'Travelling Behind Glass', for instance, we hear her ask for 'a sea/to be accommodating,/to warm me, obey me,/accept me like an arm;/in time to release me/entirely, as nothing at all./As belong-ing to nothing at all.' As her work develops, she finds a bolder and more subtle solution to her dilemma – one that involves her in making repeated efforts to distinguish between a thought-filled response to the world, and one that depends on more sensuous kinds of appreciation and involvement.

We can see the differences being weighed in the aptly titled 'Small Philosophical Poem', which sets 'the pleasure of thought' experienced by Dr Animus against the more material existence of his wife, Anima. Short as it is, this lyric establishes the integrity as well as the aridity of the doctor's position, and the warmth (the 'love') as well as the vulnerability (the 'fear') of his wife's – implying at its close that although Anima must bear the burdens of her consciousness, they nevertheless connect her with the world in more valuable ways than any her husband has at his disposal. A similar point is made in the elegy for Anne Pennington, 'Dreaming of the Dead', where Stevenson says 'I am what I see and know,/But no other solid thing's there/Except for the terrible glow/Of your face and its quiet belief,/Light wood ash falling like snow/On my weaker grief.'

Such poems form the bedrock of Stevenson's work because they prove that her final commitment as a writer is to the ragged, volatile and familiarly uncertain world, not to a version of experience that has been tidied up to fit a controlling idea. But it is also a mark of her quality as a poet, and further proof of her need for continual self-testing, that this commitment is never entirely fixed and settled. The surfaces of her best work, which are always impressively alive to the significance of things-in-themselves, are repeatedly disturbed by incursions from the thinking mind. These make her in the best sense an uncomfortable writer – one whose inheritance (which promoted notions of honesty, austerity and philosophical rigour) has led to her cautious acceptance that art can look faithfully at the evolutionary fleetingness of human life without paying lip-service to a righteous God or a benevolent-minded Designer. As she has said herself, 'If my poems have any value as art, it is because they ARE art. What I really learned from Elizabeth Bishop (and from Sylvia Plath too) is that poetry matters when content, form, passion unite in language that speaks to the ear and heart as much as to the mind – to body and soul, you might say, as a single, always threatened, always perishable entity.'

It's not just that Stevenson refuses to settle for easy conclusions about what makes a personality complete, and about what makes life bearable; she is also and often agitated by the act of writing itself – debating how it can best shoulder its responsibilities, and manifest the contradictory truths of nature. In the majority of her poems, these agitations are given a local habitation and a name: they arise in particular relationships and particular landscapes. They also stand clear in a handful of poems about writing itself. Some of these question the ability of language to capture what it seeks to express – 'the inescapable ache/of trying to catch, say, the catness of cat/as he crouches, stalking his shadow,/on the other side of the window'. Others (and especially in her book *The Fiction Makers*, 1985) call the entire business of writing into question: 'In the event/the event is sacrificed/to a fiction of its having happened'. Others again, and particularly those that mention her increasing deafness, go so far as to wonder whether her faith in seeking to comprehend the world through the senses is in fact well founded. But while these questions are posed in all seriousness (or seriously laughing) they are never allowed to undermine her faith in first principles. The devastations of philosophy always prove weaker than the consolations of mystery, form and sympathetic wit – as we can see in her typically courageous short poem 'On Going Deaf':

> I've lost a sense. Why should I care?
> Searching myself, I find a spare.
> I keep that sixth sense in repair
> And set it deftly, like a snare.

A part of what Stevenson means by 'that sixth sense' is the imagination itself, and it is right and proper that any introduction to her poems should end by insisting on its authority throughout her work. She is not much given to plundering her unconscious (however interested she might be in dream-stories), and neither does she often yeast up her language to evoke surreal states of mind. But she does continually animate her acts of clear-seeing by connecting the exterior world with her interior states. It is, of course, a connection that all poets make to a greater or lesser extent, but in her case the fusions have a particular resonance. They are the means by which Stevenson stays true to her inheritance even as she extends it. They are proof that she is a puritan writer who is both at peace and at odds with herself. Her work is continually fortified by that contradiction, for reasons that she makes plain – appropriately enough – at the end of her kindred-spirit 'Letter to Sylvia Plath':

> We learn to be human when we kneel
> To imagination, which is real
> Long after reality is dead
> And history has put its bones to bed.

Bob Dylan

1 Going Electric

Remember the famous Albert Hall concert in May 1966, when Bob Dylan's folk supporters booed him for converting to electric music, and one of them shouted 'Judas'? Anyone answering 'yes' to that is a liar. Dylan did tour England in the spring of 1966, and he did play the Albert Hall – but the notorious 'Judas' episode happened in Manchester, at the Free Trade Hall. For many years the evidence existed on a bootleg; now this recording is commercially available, the facts are more generally known.

The trouble that overflowed in England had been brewing for a while. During the previous four years, Dylan kept feeling increasingly hemmed in by the very thing that had shaped his style in the first place – the folk tradition which, as rock and roll started to take off, became more introverted. His initial response was to adapt his style comparatively modestly. But the more insistently folk-purists urged him to become their Messiah, the more deeply he committed himself to the 'beat' alternative. When Dylan himself wrote about this in a note to *Biograph* he made no effort to conceal his frustration: 'There was just a clique, you know', he said. 'Folk music was a strict and rigid establishment. If you sang Southern Mountain Blues, you didn't sing Southern Mountain Ballads and you didn't sing City Blues. If you sang Texas cowboy songs, you didn't play English ballads. It was really pathetic. You just didn't.'

Electricity offered a way out, as Dylan proved on *Bringing It All Back Home* (1965), half of which is hard-edged rock and roll, half solo acoustic, and then again, even more emphatically, on 'Like a Rolling Stone', which he described as 'a long piece of vomit' before adding pointedly, 'I knew I had to sing it with a band.' When the band (eventually *The* Band) turned up and plugged in their instruments, the reaction was just as Dylan expected. At Newport – the 'Mecca of the American Folk Revival', as C. P. Lee calls it in *Like the Night* (1998) – his set was greeted with tears of rage. When he began a world tour in 1966, playing in America and Ireland before coming to England in May, the same thing happened. His change of direction was 'a betrayal'. In Liverpool someone in the audience shouted, 'Where's the poet in you? Where's your conscience?' In Sheffield he heard, 'Traitor! We don't need you! Go and play with the Rolling Stones.' 'Judas', clearly, was an insult waiting to be hurled.

The first half of the Manchester gig was an acoustic set of seven songs, the second a series of controlled explosions. Because the rumpus of this second part has attracted so much attention, it's easy to forget the wonderful poetic force of everything that precedes it. Dylan's voice, at once thin and robust, and full of relish for its extraordinary habit of seeming to italicize individual words, sounds almost disembodied – lost in space.

For instance, in the opening song 'She Belongs to Me', his delivery exactly suits the entrancement of 'the Egyptian ring, which sparkles before she speaks'. And everything about his singing is then complemented in turn by the long-drawn-out harmonica passage that ends it. Here, as elsewhere, he is simultaneously disciplined and abandoned, crisply dry and mouthily wet.

The mixture of sense and surreality in 'She Belongs to Me' appears again and again in what follows, especially in the 'visions of Johanna which conquer my mind', and the dystopian 'trance' of 'Desolation Row' (which is sung in a light drawl, across a lightly strummed guitar). The effect, combining with the generally hollowed-out feel of the recording, is one of tremendous delicacy – much more so than on the *Unplugged* album, where 'Desolation Row' is masterful but weighty, a shade too conscious of its own doom and confusion.

Maybe the pressures surrounding the concert made Dylan exaggerate the two sides of his personality. It's certainly true that the second half is as earthy as the first half is ethereal: loud almost to the point of brutality, creating a background cascade from which Dylan's voice rises with surprising authority. And with surprising subtlety. Even at its most harsh (on 'Baby Let Me Follow You Down', and the relentless twelve-bar boogie of 'Brand New Leopard Skin Pill Box Hat'), he is able to inflect things so that they seem alternately sardonic, tender, wistful, dismissive and amused.

Not that some of the audience noticed. Through the whole of this second part, in the breaks between the eight songs, we hear dissent gradually accumulating, rising through catcalls and slow hand-claps to general barracking until the climatic 'Judas!' Even though Dylan was used to complaints by this time in his tour, his silence following the accusation is shocked. Eventually, he comes to the microphone and slowly drags out: 'I don't believe you. [Pause.] You're a liar.' Then he smashes off into 'Like a Rolling Stone', the song that crystallized all his trouble.

'How does it feel – to be on your own?' the song famously wants to know. This concert is the answer. It feels lonely and oppressed and fractured, but at the same time defiant and unrepentant. There's something in Dylan, as there is in all great innovators, that thrives on opposition and disbelief, that enjoys confrontation, and that doesn't mind the bewilderment of fans who can do nothing but rock along in his wake.

This is what makes the album so fascinating: listening to it, we follow Dylan the protest-singer into a storm of protest, knowing that he will emerge triumphant. Does that make the value of the music sound too purely historical? It would be a pity if it did. Because what's 'interesting' about the album can't be separated from what is simply unforgettable: the tremendous beauty and subtlety of the songs, and the matchless voice that sings them.

2 Drawn Blank

Bob Dylan is one of the few great artists whose work is as highly valued in one form as it is in another. Right from the beginning of his career, his words garnered as much praise as his music – to the

The Drawn Blank Series (Halcyon Gallery, London, 2008)

extent that questions about whether he could be considered 'a poet' and/or 'a song-writer' soon became redundant. He is both, in ways that are at once free-standing and mutually dependent.

And that's not all. He is also a draughtsman and painter. But whereas Dylan's reputation as a writer has always been reinforced by the publication of solo texts (his novel *Tarantula*, his sometimes extensive sleeve-notes, his autobiography *Chronicles*), his work as a visual artist has emerged more gradually. Dylan himself places its origins in the early 1960s. 'What would I draw?' he asks in *Chronicles*. 'Well, I guess I would start with whatever was at hand. I sat at the table, took out a pencil and paper and drew the typewriter, a crucifix, a rose, pencils and knives and pins, empty cigarette boxes . . . In a strange way, I noticed that it purified the experiences of my eye.' Although some of this work reached the public – on the sleeve of The Band's *Music from Big Pink* (1968) and his own *Self Portrait* (1970) – and although certain songs alluded to it – 'When I Paint My Masterpiece' – it wasn't until 1994, when he published ninety-two drawings made between 1989 and 1992, while touring America, Europe and Asia, that the extent and skill of his work became apparent.

Dylan called his selection *Drawn Blank*, a title that appropriately suggested an interest in absence but also implied that, for all their self-sufficiency, his drawings contained a certain degree of un-finishedness. Dylan evidently thought so, anyway, and when he was contacted over twenty years later by Ingrid Mossinger, the director of the Chemnitz City Art Gallery in Germany, and invited to 'complete' his pieces, he didn't hesitate. 'I was fascinated to learn of Ingrid's interest in my work', he said, 'and it gave me the impetus to realize the vision I had for these drawings many years ago.' In an intense burst of creative concentration, he transferred photographs of the drawings onto larger-than-original deckle-edged sheets of paper, and worked on them during a period of eight months.

These versions of the *Drawn Blank* series were shown in Chemnitz last year – but they turned out to be another stage in a journey, rather than a final resting place. With the same kind of inventiveness and daring that he brings to his songs in performance, Dylan has now visited the images yet again, re-colouring, re-configuring and re-imagining them. It is an extraordinary collection, at once a significant independent achievement, and a fascinating extrapolation of themes and images that haunt his music. It's hard to think, in any previous century, of an artist whose work is so impressively diverse, yet so all of a piece.

The main difference between the previous versions of the pictures and those seen here has to do with their colouring. The dress worn by the *Woman in Red Lion Pub*, for instance, which started life as a delicate pencil sketch, first blossomed into red, then got tangled up in blue, and is now a pulsating yellow. But as this powerful image reminds us, to speak of colour is also to speak of mood, atmosphere, emotions and ideas. The woman's place in the world changes as Dylan's palette changes, fluctuating between weariness and sexiness, independence and neglect. The versions allow for ambiguity, and make a virtue of reaching no firm interpretive conclusion.

In this respect, *Woman in Red Lion Pub* is typical of the series as a whole. It is a set in which we see human life caught in the act of ebbing and flowing, coming and going, leaving and arriving. The characteristic settings are provisional: hotel bedrooms, bars, cafés; the point of view is akin to a bird's eye – with its concomitant air of detachment; the recurring shapes are often barriers that might also be thresholds (verandas, balconies); the focus is unflinching but also un-centred, which means the viewer is left searching for a governing shape, a controlling form.

South Dakota Landscape is a good case in point. The view is taken at standing height, from inside what appears to be a hotel room – cheap metal-frame windows, a flimsy curtain, part of a car disappearing stage left past part of a house, a log pile in the foreground and some pygmy pines beyond it (which will presumably soon become logs themselves), and a gigantic truck travelling along the horizon like a creature from pre-history. At various stages in its life, Dylan has changed the colours in this image dramatically – the curtains from red through yellow to lilac to brown, and the sky from a wintry to a warmer blue. This encourages us to detect a mellowing in the mood of the picture (the same tonal shift is noticeable in many of the other images), but the fundamental point remains the same. Everything speaks of the transitory, the travelling, and the impermanent, and therefore also of sadness. But at the same time there is a conviction in the colour, and a steadfastness in the gaze, which exerts a counter-balance (and fits with Dylan's remark that his drawings were made to 'refresh a tired mind').

In other words, Dylan's pictures pull off the difficult trick of being simultaneously settled and unstable – both in their themat-ic concerns, and in their forms. The outlining sometimes recalls Van Gogh and the German Expressionists, the postures Degas, the coloration Matisse and Cézanne. Yet these references and quota-tions are assimilated to a rolling stone's view of the world that is entirely individual, and entirely in keeping with the way Dylan's songs also often refer to other and sympathetic material. But does this mean they offer a vision of the world without firm conclu-sions, in which there is nothing to lean on? Appropriately enough, the pictures suggest two answers at once. One derives from the portraits, the generally single figures, some comparatively formal, some erotically charged, in which the restless eye that habitually roves across landscape and domestic interiors is stilled, fixed, and satisfied. In *Portrait of a Woman Smiling*, for instance, where the sideways smiling, lush-lipped, scantily strapped subject, whose features are rendered with excited flourishes and emphatic shad-owing, shares her beauty and self-confidence with the viewer and, by implication, with the painter too. Or *Portrait of Tom Clark*, in which we see a gaze as rewarding in its candour as the complicit smile of the woman. In the swirl and muddle of the everyday, these two portraits suggest that human intimacy is a reliable haven; they are not alone.

The other sense of certainty derives from a paradox: from the way in which the pictures feel at ease with their lack of ease. This isn't to say they're complacent, or shallow in their apprehension of what is fugitive; rather, that they reflect a mind that is able to stare fairly and squarely at the hard facts of existence (as well, some-times, at its pleasures) and record them with an appropriately tough simplicity. The empty chairs, the single rooms, the windows overlooking parking lots and back alleys: they all speak of reasons to be melancholy, but their voices come nowhere near drowning the sense of excitement generated by the pictures' energy, their delight in sculptural shapes, and their bold colours. In this sense, they strike a balance that is equivalent to the method by which they have been new-made and new-minted. 'I like to stay a part of that stuff that don't change,' Dylan wrote in the notes to *Biograph*. Exactly. Here, as in the songs, his past and present form parts of a continuum, as do the reasons to celebrate and be sombre.

AFTERWORD

My parents were country people, not bookish, and as a teenager I felt impatient with my inheritance. I wanted to make my own way, and to insist that writing and thinking and criticizing were as important as the things my family and their friends enjoyed. Because my first independent loves were reading and writing, books became the focus of my rebellion: they allowed me to imagine, and eventually to discover, my own different life.

Pictures might have done the trick equally well, supposing my school English teacher Peter Way had taught me art history not literature, and supposing I'd known where to find them. I was seventeen before I went to an art gallery, and the paintings at home were nothing much. In the dining room and hall we had half-a-dozen large gloomy portraits of ancestors – my father's, mostly: a couple of swan-necked young women, a crone stooped by the weight of a seagull-bonnet, my great-grandfather in a high collar and spotted bowtie, and my grandfather in his Captain's uniform looking understandably relieved that he'd survived the trenches. Elsewhere – in the downstairs lavatory, on the top landing, in the spare room, and in the bedroom I shared with my brother – there were horse pictures. Six sludgy-green episodes from 'The Midnight Steeplechase'. Hunting scenes (including one painted as though on horseback, with the horse's ears in the foreground and the fox and hounds racing into the middle distance, which was called 'The Finest View in Europe'). A stiff little portrait of my mother, my brother and myself, posed in the field outside the house on Serenade, Musket and Lollipop.

The drawing room was different. It was a pretty space, with a floor-to-ceiling French window overlooking a strip of garden and a rose-bed, then the field where we'd sat for the horse-portrait. All day, whatever the weather, light poured across the big green sofa and two comfy armchairs, gradually softening the cloth and bleaching the colours. It might have bleached the paintings too, since they hung within range either side of the fireplace. But this didn't happen, my mother explained, because these weren't real paintings, they were reproductions, and wouldn't fade.

They were a pair, almost identical, by a Dutch painter my mother said was famous, though none of us could remember his name. About eighteen inches by twenty-four. Flower pictures. Blood-red tulips with cream streaks in the petals, a few carnations, and sprays of writhing greenery. They needed the greenery because apart from the flowers, and the white-and-blue vases almost entirely hidden by dangling leaves, there was nothing else. Just a shiny black background, surrounded by a thin and even shinier black frame. I liked flowers, especially the ones my mother grew in the herbaceous border that curled along one side of the garden around the corner from the sitting-room window, but these Dutch ones were baffling. My parents preferred wild and natural things that were close to home: how could they bear to spend their evenings looking at anything so boring and artificial and foreign?

Of course they didn't really look at them, and neither did I. They were just *there*, silently proving that art was different from life, and had its own separate values. Values which were not ours, and could easily be ignored, but evidently had their place (the drawing room was where we sat with visitors, and gathered *en famille* every evening for supper on our knees).

So why did they suddenly disappear? I have a guilty feeling that as I groped forward into adolescence, I might have said something disparaging about them. My mother would have had mixed feelings about this. Relief that I was 'taking an interest', and annoyance that I was criticizing something she and my father found perfectly acceptable. In any event, when I came home for the summer holidays shortly before my seventeenth birthday, she took me into the drawing room with a certain amount of ceremony, and showed me that the wall to the right of the fireplace was now blank, while on the wall to the left, above her desk, was a surprise. A reproduction of Claude Monet's *The Poppy Field*.

Not that she called it that. 'It's French,' she said. 'By one of the Impressionists. I got it in Braintree, which is pretty good for Braintree. I thought you'd like it.' When I told her I did, I was trying to do two things at once: to prove that I had at least some knowledge of things I considered high-brow, and to thank her for showing that she was on my side. 'Perhaps you'll tell us what it means?' she went on, half smiling so I reckoned she might be pulling my leg. 'Of course,' I told her, hoping I hadn't missed a beat, and over the next few days I looked into the Thames and Hudson book on Impressionism that I had in my bedroom. I discovered that Monet was thirty-three in 1873, when he did the painting (which was in fact called *Coquelicots, environs d'Argenteuil*) and exhibited it at the first Impressionist show the following year. Argenteuil was a village outside Paris, close to the Seine, and Monet moved there in 1871, the year the Franco-German war ended; he stayed until 1878.

This didn't have much to do with 'meaning' but it was a start, and helped me to feel the picture had been painted by a real person, living in real time, when I sat down to stare at it. It seemed mysterious, but I told myself not to panic: I had to go at it like Mr Way told me to go at poems, using my eyes and my imagination at the same time. Almost exactly half was sky, a mid-blue but warm-looking (in spite of the clouds) which was only right, considering everything in the bottom half of the painting told me it was summer: the line of blob-leafed trees, the tall whispery grass, the two couples (a woman and a child in each case) wearing hats, and poppies flowering along the slope which filled the left-hand side. I'd been right not to panic; it wasn't mysterious at all. It was a picture of people out walking on a sunny day. Why did my mother think it needed explaining?

But she was definitely on to something. The longer I looked, the more puzzled I felt. That house, for instance, just to the right of centre. Was that where the women and children lived? Probably not, or maybe only one of the couples. And why, if it was a home, did it look so closed-up? The dark little windows, and the fawn stone – it felt like a place that wouldn't welcome them when they got back, and brought something cold into the picture, even though the weather was good. The same went for the slope, which kept one woman-and-child apart from the other. What was it? A natural fold in the ground? Or an embankment of some kind: if I jumped up, would I be able to look down into the left-side corner, and see it was really a levee, and the couple walking along the top were in fact strolling along the edge of the Seine? Now I thought about it, the two couples weren't so straightforward either. For one thing, they might not be mothers and children, but nannies or guardians and their charges. And in any case, what sort of people were they? What did they feel like, taking their stroll? Were they happy or sad or something in between? Why were there no men? Because it was a weekday and men were off working, or for other and more sinister reasons? It was impossible to tell: I couldn't read their expressions, and the child in the foreground was disappearing into the grass – only the top half of his sailor-suit, his small blurred face, and his hat were visible. Those things, and the bunch of poppies he was holding.

I'd left the poppies to last. They were the main subject – the title said so – and I expected them to make the meaning clear. But they didn't. On the one hand they were beautiful: signs of summer, and nature going about its business. On the other, I couldn't look at poppies without thinking about the First World War, even though I realized Monet couldn't possibly have seen it coming in 1873. In any event, they weren't just pretty, they were spots of blood, and the way they spilled down the slope between the two couples seemed to connect them. Were they signs of what Mr Way called 'our common humanity'? Were they meant to make me think about women and menstruation and begetting? If so, was that why one of the trees – the one growing on the river bank (if that's what it was) behind the left-hand mother and child (if that's what they were) – was so phallic? I couldn't be sure. As Mr Way said, one could be too ingenious.

I decided to play safe, and tell my mother only what I thought she'd like to hear. Yes there were ambiguous things about the painting, but essentially it was a happy scene, an afternoon wander, and you could see that everyone was enjoying themselves because it was a pretty place, and the woman nearest us had her parasol tilted behind her, which showed she felt relaxed. Her blue parasol, like a seven-sided chunk of the sky. That was enough for my mother, and we let the subject drop. We'd never had this sort of conversation before, and it was vaguely embarrassing for both of us. Paintings weren't work; they were there to be enjoyed. That's why she'd bought it.

The sense that I'd failed her, and failed the painting too, haunted me for a long time after we'd turned to other things. It became a kind of talisman – a sign that my life-to-come lay elsewhere, and also an annoying reminder that I couldn't reach it yet. I didn't know enough; I wasn't clever enough. The only consolation was thinking that, as time went by, I might finally sort things out and get what I wanted: a definite meaning.

It made me start almost to dislike the painting, hanging there hoarding its secrets, pretending to be sunny when really it was full of darkness, while my days rolled slowly forward. When my parents' friends dropped by, arguing with me about my clothes and the length of my hair (it was the 1960s), the trees stayed locked in their shiny stillness. When we spent ordinary evenings in front of the telly, watching the news and nature programmes, the whiskery grass stayed at exactly the same angle while the breeze poured across it. When my mother had her accident and disappeared into hospital, the women stayed beside their children as though nothing had changed. When she was ferried home in an ambulance one Sunday, and the local vicar performed the ceremony of The Laying On Of Hands, the poppies never blinked their red eyes. When I left for university – and effectively moved out for good – the painting stayed put. It was a part of me because I remembered it, but it hadn't exactly melted into my life. I couldn't answer the questions it asked, and that kept me at a crucial distance.

Thirty-odd years later, in my early fifties, with my mother long dead and the house long sold, I went to Paris for a weekend and visited the Musée d'Orsay. I'd visited before, but always to look for particular things. This time there was no hurry, and I wandered off into side galleries on the ground floor as I was leaving. I'd forgotten (if I'd ever known) that I might see *Coquelicots*; suddenly there it was, glowing at the far end of an almost empty room. At the far end, yet seeming to rush towards me, so everything around it suddenly blurred while its own particular sky and trees and grass and women and children and poppies all stayed clear. It was like bumping into a lost friend, miraculously unchanged by time. Except as I stepped towards it – dream-walked towards it, rather – I realized it had changed. It was more compact than I remembered, and the colours were more intense, as though the whole surface was covered by a gigantic but invisible magnifying-glass. That wasn't all. The surrounding air undulated with details of home: my mother's desk, the pale grey wallpaper, the grandmother clock on the mantelpiece, my mother herself relaxing in her green chair, with her feet up on the long stool she'd just finished embroidering. The whole last part of my childhood, intact but at the same time smashed into atoms.

I stood in front of it, gazing, and gradually the atom-storm subsided. The picture hadn't changed; it was me that had changed. I was older. I knew different things about life and more about painting. As I began to remember what I'd said to my mother, when she'd asked me what it meant, I hurriedly abandoned some ideas and hung onto others. In the process, I waited for the sense of mystery to return, along with the feeling of annoyance it had led to. It didn't come. At least, I had the same sense of puzzlement, but it didn't bother me. These women: did it matter whether they were mothers or guardians? And what of the distance that separated them, the voracious grass, the shut-up house, the trees, the poppies? The important thing was not to give them a hard-and-fast significance, but to connect everything that was obviously fixed and intended in the painting with everything these things meant to me individually. And what they meant was several different kinds of uncertainty. It was a painting about ease and pleasure and time off, as well as impending troubles and divisions and death. It showed how nature consoles us, and also how it will consume us eventually (the child vanishing into the long grass). It suggested that people need to live with degrees of separation in their lives, but at the same time proved a longing for community. Mystery, which had made me panic thirty-odd years before, now seemed the be-all-and-end-all, or something very close to that. I welcomed it. It felt true to life.

Ever since I'd left home and started going my own way, the pictures I'd most enjoyed seeing, and the poems I'd most enjoyed reading, had led me to the same end. This time it connected my childhood with my later life in ways that were uniquely definite. Being in two minds, or more than two minds, made me all-of-a-piece. I walked out of the gallery into the white light of early afternoon, and went to look for lunch.